MY DAYS AND DREAMS

BEING AUTOBIOGRAPHICAL NOTES

BY

EDWARD CARPENTER

Author of "Towards Democracy"
"Civilization: its Cause and Cure," &c.

WITH PORTRAITS AND ILLUSTRATIONS

LONDON: GEORGE ALLEN & UNWIN LTD.
RUSKIN HOUSE, 40 MUSEUM STREET, W.C. 1

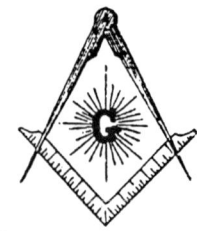

E. C. (1857), AGE THIRTEEN.

First published . June 1916
Second Edition . October 1916
Reprinted . . February 1918
Third Edition September 1921

PREFACE

OLD St. Pancras Churchyard even now, though dominated by the huge gasometers of Wharf Road and backed against the roaring traffic of the Midland Railway, preserves something of the sylvan beauty which a hundred years ago made it the frequent trysting-place of Percy Shelley and Mary Godwin. As it happened, in the summer of 1890, when staying in London, I used to make the garden my resort for writing purposes ; and one day in July of that year I started some autobiographical notes. In a very casual way, and with long intervals between, the notes have been continued down to the present time. The volume therefore to which this is the Preface has been composed in somewhat disjointed fashion ; and the discerning reader will probably perceive slight differences of style and outlook in its different portions, and perhaps also experience some uncertainty as to the proper chronology of the events which it records. In order to mitigate the latter trouble I have from time to time inserted in square brackets the date of the year in which the corresponding portion was written.

Edward Carpenter

May 1916

CONTENTS

ILLUSTRATIONS

MY DAYS AND DREAMS

I

BRIGHTON

My life hitherto [7th July 1890] divides into four pretty distinct periods—first, my early life up to the age of twenty, during which time I lived mainly at Brighton, embedded in a would-be fashionable world which I hated; secondly, the period from '64 to about '74, during which time I was mostly at Cambridge, in a more or less intellectual atmosphere; thirdly, from '74 to '81, when I carried on the Extension lectures and made acquaintance with the manufacturing centres and commercial society of the North of England; and fourthly, for the ten years from '80 and '81 down to the present time, when I have lived almost entirely among the working masses, and been largely engaged in manual labour.

It may seem ungrateful to say so, but my abiding recollection of early days is one of discomfort. Not but that I had on the whole good times at school, in the classes and in the games; not but that at home I was lapped in the ease and attentive service of a well-to-do household, and had a hundred advantages denied to an ordinary child of the people; but that after all at home I never felt really at home. Perhaps I was unduly sensitive; anyhow I felt myself an alien, an outcast, a failure, and an object of ridicule.

The social life which encircled us at Brighton was artificial enough ; but it was the standard which we children had to live to. My parents were the best people in the world, but they could not fly out of the conditions in which they belonged. I hated the life, was miserable in it—the heartless conventionalities, silly proprieties—but I never imagined, it never occurred to me, that there *was* any other life. To be pursued by the dread of appearances—what people would say about one's clothes or one's speech—to be always in fear of committing unconscious trespasses of invisible rules—this seemed in my childhood the normal condition of existence ; so much so that I never dreamed of escaping from it. I only prayed for a time when grace might be given me to pass by without reproach. I was never a daring or rumbustious child. Timid and sensitive, my spirit was sadly lacking in the inestimable virtue of revolt. I suffered and was stupid enough to think myself in the wrong.

There was a curate at one of the churches to which we used to go—a smooth-haired, carefully shaven, meek young man, probably of feeble mind ; but all I knew was that people praised him : such a good-looking, well-mannered fellow he was, and preached such nice sermons ! "Happy Mr. Cass," I used to think, for even now I remember his name—"Oh, happy Mr. Cass, if only I could be like *you* when I grow up." I was then about fourteen, and I fancy that the mere sight of Cass in his spotless surplice must have worked upon me, for it was about that time or a little later that I began to make up my mind to take Orders. No doubt from the first there was a fatal bias towards religion.

I remember distinctly—and it must have been about the same period—thinking as I lay awake in bed at night that if the house were on fire I would save my *prayer-book* ! I saw myself in my mind's eye in heroic attitude rushing into my mother's room where the sacred volume lay, and bearing it out through flames and smoke into the street. It was not my mother or sisters that I was going to save . . . but my prayer-book ! Alas ! what a defect of nature, or of teaching, must have been there !

Curious, the covered underground life that some children lead ! I never remember, all those years at Brighton, till I was nineteen or twenty, a single person older than myself who was my confidant. I do not remember a single occasion on which in any trouble or perplexity I was able to go to any one for help or consolation. My mother, firm, just, and courageous as she was, and setting her children an heroic example, belonged to the old school, which thought any manifestation of feeling unbecoming. We early learned to suppress and control emotion, and to fight our own battles alone : in some ways a good training, but liable in the long run to starve the emotional nature. Masters at school in those days did not "draw boys out" ; education was mainly a nipping of buds ; older friends outside the family, who may so often play a useful part in the development of boy or girl life, never came—that I remember—to the rescue ; and so my abiding recollection of all that time is one of silent concealment and loneliness.

Nevertheless of course there were joys. Though a town-house is not a congenial nursery for a child, yet we were comparatively fortunate. There was a large space at the back, where we kept, in succession, endless pets—pigeons, seagulls with clipped wings, rabbits, tortoises, guinea-pigs, and smaller fry (I was especially fond of an aquarium) ; while in front was the large garden of Brunswick Square, overrun, despite the efforts of the gardener and other authorities, by all the children of the surrounding houses. A fearfully active family, boys and girls, we kept a sort of proud superiority over the other children in running races, prisoners' base, etc. ; while inside the house, and for wet weather, we had a sport entirely our own, and which consisted in one pursuing the others up the front stairs and down the back stairs, or *vice versa,* with endless shrieks and uproar—a terrible affair, which nothing but the noblest self-sacrifice could have ever nerved our parents to endure ! Also there was hide-and-seek in the dark, a grisly game, dangerous both to limbs and to furniture ; and occasionally a battle of the giants—as when, on one occasion, an elder sister having with the greatest care built up a beautiful dummy man round a long smooth pole, my eldest brother came on the sly and drew the backbone out ! Then there was earth-shaking conflict, which I, quite a small boy, witnessed from a distance, and with quaking limbs.

As to school life, I suppose it is a general experience that what one learns at school does not count for much. At the age of ten I began at the Brighton College. My eldest sister had taught me a little Latin grammar before that. My eldest brother Charlie was already at the College. He was a kind of hero there. At that time (or possibly a year or two later) he was easily first in *everything.* In mathematics, classics, foreign languages, in cricket, football, athletics—no matter what it was—he took all the prizes. Withal he was so friendly, so sociable, that he was a universal favorite ; so generous and so humorous—so naturally full of fun and comedy—that I really think he disarmed all jealousy in others—nor felt a spark of jealousy or vanity in himself. Seldom I should think has there been such a boy; and when at the age of nineteen or twenty he took his final leave in order to join the Indian Civil Service, his memory lingered long and long behind him in the school.[1]

My reception under those circumstances was naturally favorable. One day, shortly after my arrival, I was playing by myself in a corner of the entrance hall, when a big boy with a pleasant face came up to me and, making a suitable gesture, said, "Sweep up the Chips, sweep up the Chips." Then I knew that my nickname was Chips—a family nickname indeed, since my father and my brothers at different times bore it.

The College was a large school of 150 or 200 boys—on public school lines. I went through the

[1] In India he rose rapidly through the early grades of the Service. The Mutiny of 1857 was just over, and administration was being reorganized in various directions. He was stationed at Futtehpore, Saharanpore and various places in the N.W. Provinces; and then at Allahabad, where he became Settlement Officer and something of an authority on Land and Irrigation questions. Afterwards he was transferred to the Central Provinces and made full Commissioner first at Jubbulpore and then at Nagpore. It was at the last-named place that a fatal accident overtook him while riding in a steeple-chase; and a career of great promise was cut short. This was in March 1876. The *Pioneer* of the 7th of March said: "His public career, though now but commencing, was full of the highest promise. Sound, cool, and cautious in deliberation, he carried into action the promptness and decision which are born of self-reliance and of a healthy vigorous *physique*. His was emphatically *mens sana in corpore sano*; and he himself an officer of rare judgment and of most sterling merit."

See *A Memoir of C. W. C.*: a little brochure (privately printed) written by my eldest sister after his death.

classes in due order from the lowest upwards; and the personality of each master in turn impressed its unconscious weight upon me. I remember distinctly the agonized effort and the triumph of passing the "Asses' Bridge" in Euclid. The name of the master who got me over was Newton, and for some years I firmly believed that he was no other than the celebrated Sir Isaac. I joined in the games and athletics—and not without success, though I was never very partial to cricket; I climbed slowly up through the classes; I rubbed shoulders with all the queer, red-haired, pock-marked, fat, lean, mean, generous, handsome, clever, tyrannical, cross-eyed, gentle, good-natured, specimens of fellow humanity—the other boys—whose influence on one at that age is so strange and incalculable, and whose characters and deeds appear at the time so mysterious and inexplicable; though when one looks back upon them at a later date, they seem transparently clear and simple. I cannot remember anything very heroic that I did, though I can remember some mean things. I remember joining with the others in teasing the French master—that ever defenceless quarry; and I remember what was much worse, taking a kind of delight in privately tormenting an idiot boy. That was indeed a strange experience. I don't know why the boy was allowed in the school; he was certainly quite weak-minded and incapable; and besides there exhaled from him an odd and fearsome odour. That boy convulsed me with alternate rage and pity. At one moment I was seized with the greatest sympathy for his weakness, and the next I was filled with wrath at his odour and his idiocy, and found or invented excuses for slapping him! Then after that I would sometimes lie awake at night remorseful over my conduct, and planning little schemes of reparation; but in the morning the sight of him would launch me on the waves of irritation again. It was quite a little tragedy to me—and I mention it because this savage and instinctive dislike of anything malformed, which is so very marked in boys, no doubt accounts for much of their cruelty. It remains in the mind of course to a much later age, but is gradually covered over by the growth of sympathy and understanding. As a rule my better deeds were done in defence of the weak. Timid for the most part, I regained my courage on these occasions—as in delivering a small boy from a big bully; or once in sticking up for two brothers, the dirtiest and most stupid boys in the class, against the gibes of the master; or another time in helping a poor man in the street with his bundle—on which last occasion the said Sir Isaac Newton passing by, instead of scolding me as I expected, actually said, "That's right, my boy"—a remark for which I felt ever so grateful to him—for indeed I was feeling rather ashamed of myself.

I think that was about the only occasion on which a master exercised any directly helpful influence. Schools were odd places in those days. The idea of really reaching the boy and drawing out his interest seems never to have occurred to the masters. When I arrived in the Sixth Form, the Headmaster was a certain Dr. Griffith—a burly, headstrong, muddle-headed, perhaps rather good-natured man. As often as not he would arrive in the class-room late, with his hair a-tumble, and looking as if he had not slept all night, would complain that some naughty boy in the Fourth Form was preoccupying his mind, and would leave us again alone with our books. Then presently his study door would open, and he would push the said boy into the room, saying,

"I wish one of you gentlemen would *cane* this boy," and throwing a cane in over the boy's head would close the door again. Once, drawing a handful of silver and gold out of his pocket, he asked me to cane a boy for him—and afterwards I felt sorry I had not accepted the bargain. I think he must have been a little touched in the head. It is certainly aggravating to think that we used to read Homer and Virgil and the Greek plays, and *never* that I remember was any attempt made to make us understand the subject or the plot or the literary interest of these works—nothing but grammar and syntax. As to mathematics the neglect was worse—and I left school at eighteen or nineteen having done nothing beyond Euclid and Algebra.

My record in the classes was on the whole, I suppose, good—though nothing remarkable. I gained the usual number of prizes, and kept about an equal interest in classics and mathematics. With regard to the former, my father—who had progressive ideas on such subjects—gave me a word for word *crib* to Horace, saying that the best way to learn a language was to use such a crib. Naturally after that I rejoiced in it freely in my preparation-work at home of an evening. But one day I could not resist taking it to school and showing it to some of my class-mates. Of course we were pounced upon, and the crib confiscated. The form-master at that time was E. C. Hawkins—a really fine type of man, father of Anthony Hope Hawkins the novelist. But when he asked me where I got the crib from, and I replied quite truthfully and simply "My father gave it me," he was struck dumb! He certainly thought I was lying, but could make no reply. And for a long time after that would hardly speak to me.

Cricket I never took to much. Being a bad player

I voted it 'slow.' Probably it gave too much rope to my dreamy tendencies, and I got into trouble missing unexpected catches. But hockey and football I was fond of, and fives, as being more lively.

When I was about thirteen an event important to us children happened, which I must not pass by. My parents determined to spend a year in France, and they actually transported the whole household, nine children (i.e. all except my brother Charlie) and two servants, to Versailles. I remember only too well that awful night journey by Newhaven and Dieppe, the raging sea, the arrival drenched, the dim lights of the Customhouse, the cries of lost children, the journey by train to Paris and onwards. How my mother survived it I do not know. We settled in a house in the Avenue de Sceaux, amid barracks, and continual fanfaronades and trampings of military, near the great Palace with its endless galleries, and the Park with its fountains and music. All very exciting and delightful. And we found some good and friendly French neighbours. At first they did not the least understand our household. It never occurred to them for a moment that it was all one family, and for some time it was supposed that my father and mother kept a school! But when the truth at last dawned upon them, their delight and amazement knew no bounds, and we became the centre of the greatest interest. I and my younger brother, Alfred, went as day-boys to school at the Lycée Hoche (then Imperiale)—a great place of five hundred boys—where we learned French by sheer necessity. I do not think we learned much else. In the matter of lessons the instruction was much on a par with that at the Brighton school, and the playground life and social organization of the boys were far less pregnant of good influences.

I don't know how the Lycées are now, but at that time the school methods were only poor. The boys sat an outrageously long time at their desks—ten hours a day or more—either construing or preparing lessons; but got through very little work, spending most of their time in furtive games or conversations with each other. Everything was done in set and military style—marchings along corridors from class-room to class-room, or from class-room to refectory, or from refectory to playground. In the latter a master (always called 'pion') was present to see that there was no bullying, or to disperse knots of boys (who might of course be talking sedition) or to prevent individuals approaching the playground wall within a set distance (lest they should escape). The games were limited and regulated. Everything was regulated. It was said that the Minister of Education at Paris could at any hour of the day place his finger on the line of Virgil that was being translated, or the proposition of Geometry that was being proved at that moment in all the Lycées alike over the face of the land. One very curious custom prevailed, which has probably now gone out of date, but which had a strong suggestion about it of the Church system of Indulgences. At the end of the week the marks gained by each boy during the week were added up and announced by the master. Then those boys who were credited with more than a certain number of marks were told they might write out for themselves a certificate of satisfaction, good for exemption from one, two, or even three hours' punishment, according to circumstances! Great excitement prevailed. You cut yourself a neat square of paper, adorned it with lines and flourishes, and inscribed on it "Témoignage de Satisfaction—Elève Carpenter—bonne à une heure"—and left a space at foot for the signature of the master. When signed you treasured this up in your desk—and at some later date when the hour of punishment came, produced it, and unless your crime was very heinous were duly let off! It was a curious arrangement, but one which had perhaps the advantage of discouraging a boy from being *too* good—since obviously, it would be a mistake to collect a greater number of such tickets than you were likely to make use of.

My brother and I, as day-boys, escaped a good deal of the general school routine and regulation, and on the whole had not a bad time. The boys received us decently, and as we could play leap-frog or prisoners' base (Les Barres) as well as any of them, paid us due respect; and one of the masters, Llandais by name, was quite kind and thoughtful towards me. Out of hours we careered through the woods of Satory, watched military evolutions on the plain above, or at dusk chased and caught the great stag-beetles—a thrilling joy. We wandered through the huge statue-adorned Park and the shady Bosquets of diamond-necklace celebrity, and learned swimming—as did also my sisters—in the fine open-air swimming bath, which used to be the bath of the pages of Louis XIV's Court. After a year thus spent, the family returned to England, and we boys to the Brighton College.

As I say, it is probably a common experience that mere school teaching does not leave a very deep impression. Probably a good deal really *is* learned—but these are the more indirect things which slip into the background or foundation of the mind and character and so pass comparatively unobserved. Only three or four subjects of interest stand out in my memory as belonging to my school-days, and these all lay outside school proper. The earliest of these was music. At the age of ten I desired mightily to learn the piano ; but music was not considered appropriate for a boy—besides there were six sisters who had to be taught, poor things, whether they liked it or not—and so my appearance on the music stool was treated rather as an intrusion, and I was generally hustled off again forthwith. However I got my way by playing late of an evening, when they were all upstairs in the drawing-room ; I never had any regular teaching, but my mother took pity on me and taught me my notes ; and from that time I stumbled through the "Marche des Croates" and the "Nun's Prayer" till at last I emerged on the far borderland of Beethoven's Sonatas. This hour of piano practice to myself was for a long time one of the chief events of my day. Indeed, it is curious, but I took to composing, or attempting to compose, music before ever I thought of composing or attempting to compose poetry. Of course with a juvenile mind, and no musical training, nor even a particularly keen ear, my compositions were of no value, and I hardly ever troubled to write them out ; still the habit of making up pianoforte pieces, and the love of doing so, continued all my life, and forced its way out from time to time. It is only in quite late years that, with more technical knowledge, I have written some of these down—perhaps twelve or twenty in all—and even occasionally thought of printing them.

I was also fortunate enough, when I was about fifteen, to come in for the reversion of a cupboard full of chemical apparatus, which had belonged to my eldest brother, and here in a little room with retorts and test-tubes I spent many a half-holiday, carrying out important experiments and prosecuting valuable inventions, which ended almost invariably in bad smells and worse headaches. Perpetual motion, as usual in such cases, was one of my chief objects; and I could not for the life of me tell why a solid cylinder of wood, placed with its axis horizontal in the side of a box containing water, and so carefully fitted that it would turn on its axis without allowing the water to run out, would not revolve perpetually—seeing indeed that the one half of it which was in the water, being lighter than water, would continually tend to rise, and the other half of it which was in the air would continually tend to fall. I invented an arrangement for the pianoforte after the Morse telegraphic system, by which extemporaneous effusions could be written down in the act of playing—an invention which luckily has not been generally adopted; and was engaged on various other little patents at different times. Sometimes I gave a lecture—though it must be confessed that it was with difficulty that any of the household could be induced to attend! The lecture was small, but the danger from explosions and horrible smells was great. My remarks were not very lucid or explanatory, but consisted mainly of expressions like "Now I will show you something else" or "You needn't be frightened, there is no danger." These investigations were however very absorbing and excited far more interest in my mind than anything I learned at school; and I remember that they led me to think quite seriously about being a doctor (I suppose from some vague notion about the connection between chemicals and medicine)—a profession which my father was inclined to recommend to me, and which I have sometimes regretted that I did not adopt.

Towards the later part of my time at Brighton the natural *épanchement* of youth led me often to seek consolation and an escape from the wounds of daily life in intercourse with Nature. The Brighton social life—with its greetings where no kindness is—was to me chilly in the extreme, and I often used in later years to feel that I "caught cold" (morally speaking) whenever I returned to it. The scenery and surroundings of Brighton are also bare and chilly enough; and trees, whose friendly covert I have always loved, do not exist there; but the place has two Nature-elements in it—and these two singularly wild and untampered—the Sea and the Downs. We lived within two hundred yards of the sea, and its voice was in our ears night and day. On terrific stormy nights it was a "grisly joy" to go down to the water's edge at 10 or 11 p.m.—pitchy darkness—feeling one's way with feet or hands, over the stony beach, hardly able to stand for the wind—and to watch the white breakers suddenly leap out of the gulf close upon one—the "scream of the madden'd beach dragged down by the wave," the booming of the wind, like distant guns, and the occasional light of some vessel laboring for its life in the surge.

But the Downs were my favorite refuge. On sunny days I would wander on over them for miles, not knowing very clearly where I was going—in a strange broody moony state—glad to find some hollow (like that described in Jefferies' *Story of my Heart*) where one could lie secluded for any length of time and see only the clouds and the grasses and an occasional butterfly, or hear the distant bark of a dog or the far rumble of a railway train. The Downs twined themselves with all my thought and speculations of that time. Their chaste subdued gracious outlines and quiet colour have a peculiar charm. Their strongest line is generally some white edge of cliffs or curve of the shore itself, their deepest tint the blue of the sea or occasionally a field of red clover or one overgrown with charlock. For the rest they wear the faint blue-green colour of thin turf through which the chalk almost shows. Over the velvety sward and among the fine herbage cropped by plentiful sheep run innumerable tiny flowers dwarfed by salt wind and scanty soil—thistles, whose chins rest on the ground out of which they grow; patches of sweet thyme which the wild bees love, of pink centaury and thrift and madder and dwarf-broom, and that sweet yellow lotus or bird's-foot trefoil, which runs all over the world, in Siberia and Alps and Himalayas the same, one of the commonest and friendliest of all the flowers that grow. Overhead the lark sings, the clouds drift through the untampered blue, the bee and the butterfly sweep past on the breeze. Three or four miles from Brighton, and one is in a world remote from man. Except an occasional shepherd there is hardly a human to be seen. Here and there in a hollow nestles the tiniest hamlet—an old farmhouse, one or two cottages, a dwarf church faced with rough work of flints, a few trees and a well. Taking its character from the sky—as all chalk and limestone countries largely do—this land has an ethereal beauty in summer weather; but on wintry and gray days it is monotonous and sad. The shepherd then huddles himself in his cloak in the lee of the gorse-bush, the cloudy rack drives over the backs of his sheep, line behind line the Downs stretch, colorless, unbroken by any hint of tree or habitation; the wind whistles among the thin grass stems with a peculiar shrill and mournful pipe, and in its pauses the sullen and distant roar of the sea is heard.

How can I describe, how shall I not recall, the

thoughts which came to me as I wandered, towards the close of my school time, over these same hills—the brooding ill-defined, half-shapen thoughts? The Downs were my escape; even in their most chill and lonely moods they were my escape from a worse coldness and loneliness, which, except for a few boy-friends at school, I somehow experienced during all that time. Nature was more to me, I believe, than any human attachment, and the Downs were my Nature. It was among them at a later time that I first began to write a few verses. But at the time I mention, and till quite the end of my school days, I never wrote anything at all. If the thought of writing had occurred to me I should have deemed it, in my then state of mind, monstrous presumption—but I doubt whether the thought ever did occur to me. I did not even read poetry. Mozart and Beethoven were familiar to me, but I must have been eighteen years old before I was roused to any interest in Tennyson (the poet of the day) by a lecture at school on "In Memoriam." After that I read "In Memoriam" and loved it well. This was followed (at Cambridge) by Wordsworth; and then by Shelley, who excited in me the same passionate attachment that he has excited in so many others. After that Whitman dominated me. I do not think any others of the poets—unless Plato should bear that name—have deeply influenced me.

As to friends—that absorbing subject—I can trace the desire for a passionate attachment in my earliest boyhood. But the desire had no expression, no chance of expression. Such things as affection were never spoken about either at home or at school, and I naturally concluded that there was no room for them in the scheme of creation! The glutinous boy-friendships that one formed in class-room or playground were of the usual type: they staved off a greater hunger, but they did not satisfy. On the other hand I worshipped the very ground on which some, generally elder, boys stood; they were heroes for whom I would have done anything. I dreamed about them at night, absorbed them with my eyes in the day, watched them at cricket, loved to press against them unnoticed in a football melly, or even to get accidentally hurt by one of them at hockey, was glad if they just spoke to me or smiled; but never got a word farther with it all. What could I say? Even to one of the masters, I remember, who was a little kind to me, I felt this unworded devotion; but he never helped me over the stile, and so I remained on the farther side.

I often think what a fund of romance, and of intense feeling, there is in this direction latent in so many boys and capable even of heroic expression—and how much will have to be done some day in the matter of directing and giving a constructive outlet to it. Already however there is a great difference in the tone of the public schools themselves on this subject, from what there was twenty-five or thirty years ago. The trouble in schools from bad sexual habits and frivolities arises greatly—though of course not altogether—from the suppression and misdirection of the natural emotions of boy-attachment. I, as a day boy, and one who happened to be rather pure-minded than otherwise, grew up quite free from these evils: though possibly it would have been a good thing if I had had a little more experience of them than I had. As it was, no elder person *ever* spoke to me about sexual matters—no mother, father, brother, monitor or master ever said a word. I picked up the usual information from the talk of my companions, and made up my own mind unbiased by any person or book. I suppose it was in consequence of this that I never saw anything repellent or shameful in sexual acts themselves. From the earliest time when I thought about these things they seemed to me natural—like digestion or any other function—and I remember wondering why people made such a fuss about the mention of them—why they told lies rather than speak the truth, why they were shocked, or why they giggled and stuffed handkerchiefs in their mouths. It was not till (at the age of twenty-five) I read Whitman—and then with a great leap of joy—that I met with the treatment of sex which accorded with my own sentiments.

Nevertheless though these desires were never to me unclean, yet during all that time of later boyhood and early university life they were strangely discounted by that other desire of the heart. I could not think much of sex while the hunger of the heart was unsatisfied—and *that* for the time being occupied all the foreground of my life. Indeed at times it threatened to paralyse my mental and physical faculties. It was like an open wound continually bleeding. I felt starved and unfed, and unable to rest in the chilling contacts of ordinary life. As to the usual attractions set before the eyes of middle-class youth, the hopeless, helpless young ladyisms, or the bolder beauties of the gutter, they were both a detestable boredom to me.

For indeed the life, and with it the character, of the ordinary "young lady" of that period, and of the sixties generally, was tragic in its emptiness. The little household duties for women, encouraged in an earlier and simpler age, had now gone out of date, while the modern idea of work in the great world was not so much as thought of. In a place like Brighton there were hundreds, perhaps, of households, in which girls were growing up with but one idea in life, that of taking their "proper place in society." A few meagre accomplishments—plentiful balls and dinner-parties, theatres and concerts—and to loaf up and down the parade, criticizing each other, were the means to bring about this desirable result! There was absolutely nothing else to do or live for. It is curious—but it shows the state of public opinion of that time—to think that my father, who was certainly quite advanced in his ideas, never for a moment contemplated that any of his daughters should learn professional work with a view to their living—and that in consequence he more than once drove himself quite ill with worry. Occasionally it happened that, after a restless night of anxiety over some failure among his investments, and of dread lest he should not be able at his death to leave the girls a competent income, he would come down to breakfast looking a picture of misery. After a time he would break out. "Ruin impended over the family," securities were falling, dividends disappearing; there was only one conclusion—"the girls would have to go out as governesses." Then silence and gloom would descend on the household. It was true; that was the only resource. There was only one profession possible for a middle-class woman—to be a governess—and to adopt that was to become a *pariah*. But in a little time affairs would brighten up again. Stocks went up, the domestic panic subsided; and dinner-parties and balls were resumed as usual.

As time went by, and I gradually got to know what life really meant, and to realize the situation, it used to make me intensely miserable to return home and see what was going on there. My parents of course were fully occupied, but for the rest there were six or seven servants in the house, and my six sisters had absolutely nothing to do except dabble in paints and music as aforesaid, and wander aimlessly from room to room to see if by any chance "anything was going on." Dusting, cooking, sewing, darning—all light household duties were already forestalled; there was no private garden, and if there had been it would have been "unladylike" to do anything in it; *every* girl could not find an absorbing interest in sol-fa or water-colours; athletics were not invented; every aspiration and outlet, except in the direction of dress and dancing, was blocked; and marriage, with the growing scarcity of men, was becoming every day less likely, or easy to compass. More than once girls of whom I least expected it told me that their lives were miserable "with nothing on earth to do." Multiply this picture by thousands and hundreds of thousands all over the country, and it is easy to see how, when the causes of the misery were understood, it led to the powerful growth of the modern "Women's Movement."

During my school-days, however, this tragedy had, so far as our household was concerned, hardly developed itself, or at any rate become at all serious; and a charming recollection of that period is that of my companionship with two of my elder sisters. With one of these—my sister Ellen, afterwards Mrs. Hyett—I used to go long country walks. She had an eye for landscape and animal painting, and sometimes brought her sketch-book with her. Occasionally on hired hacks we rode together over the Downs. Her mind had an adventurous outdoor quality about it; and our conversation turned mainly on what we saw on our explorations, and on speculations about foreign lands. The other sister (Lizzie, afterwards Lady Daubeney) was never much of a walker; but she stayed at home and played Beethoven's Sonatas, and these were a continual delight to me. I stood quietly by and turned over the pages by the hour. The "Sonata Appassionata" was a dream of wonder. This sister had a highly poetic, sensitive temperament. When the younger ones of the family were children she told us absorbing fairy-tales. At the time I speak of she was the one in the household who gave to the atmosphere a touch of sympathy, tenderness and romance; which was of priceless value. As my mind expanded we even talked a little poetic philosophy together, and discussed Tennyson and Shakespeare.

My younger brother, Alfred, who was my schoolfellow at the Lycée at Versailles, went to the Brighton College with me (I joining for the second time) when the family returned to Brighton in 1858. But at an early age (fourteen) he joined the Navy, and after a preliminary year on board the *Britannia* training-ship, went away to sea. Consequently he was not so much at home during those early years. The sea-life suited him, I think. With a rather dare-devil temperament as a boy he was always getting into scrapes at school [Once, I remember, he had the brilliant idea of lighting a fire in his locker in the schoolroom, and then sitting, all innocence, on the seat—until the crackling of sticks and the curling smoke drew all eyes that way, and he was discovered like the phœnix in apparent peril of being consumed!] In the Navy, at an early period, he distinguished himself by saving life under risky circumstances. In one case a man had fallen overboard at night in the Tagus from another ship, and in the darkness was being swept by the current seawards past the *Warrior*, on which ship my brother was—when the latter, who was on deck at the time, jumped in to the rescue, at the same time calling to some of the bluejackets to man a boat and follow. Of course he and the drowning man were immediately lost to sight in the gloom, and when the boat did get under weigh it was only by his distant shouts that its crew could be guided. The two men had drifted half a mile or more before they were picked up; but it was not too late, and their rescue was safely effected. In another case off the Falkland Isles he swam to the rescue of an ordinary seaman under even more perilous conditions, and for this act gained the Albert medal—which may be called the V.C. of life-saving medals.

At a later period [1875-76] my brother Alfred was lieutenant on board H.M.S. *Challenger*, and it was under his management that the deepest sounding effected up to that period was taken. He obtained 4,475 fathoms, or nearly 27,000 feet in the vicinity of the Ladrone Islands. After the *Challenger* he had several commands in China and elsewhere, including charge of the Marine Survey of India; and as commander of the *Investigator* he spent several years surveying and making charts of the coasts of India and the Andaman Islands. In 1885, in connection with the Burmese expedition against King Thebaw, the important duty was assigned to him of leading the War Flotilla up the river Irrawaddy. As an officer he was well liked, being considerate of the men under him, but firm in their management, and in moments of danger plucky and reliable.[1]

[1] His son, Francis, followed my brother into the Navy, thus representing a fourth generation of Carpenters in a direct line in the same profession. He is now [1915], though still young, occupying a high position in the North Sea Fleet, and has distinguished himself not only like his father by saving life, but also by bringing out important inventions which have been taken up by the Admiralty.

Such, roughly summed together, are the main outlines of my early days—full after all of tenderest recollections. A large family is a roughish training school, but it is a valuable one. Over-sensitive and of a clinging disposition by nature, I early learned the profound lessons of suffering and of self-dependence. My spirit concentrated itself, and partially overcame its inherent vagueness and weakness in years of silence. The tension of those early days, the unexpressed hatred which I felt, though I did not understand it, for the social conditions in which I was born, was destined, when its meaning gradually realized itself in my consciousness, to become one of the great directing forces of my after life.

II

MY PARENTS

MY father (born in 1797) had a curious early life. He came of a family which had lived in Cornwall (Launceston) for some generations. He was the eldest son—though he had three sisters—of an Admiral in the Navy, and appears to have taken to his father's profession, when a boy, as a matter of course. He was not, however, at all suited to it, for he was of a rather studious temperament, and the rough life of the Navy of those days was probably very distasteful to him. He was in one or two skirmishes with the French off the American coast, and I remember his telling me of the painful feeling which he experienced once when being in a small boat and coming across some French sailors in another small boat he had to take aim and fire at them. To his relief, however, no one was hurt!

When he was twenty-three or twenty-four my father began to learn German and read philosophy in his spare hours, which did not look as though he were destined to remain long on board ship! As a matter of fact he left the Navy when he was about twenty-five. The bad climate of Trincomalee, where he was stationed for two years, damaged his health. He came to London and set about reading for the Chancery Bar. In due course he was called and for some years practised with success—so much so indeed

MY FATHER: CHARLES CARPENTER.

that on his retirement he was greatly complimented by the presiding judge. In 1833 he married; and this it was which, curiously enough, led to his retirement from the Bar. For his father-in-law—Thomas Wilson—who had also been in the Navy, and who was then a widower, only consented to the marriage on condition that his daughter should remain at home, and that the married couple should therefore take up their abode at his house at Walthamstow. This they did, and the distance from London, a considerable matter in those days, combined perhaps with a little anxiety about my father's health, which still remained unsatisfactory, brought about the abandonment of his profession—a great mistake as it appeared, for of course as soon as he lost his regular occupation he began to worry badly. Then, when Mr. Wilson died, in 1841, a move to Brighton (which just then was growing into importance, and yet retained some of its old-world character) was thought advisable, both for my father's sake and for that of the little family which now had to be considered. But as far as my father was concerned this did not mend matters, and my mother has often told me that this was the worst period of their married life.

He got more and more anxious and restless—to a degree which seemed almost a danger to his mind—till at last my mother induced him to let himself be appointed magistrate and take his seat on the Brighton bench; after which his serenity returned, and he remained one of the most active and probably the most public spirited of the members of the Brighton and afterwards of the Hove magistracy till a year or two before his death. The death of his own father in 1846 freed him from any real cause for pecuniary anxiety—though from time to time all through his later life he was liable to fits of considerable depression and nervousness about his monetary concerns. He settled down permanently at Brighton (No. 45 Brunswick Square) into the life of the respectable *rentier,* with its usual aims and ideals as far as his family was concerned, though for himself his aims were very different from those of the society round him, and his conception of life was as broad as it could well be upon the foundation of that particular social status to which he belonged.

His early life in the Navy had given my father that honest, somewhat simple, cast of mind which belongs to sea-faring folk. He was always ready to be impressed by a tale of distress—especially if it came from the lips of one of the fair sex. At the same time his active brain had carried him far in most fields of thought. Though having a strong religious feeling, he soon emancipated himself from current orthodoxies in religion, and seldom in later life went to church—a fact which to the mild respectabilities around us was a sufficient justification for calling him an Atheist. For Frederick W. Robertson, who was then preaching at Brighton, and who not unfrequently came to our house, and for Frederick D. Maurice, however, he had a great admiration; and his own views were—as far as I remember what he said when I was a boy—a kind of Broad Church mysticism, derived at first from reading S. T. Coleridge (whom he had met occasionally in former years in London), and gradually broadening out under the influence of Eckhardt, Tauler, Kant, Fichte, Hegel and others into a religious and philosophic mysticism without much admixture of the Broad Church at all.

In politics he was a strong Liberal—indeed in his most active period a philosophic Radical of the Mill school, and gave strong support to Henry Fawcett during the time when the latter represented

Brighton. Though occasionally asked to stand himself he never as far as I know felt inclined to do so, and indeed a certain lack of glibness and difficulty of expression which he experienced always made him disinclined from taking part in any kind of public speechifying. In his quite latest years he veered round to the support of Beaconsfield's Government; but this, if partly due to the reactionary tendency of old age, was also caused by his keen perception of the hypocrisy (unconscious or otherwise) of Gladstone, whom in the last few years of his life he never ceased to vilify.

Almost all general literature interested my father—especially works on natural history, travels, and science of any kind; but art and music were never much in his line. Any tale of heroism, or prodigy of science would bring ready tears to his eyes; and his love of reading—as in the case of his own father—lasted to the latest years of his life; for when he was over eighty years of age he would not unfrequently sit up till one or two in the morning, conning the last new book or running over favorite passages of his philosophical authors.

In a letter of his (written in '73) I find the following passage: "Circumstances have been leading me to think a good deal lately about Instinct. I do not see how any distinction can be drawn between what we call Instinct in the lower animals—such as the insect when she deposits eggs and then brings to the place of deposit the food needful for the support of her offspring grub, and covering them up (eggs and food) together, flies away to perish—and that power in Plants that causes them to send forth their roots often to a great distance and in a special direction, in search of the material needful for their nutriment, the mineral perhaps without which they could not live. This can only be understood, as it seems to me, upon the assumption of there being a Life, an intelligent Life, in the Plant or Insect, of which they are unconscious. Think of the Swallow going to Egypt perhaps, and then at proper season returning to its old nest under the eaves of some cottage in England. The possession of sense-organs, therefore, does not expel from the Bird or Fish this Intelligent Life within them, which orders their migrations, etc., but of which they are unconscious. And why should it be otherwise with man? That he should be conscious of this life will one day be his highest blessing."

And in another letter (of 1876): "Surely the true meaning of Nirvana is that at some future stage of our being man will be so conscious of the indwelling and inworking of Deity, that he will ascribe every movement, whether of his body or mind, to the One Will, the One *Vernunft*, the One Life, and thus think of himself as swallowed up by and absorbed, as it were, in that Being."

These extracts will show what a priceless debt I owe to the early contact with his mind.

How strange and far-back all that early life seems now—and yet so vivid—I can see it all in brightest detail! Of an evening, after dinner or supper, how we sat round the drawing-room table, or in scattered chairs, reading. My father would get out his Fichte or his Hartmann and soon become lost in their perusal. Occasionally he would, when he came to a striking passage, play a sort of devil's tattoo with his fingers on the table, or, getting up, would walk to and fro quarter-deck fashion, with creaky boots, and reciting his authors to himself. Then my mother or perhaps my eldest sister would remonstrate, and after a time he would settle down again. Sometimes if he was very quiet one might look up from one's book and see from his upturned eyes and half-open lips that he had lapsed into inner communion and meditation.

His was a very religious nature, and it was his habit to think of the divinity as clearly present—as he would say: "When I am taking my bath or even when I am breathing I say to myself, 'This is God working within and around me.'" In later years, however, his liability to extreme worry and anxiety would return; and there were times when even his books failed to save him from the sleepless nights and despondent days occasioned by the failure or possible failure of some Stock Exchange speculation. At such times reports of railway companies, maps, gazetteers, newspaper cuttings, etc., were got out and studied and restudied; I was called in to take part in the investigations ("put in the stocks" as I used to call it), and had to sit up till the small hours of the morning in attitudes of painful suspense and tension. The troubles, however, would pass away in due time, and on the whole my father was (owing chiefly to the care and thought he gave to them) very successful over his "investments."

The rest of the family spent the evening, as a rule, in reading—of which we were all fond. My sisters would play or sing a little; and when they ceased, the sound of the near sea would reassert itself, or the roaring of the wind in the chimney. My mother sat on a low chair, with a book on her knee and some knitting in her hands, but occasionally, tired with the work of the day, would drop asleep; at ten o'clock the servant brought up wine and biscuits, and shortly afterwards we would all—except my father—retire.

Of my mother's life how can I say anything? That which is so vital to one, so intimate, how can one disengage it from oneself? There was an unspoken tragedy in those beautiful gazelle-like eyes —the tragedy as of dumbness itself. The tender loving spirit which beamed forth from them never found direct utterance in this world. It was the look of a prisoner. Her mother was a Scotchwoman. A baneful parental influence—Scottish pride and puritanism—had rested on my mother's young life, making all expression of tender feeling little short of a sin; and this reserve, inculcated in youth, became in later days involuntary and inevitable. My mother had a sister to whom she was much attached, but who had offended my grandmother by marrying a man who was considered undesirable. The sister was never forgiven, nor even acknowledged again. She died soon after her marriage; and her death, with all the accompanying circumstances, was a great blow to my mother; but of it—as of other things which touched her nearly—she would never speak.

Her nature was not so much intellectual or imaginative as practical and prompt to act, with a kingly sense of duty and courage. Her life was one long self-sacrifice—first to her parents, then to her husband and children. All day and much of the night, without haste and without rest, she went about the house attending to our young wants, to my father's comfort, and to the organization of a large household—wearing herself daily to a thinner and slighter frame, which even in age seemed by this means to maintain its activity—till at last when her children were grown up, and her husband's growing infirmities demanded the services of a trained nurse, there came upon her the grievous sense—not the less grievous because wholly unwarranted — that she was "no longer of any use in the world." Twice, I remember, she repeated these fatal words ; and then, not long after, a brief attack of bronchitis parted easily the thread of life, already worn so fine. The manner of her death was as heroic as that of her life, with thought in lucid intervals for all around her, servants, and everybody in the house ; and with closing smile, and words of calm, "All is as it should be."

When my mother died (in January 1881) my father—who had been for the most part absorbed in business or philosophic speculations, and who had given indeed too little time to personal matters—suddenly became aware of the greatness of the loss he had sustained. He woke up from dreamland when it was too late. My mother's silent and untiring forethought had unconsciously to himself been the great support and directing power of his life ; and now he ceased not to say, "The mainspring is broken, the mainspring is broken." His infirmities, which at eighty-three years of age were the natural ills of senile decay, rapidly gained upon him, and a year afterwards, in April 1882, he died and was laid in the same grave with her—in Hove cemetery, between the sea and the Downs, close to the little church to which, years before, we as children had trudged with these our parents every Sunday by the fields and footpaths which then separated the village of Hove from the growing West of Brighton.

My mother had very gracious manners, of gently-smiling dignity, yet her inflexible sense of truth and justice—inflexible especially as regards her own life and conduct—was easily apparent beneath the gentle exterior. Her ideas of social demarcation, etc., were of course of the old school ; and she looked upon it quite as a duty to keep up a certain position in society—as the phrase is. Indeed, though much of the social life of Brighton was in reality irksome to her, I think that she never questioned the duty of conforming to it. But then—unlike many modern mistresses—she never questioned the duty of attending to the wants of dependents ; and her care for the interests of the household servants, and others whom misfortune might bring to her door, was most unfailing and most sincere. The servants in fact were as a rule much devoted to her—though she was by no means lax in matters of discipline and daily superintendence.

A great feature of my mother's character was her love of animals, especially dogs and horses. Outdoor and garden occupations she was also fond of—and I believe her natural inclination would have led her to a rural life. But Brighton offered nothing in this direction—and here again the promptings of her nature were destined only to be thwarted.

MY MOTHER: SOPHIA WILSON CARPENTER (ABOUT 1864).

III

CAMBRIDGE

BETWEEN school and College days I went to Germany for some months. I was already nineteen when I left school, full old enough to go to College, but it did not seem to be decided what was to become of me. I inclined to go into Orders. Possibly my father, dreading this, thought Heidelberg would be an antidote! At any rate I could learn German there. So off I went, lodged with a professor and his Frau for five months, wandered through the woods and over the hills of Heidelberg, heard Bunsen and Kirchhoff lecture on Physics and Chemistry, attended the English church on Sundays, and ate sausages with the Professor and his friends on weekdays. An odd secluded life, seeing but little of the Germans and less of the English, what I chiefly remember of it is those long moony rambles through the woods —not very clearly thinking about anything that I can make out, but wondering, and just waiting—and every now and then chancing in some secluded glade or gorgeous sunset scene upon something that caught my breath and held me still. Indeed on one occasion I perpetrated some rhymes in German about the Neckar—the first verses that I ever wrote. The Professor and his wife chaffed me about my odd ways. I even wore a tall hat to the English church on Sundays! He argued with me about the Bible and about the idiotic habits of my countrymen and women. I resisted his arguments, but secretly they touched me. Ultimately I gave up attending the church, and became so disgusted with my tall hat that when I returned to England I placed it in my carpet-bag ! So I learned something besides German at Heidelberg.

Then came Cambridge. When my father after some hesitation consented to let me go to Cambridge, and asked me which College I would prefer, I said " Trinity Hall," and for my reason that it was a *gentlemanly* college. My father laughed, as he certainly was justified in doing—and I can only wonder now what sort of animal I was then. At any rate the answer shows that notwithstanding all my sufferings at Brighton I had not yet realized what was the true cause of them. There were however other reasons for my choice. One was that Romer, the last Senior Wrangler, was a " Hall " man ; the other was that the same College was now Head of the River. Both events had brought Trinity Hall into notice.

So thither I went, and found myself immediately in the thick of a boating set. The whole College was given up to boating. Not to row or help in the rowing in some way or other was rank apostasy. A few might read besides, and a few—a dozen or two at most—did so. I boated and talked boating slang ; was made stroke of the second boat, and it went down several places ; became Secretary of the Boat Club ; and for two years wore out the seat of my breeches and the cuticle beneath with incessant aquatic service. At the end of that time I got sadly bored with the business, and gave it up. Indeed I was obliged to give it up ; for reading pretty hard for my degree, as I was later on, the two strains together were too much, and my health was breaking down. But so far perhaps boating had not been a bad thing. It was healthy exercise, and brought me in with healthy muscular companions who bothered their heads about no abstruse problems, and for the most part rarely read a book. Fives and rackets too occupied some of my time ; but in athletic sports I was not so successful as I had been at school. At Brighton I had been a good high-jumper, having cleared 5 ft. 3 or 4, a good height in those days—but at Cambridge, probably owing to the relaxing quality of the air, I failed to make any mark. Thus, with games and wine parties and boat suppers, life slid easily onward.

Certainly nothing could be more unlike what I had expected. I had imagined a university where folk would talk Latin naturally and where I, lamely taught at school and late coming from loafing in Germany, would be an outcast and an object of contumely. I found myself at the end of the first term easily head of my year in the College examinations. Myself and another. He, Yate, was the son of a country doctor—keen on boating, but a fellow of some originality and thought as well and of singular gentleness and candour. A friendship sprang up between us ; and for the next year or two we were always together. In examination honours (such as they were) we were quits, and it was sincerely I believe a matter of indifference to both of us which might win the prize. Then he fell ill of rheumatic fever, and ultimately died without taking his degree—my first experience of loss of this kind.

Other friends of this period were Ernest Gray—a very dear and affectionate creature who afterwards became the Vicar and very fatherly pastor of a country parish ; Harry Spedding, son of Anthony Spedding of Bassenthwaite, and nephew of James

Spedding of Baconian fame; and Francis Hyett of Painswick, who afterwards became my brother-in-law. Harry Spedding was one of those extraordinary beings who though quite unable to row himself cherished an immense enthusiasm for boating. Long and thin and weak-chested, hard work in the boats would probably have been fatal to him, but on the banks, running beside the boats and cheering the crews in the races, his pluck and lively humour never failed. Hyett did not take to the river, but kept to racquets and his law-studies, and was really one of the few undergraduates who took any interest in political affairs. In later years he has done much administrative and literary work in connection with his own county.

In coming up to Cambridge it had never occurred to me at the outset to go in for an honour degree; my opinion of the university was too high for that. But after a term or two the tutor to my surprise seriously recommended me to read for the mathematical tripos. I was of course frightfully behindhand in my subjects, but I took a private 'coach,' went through the routine of cram, and ultimately obtained a fellowship.

Mathematics interested me and I read them with a good deal of pleasure—but I have sometimes regretted that three years of my life should have been —as far as study was concerned—nearly entirely absorbed by so special and on the whole so unfruitful a subject. I think every boy (and girl) ought to learn some Geometry and Mechanics; without these the mind lacks form and definiteness, and its grip on the external world is not as strong as it should be; but the higher mathematics (certainly as they are read at Cambridge) are for the most part a mere gymnastic exercise unapplied to actual life and facts, and easily liable to become unhealthy, as all such exercises are.

After my degree, though retaining a certain general interest in the subject, I never again opened a mathematical book with the intention of seriously pursuing its study. I worked however at one time on "Taylor's theorem" in the Differential Calculus, with the object of finding a simpler and more direct proof than Homersham Cox's (the one usually adopted). But not being able to complete the proof, I handed it over to my friend Robert Muirhead, who has adopted and worked it to its conclusion in a contribution to the Proceedings of the Edinburgh Mathematical Society (Vol. 12, Session 1893-4).

It was just about this time of my degree (and curiously late) that my attention began to be turned towards literary production. I had won as an undergraduate—and to my surprise—two College prizes for English Essays (one, by the way, on Civilization); and shortly after my degree, in 1870, I was awarded a university prize (the Burney), £100, for an essay on "The Religious Influence of Art." Meanwhile I kept scribbling, just for my own satisfaction, quantities of verse, very formless and incoherent—but which formed an outlet for my own feelings in the absence of any more tangible way of expressing them.

How well I remember going down, as I so frequently did, alone to the riverside at night, amid the hushed reserve and quiet grace of the old College gardens, and pouring my little soul out to the silent trees and clouds and waters! I don't know what kind of longing it was—something partly sexual, partly religious, and both, owing to my strangely slow-growing temperament, still very obscure and undefined; but anyhow it was something that brooded about and enveloped my life, and makes those hours still stand out for me as the most pregnant of my then existence.

Here are some verses (written in '68) which I give as a specimen of the kind of thought and the half-formed emotional atmosphere in which I brooded, as well as of their juvenile style.

O pale and wan with watching, starless night!
    Far, far beyond thy cloudy banks
    Pass and repass in serried ranks
The flaming watchfires of the infinite—
Gliding and streaming through the realm of space
    In breathless adoration round
    The burning throne whose base profound
Knoweth no resting-place.

To thy deep silence through the moving years
    Cometh no cry of misery,
    No sound of all the things that be,
Upborne from this dark field of feverish tears;
But all the myriad worlds thou dost enfold
    Move on before their Monarch hushed,
    And, looking forth, my soul is crushed
Beneath a weight untold.

O great Humanity, that liest spread
    Beneath the gaze of the sleepless night,
    Who is there who will dare to fight
To raise the tresses of thy drooping head?
Who cares through the immensity of suns?
    Which of the angels shall arise?
    Oh! heavy and dark the burden lies
On all thy noblest ones.

Far off the morning stars may shout and sing,
    For there is Love and Joy and Peace,
    And Life—true life that cannot cease—
But here the ghastly shuddering of Death's wing.
And here faint whispers only come to die
    Upon the threshold of our hearts,
    Voices at which the sad soul starts
With a half-uttered sigh.

O hanging cloud, O scarcely stirring trees,
O velvet waters moved to sound
By the gliding fishes' bound,
O Willow, whispering to the fitful breeze,
O gentle touch of the sweet summer air,
O solitary owl, alone,
Nursing thy joy in low weird tone
Within thy leafy lair!

O one and all, unveil! and let us see
The flaming soul of world-wide Love
Burning behind you, far above,
Beneath, deep-fountained life, strange mystery!
Unveil! O night that washest Earth's dark shore,
O suns, through space that ever roll,
O Love, clasping us body and soul
For evermore!

Curiously enough, as it happened, I was practically offered a Fellowship before I took my degree. The College was in want of an assistant Lecturer. There were three clerical Fellowships (the others being connected with the Bar as a profession), and one of these clerical Fellowships had lately become vacant by Leslie Stephen, who held it, relinquishing his Orders. It was understood that I was going into the Church; it seemed probable that I should take a fair degree; and for the rest, who could be found so suitable—so mild, so docile, so decently mannered and generally unaggressive—as the young man in question! Accordingly one day the tutor (Henry Latham) sounded me on the subject. I conveyed to him that I had not changed my intention of being ordained, and that I rather liked the prospect of staying on at Cambridge in connection with the College; and it became practically understood that if things turned out favorably that should be my destiny.

And things turned out accordingly. In the Mathematical Tripos of 1868 I came out tenth wrangler, which was a sufficiently high degree to justify a Fellowship at a small College ; and in the autumn of that year I came into residence at Trinity Hall as a Lecturer ; shortly afterwards I was elected to a clerical Fellowship ; and in June '69 I was ordained Deacon by the Bishop of Ely.

The story of my connection with the Church may be soon told. Brought up in the philosophical Broad Churchism of my father, with an ever-expanding horizon, my mind had at no time undergone any revulsion of feeling such as could be called a religious crisis ; no sense of antagonism to the Church and its teachings had been developed. Though quite aware that my opinions were vastly different from those of the ordinary Churchman, I perhaps hardly appreciated *how* far I had drifted ; and with an easy faith in progress, such as I had, it seemed to me that anyhow in a few years the Church, widening and growing from within, would become adapted to the times, and be a perfectly habitable and a useful institution.

As soon as I was ordained I had services in the College Chapel to read, and sermons to preach—with the usual accompaniment of winks and grins from the fellow-students, shufflings of hassocks, racings half-dressed through the prayers on winter mornings, with clicks of watches timing the performance, and all the gaping signs of unconcealed boredom ; but I thought I would like to see something more satisfactory and more definite in the way of Church work than that, and accordingly took a curacy at St. Edward's under a dry evangelical of the steel-knife and lemon-juice type, named Pearson.

If I had nursed in my mind any sentiment of

romance in connection with ecclesiastical affairs, it was soon expelled by these experiences. A peep behind the scenes was enough. The deadly Philistinism of a little provincial congregation ; the tradesmen and shopkeepers in their sleek Sunday best ; the petty vulgarities and hypocrisies ; the discordant music of the choir ; the ignoble scenes in the vestry and the resumed saintly expression on returning into the church ; the hollow ring and the sour edge of the incumbent's voice ; and the fatuous faces upturned to receive the communion at the altar steps—all these were worse, considerably worse, than the undisguised heathenism of the chapel performance.

It was not long before I began to have serious misgivings about the step I had taken. Still I did not torment myself ; and when in the following June (1870) the time arrived for my ordination as a priest, I prepared myself quite philosophically to go through the ceremony.

But here an interesting hitch occurred. In the Bishop's examination preparatory to the ordination, the candidates had among other things to write a Life of Abraham ; and such was my optimistic confidence in the breadth of the episcopal mind that I quite candidly and without any particular misgiving committed to paper the view which I had picked up, I think from Bunsen the historian, and which is also adopted by Dean Stanley in his *Jewish Church*—that Abraham's intended immolation of Isaac was a relic of Moloch-worship, and of the old practice of human sacrifices, and that the "voice of God" which bade him substitute the ram did indeed figure the evolution of the human conscience to a higher ideal of worship than that in vogue among savage nations. This paper, containing so dreadful a heresy, I sent up without a qualm ! But on arriving myself some days later at the Palace at Ely, the Bishop (Harold Browne) soon after the first greetings called me into his study and confronted me with the offending passage. At first I had some difficulty in understanding what the trouble was, but when the Bishop in grave tones began to remind me that the sacrifice of Isaac was a type—a type and a prefigurement of that greater sacrifice of Jesus, and that the whole Biblical scheme of salvation rested four-square upon this incident (not forgetting the ram), I immediately saw that the fat was in the fire, and that there was now no escaping a solemn discussion on the Atonement.

And to that it came. Our conversation, interrupted by dinner, was resumed again late in the evening; and when all the other clerics and candidates had gone to bed the reverend Father-in-God and I sat up till past twelve discussing all the main and side issues of Theology! On the latter he was easy enough. I told him plainly that I did not believe in the historical accuracy of the Old Testament; and he admitted that there were gaps! Even the Thirty-nine Articles were to be swallowed in the lump, and not in detail, so to speak. But on the Atonement the discussion narrowed. Here was a vital point. My views were woolly in outline, sadly blurred by the Broad Church mysticism of F. D. Maurice, and I confess I had some difficulty in formulating them. The Bishop merely shook his head, asked me to "say that again," and declared that he could not understand. It ended by his requesting me to *write out* my doctrine; and going to bed himself he left me sitting up for a couple of hours more for this purpose! In the morning I handed him, before breakfast, my mystic script. After breakfast he once more called me into his study, said he had read the paper, that it was thoughtful and all that, but that he could not say that he really followed it, and that he was sure it was *not* the doctrine of the Church of England.

We were then within a few minutes of the commencement of the service. I took for granted that he would not ordain me; but after a pause he said "I cannot refuse to ordain you; but I do not think your views are those of the Church." I think he hoped that *I* should then retire of my own accord. However I said nothing but took it all as settled in my favour, and in less than an hour the apostolic hands were on my head.

After luncheon the good old man, not without a certain anxiety and *épanchement,* put his arm in mine and walked with me round the garden. I remember there was a chaffinch hopping about, and a longish discourse followed on creation and suffering and vicarious sacrifice, which I listened to with due deference; but it did not seem to me to lead to any conclusion; and soon the time came for us to leave the palace, and I saw him no more.

It may be imagined that I did not find my profession any more satisfactory after being made priest than before. He of the sour knife-edge, my superincumbent, left St. Edward's, being translated into a canon of Carlisle, and was succeeded, curiously enough, by Maurice himself. That was I think early in 1871.

Of this transaction, by which F. D. Maurice became incumbent of St. Edward's, it may be worth while to say a few words. Maurice had lately come to Cambridge as Professor of Moral Philosophy. As far as his moral worth was concerned, the choice was a good one. There was an ineffable personal charm about him, of moral earnestness and deep feeling, connecting itself somehow with his lofty venerable head and extraordinary modesty. But of his philosophy perhaps the less said the better. He saw facts which doubtless it is impossible adequately to translate into language. Certainly it was impossible for him. To see him struggling with the root-ideas which he was always trying, and vainly, to express, to see him perspiring with effort, tapping his forehead with his fingers, shutting his eyes, and still only framing broken sentences, was really touching. The net result among the students was, as I have hinted, one of personal devotion to him, but of utter bafflement as to his teaching. It is said that one student hearing that the great man was giving a course of lectures on the "I" (as he was), made his way down to the *Physiological* schools and after many inquiries finding that no lectures were being given on the *Eye*, came back again with the conclusion that the whole affair was a myth!

Well, Maurice having expressed a wish to take some practical "duty" in Cambridge, and the living of St. Edward's falling vacant at that time, a movement was got up in the College to offer the living to him. The living was in the gift of the Fellows of Trinity Hall, and most of the Fellows were favorable to the proposal. But an unexpected difficulty arose in the person of the Master (Dr. Geldart). Not that the Master himself (who was an old sporting man, more than anything else) cared a button about the matter, but because his wife, Mrs. Geldart, was accustomed to attend St. Edward's and fuss round the parson there, and *she* strongly disapproved of any one so heretical as Maurice occupying the pulpit!

I was a Fellow of the College at the time, and the scenes round the table as we discussed the knotty question were most amusing. The obvious embarrassment of the old Master when the question arose as to *why* he thought Maurice so dangerous ; his mysterious references to the opinions of other people (his wife) and his candid disavowal of any knowledge on these subjects himself; the guffaws of Henry Fawcett (then Professor of Political Economy and afterwards Postmaster-General) as he called for his chop and settled himself down to enjoy a scene to which his blindness was little drawback ; the quips of H. D. Warr, one of the Fellows ; the muttered blasphemies of our Dean (Hopkins), who couldn't think why we wasted time "over such blasted nonsense" ; the ingenious surmises of the barrister fellows generally as to what Maurice's opinions might conceivably be ; and the politic expediencies of the Tutor (Latham) who at last silenced the Master and his Missus by producing a letter from the Bishop of Carlisle (Goodwin) endorsing Maurice with a friendly pat on the back : all this was as good as a play.

Maurice was installed in the living early in 1871, and thenceforth read the services and prayed and preached, with that profundity of earnest innocence which was so characteristic of him, and which contrasted strangely with the manner of his election, and more strangely still with the cheap commercialism of his congregation.

Maurice had no great ear for music. The organist and choir of flat-singing shop-girls revelled in florid hymns about the "blood-of-the-Lamb." Maurice besought me to alter this and induce them to sing again those fine old hymns like the "Old Hundredth." A nice task for an amiable curate !

It was curious that after having been brought up in and adopted Maurice's views, I should now, having become his curate, feel so uncomfortable as I did. But so it was. I had had experience in the short space of a year and a half, of three spiritual superiors—each in a sense more favorable than the last ; and yet my sense of aggravation continually increased. I saw a good deal of Maurice. He was kindness itself. I opened out my difficulties to him ; and he was I think troubled to find I could not reconcile myself to the position which *he* occupied apparently without difficulty. But to me his attitude was a growing wonder. I could quite understand his historical-philosophical view of the Creeds and the Old Testament, and that he could read into them a deep and necessary meaning, satisfactory to his own mind ; I had in fact been already, long before, initiated into this Broad Church attitude by my father. But when it came to standing up oneself in church and reciting these documents to a congregation who (as one knew perfectly well) did not understand a word of them, and practically received them in their grossest sense and in a spirit of mere superstition, then I felt it *was* necessary to draw the line somewhere ! It was not that I then, or at any time, made a trouble of the conformity of my own *views* with those of the Church ; for I thought and I think now, that if a man feels he can do useful work, and congenial to himself, in that connection, he had better remain where he is until he is kicked out ; and that seeing the variety of interpretations that Church doctrines are capable of, it is rather for the Church to decide whether *his* interpretations are within its pale, or not, than for him to do so. But the trouble to me was a practical one—namely the insuperable *feeling* of falsity and dislocation which I experienced, and which accompanied all my professional work from the reading of the services to the visiting of old women in their almshouses—who were, one could see, goaded on to hypocrisy by the position in which they were placed—and who would hastily shuffle a Bible or prayer-book on to the table, when they saw the parson coming. This sense of falsity grew on me more and more till I felt the situation to be intolerable.

It is remarkable—certainly I have found it so in my own life—how little its greater changes are one's own choice, and in a sense, how much they are forced upon one by necessity—sometimes by an outward necessity, sometimes by an inner and necessary, though perhaps unconscious evolution of one's own nature. No doubt I *thought* about this matter a great deal, argued to myself the question of my conformity to the Church, and the pros and cons of remaining in it—worried myself, passed sleepless nights—and felt generally unhinged over it; but all this conscious argument brought me no nearer to a decision. Deep below I felt that some sort of sheer necessity was driving me on. Sometimes when I was occupied with, and thinking about, quite other things, a kind of shiver would run down my back: "You've got to go, you've got to go," and I felt as if I was being pushed to the edge of a steep place.

For it was not altogether easy to face the situation. I was doing very well, in a pecuniary sense, at Cambridge, making with my Fellowship and small offices as lecturer, librarian, etc., £500 or £600 a year, and prospects good for the future; the abandonment of my Orders would probably mean the loss of my Fellowship, and possibly also that I should have to leave Cambridge altogether. And it did not seem quite reasonable to risk all this for what might after all be only a Quixotic fancy.

But blessed is Necessity which cuts all arguments short! By the middle of May 1871 I felt so ill and wretched that I *could* not stay on even a few weeks to the end of the term. I begged off my lectures, left Maurice to find another curate, and ran away!

Meanwhile other threads and clues of life were developing. Up to my degree (January '68) I had lived singularly apart from any intellectual or literary circles. As an undergraduate my companions had mostly been boating men. After my degree however I came naturally into a more literary society, consisting partly of the younger Fellows of Colleges and partly of the more go-ahead students who had not yet taken their degrees. One or two of the more thoughtful undergrads of my own College also leaned towards me. I belonged to one or two little societies which used to meet and discuss literary or other topics. To one of these, which W. K. Clifford organized, I used, after I became a curate, to rush round on Sunday evenings after church—in time to take part in the reading of Mazzini's *Duty of Man*; illustrated by a plentiful accompaniment of claret-cup and smoke! Clifford was a kind of Socratic presiding genius at these meetings—with his Satyr-like face, tender heart, wonderfully suggestive, paradoxical manner of conversation, and blasphemous treatment of the existing gods. He invented just at that time a kind of inverted Doxology which ran:—

> O Father, Son and Holy Ghost—
> We wonder which we hate the most.
> Be Hell, which they prepared before,
> Their dwelling now and evermore!

and his influence, combined with that of Mazzini, was certainly part of my education at that period. If it had by any chance come to the Bishop's ears that I attended these meetings there is little wonder about his hesitation to ordain me!

There was another Cambridge heretic with whom I not unfrequently consorted—Lock of King's—who certainly by his attainments and ability ought to have been made a Fellow of his College, but his views and the audacity with which he ventilated them proved a fatal obstacle. Having to write a 'Varsity prize-poem he sat up all the preceding night to do it, worked himself up into a kind of prophetic frenzy and managed under cover of a forecast of republican utopianism to introduce the lines :—

> Since they traded in holy things, and treated the people like beasts,
> The priests shall be slain and the kings shall be drowned in the blood of the priests.

I don't feel so certain of the exact words of the first line as I do of the second, but I hope the author of both (who was then, of course, an undergraduate) will forgive my quotation of them. It is hardly to be wondered at that in those days he was *not* made a Fellow !

One of the undergraduates of my own College with whom I made quite a friendship at this time was Anthony Beck. He came up to Cambridge, a poor student from the country district of Castle Rising in Norfolk, on the shores of the Wash—he also with his head full of rhymes and verses, which he had written since he was a boy of eight or ten, to the wonderment and delight of his widower father, who prophesied in no uncertain tone, a nook in Westminster Abbey for his poet son. Beck was a bright, capable fellow, with a slight stoop, and a stammer, and a good-humoured way of laughing at his own oddities. He took the University by surprise by carrying off, in his first year, the prize poem on Dante—having been fain, it is said, to work up the subject by reading Cary's translation (which he could not afford to buy) on the bookstalls. Then he wrote another prize poem on Runnymede, which delighted him chiefly I think on account of a misprint which occurred in the printed copy. There was an eloquent passage in the poem, describing the sunrise of freedom in England, and something about the clouds heralding the approach of morning :—

Streaks rosy-tinted vanward of the sun—

which the printer, in a materialistic mood, altered into :—

Steaks rosy-tinted vanward of the sun.

These rosy-tinted steaks gave Beck, I believe, as much pleasure as he got from all the *kudos* of his poetic success. He worked away at Classics, took a good first-class, and ultimately became a fellow and tutor of the College. But his vein of poetic feeling and romance, possibly too soon ripe, ran itself out, and he never carried on this line of production or published anything. His mind, perhaps from the same cause, took on a slightly cynical cast ; he lapsed into the ordinary channels of lecturing and coaching, then married and had a large family, and so gave himself up to the work-a-day routine of College life.

At the time I mention he and I chummed together a good deal—indeed there was a touch of romance in our attachment—we compared literary notes, went abroad together once or twice, and after he was made a Fellow, had rooms adjoining each other, and spent many and many an evening in common. He became a favorite in the general society of the younger dons and B.A.'s, on account of his brightness, naturalness and frankly avowed enjoyment of the good things of life.

As for myself, for a couple of years or so after my degree I entered with great zest into this academically intellectual existence—these chit-chat societies, these little supper parties, these lingerings over the wine in combination-room after dinner—where every subject in Heaven and Earth was discussed, with the university man's perfect freedom of thought and utterance, but also with his perfect absence of practical knowledge or of intention to apply his theories to any practical issue. It was helpful no doubt especially as a solvent of old ideas and prejudices; but after a time it began to pall upon me and bore me. There was a vein of what might be called painful earnestness in my character. These talking machines were, many of them, very obnoxious to me. And then of what avail was the brain, when the heart demanded so much, and demanding was still unsatisfied?

Looking back, I think with regard to this last-mentioned matter, that the fault was probably a good deal on my own side. Strong as had been two or three attachments of this and my earlier undergraduate period, and deeply as they had moved me (to a degree indeed which I should be almost ashamed to confess); yet for the most part, owing to my reserved habits, and the self-repressive education I had received—combined with the fatuities of public opinion—I consumed my own smoke, and did not give myself the utterance I ought to have given. By concealing myself I was unfair to my friends, and at the same time suffered torments which I need not have suffered.

As I have already said, during the time shortly after my degree I scribbled a great deal in verse form merely as an outlet to my own feelings, and without much attention to conventionalities of style and rhythms—though of course along the ordinary lines of versification. But now came my introduction to the poet who was destined so deeply to influence my life. It was in the summer of '68, I believe (though it may have been '69), that one day H. D. Warr—one of the Fellows of Trinity Hall, and a very brilliant and amusing man—came into my room with a blue-covered book in his hands (William Rossetti's edition of Whitman's poems) only lately published, and said :—

"Carpenter, what do you think of this?"

I took it from him, looked at it, was puzzled, and asked him what he thought of it.

"Well," he said, "I thought a good deal of it at first, but I don't think I can stand any more of it."

With those words he left me ; and I remember lying down then and there on the floor and for half an hour poring, pausing, wondering. I could not make the book out, but I knew at the end of that time that I intended to go on reading it. In a short time I bought a copy for myself, then I got *Democratic Vistas*, and later on (after three or four years) *Leaves of Grass* complete.

From that time forward a profound change set in within me. I remember the long and beautiful summer nights, sometimes in the College garden by the riverside, sometimes sitting at my own window which itself overlooked a little old-fashioned garden enclosed by grey and crumbling walls ; sometimes watching the silent and untroubled dawn ; and feeling all the time that my life deep down was flowing out and away from the surroundings and traditions amid which I lived—a current of sympathy carrying it westward, across the Atlantic. I wrote to Whitman, obtained his books from him, and occasional postcardial responses. But outwardly, and on the surface, my life went on as usual.

What made me cling to the little blue book from the beginning was largely the poems which celebrate comradeship. That thought, so near and personal to me, I had never before seen or heard fairly expressed; even in Plato and the Greek authors there had been something wanting (so I thought). If there had only been those few poems they would have been sufficient to hold me; but there were other pieces: there was "Crossing Brooklyn Ferry," "Out of the Rocked Cradle," "President Lincoln's Funeral Hymn," and the prose Preface [1]—and then afterwards *Democratic Vistas*.

On the whole at that time I thought most, I believe, of the prose writings. *Democratic Vistas* was a mine of new thought. Both this and the little blue book I read over and over again, and still they were new. I had read a great deal of Wordsworth about the time of my degree; then Shelley captivated and held me for a long time; portions of Plato and of Shakespeare I had read repeatedly; but never had I found anything approaching these writings of Whitman's for their inexhaustible quality and power of making one return to them.

Yet all this time, or for three or four years, I believe my interest in them was mainly intellectual—that is, they were producing an intellectual ferment in me, but I had not distinctly come into touch with the dominant individuality behind them, nor felt that

[1] It is curious how æsthetic in style this Preface is, though written in 1855, rather before the English æsthetic movement, and how, perhaps on account of its slight affectation of manner, it was abandoned by Whitman afterwards.

they were re-shaping my moral and artistic ideals. This is partly shown by the fact that I continued all these years, and up to '74 or so, writing verse along the usual lines and upon the usual subjects. Wordsworth's "Tintern Abbey" and Shelley's "Adonais" and "Prometheus" still ruled my artistic and emotional conceptions; and withal, living as I was in an atmosphere of literary criticism and finesse, mere academic technique seemed to me a great matter, and I made great struggles to attain to it.

Though I was not particularly successful in these efforts towards the conventional in literature, yet I have no doubt they were very helpful in giving me some sort of training in the power of handling words and rhythmical forms—and it was a true instinct which led me through this instead of urging me to leap at once into the ocean of metrical freedom, so difficult to navigate with success. Anyhow so it was that while (in other things as well as in literature) my inner scarcely conscious nature was setting outwards in a swift current from the shores of conventionality, under the influence of its new genius, into deeps it little divined, my external self was still busy in a kind of backwater, and working hard if by any means it might attain to a creditable or even a possible existence in these channels!

But by '71 and '72 I began to feel that continued existence in my surroundings was becoming impossible to me. The tension and dislocation of my life was increasing, and I became aware that a crisis was approaching. In May of the former year I had taken a holiday and got away from Cambridge. In October I returned to my lecturing and College work, but not to the church duties; and all '72 I continued on, going through the daily round—but in a torpid, perfunctory manner—feeling probably that I ought to throw it all up, yet without the pluck to do so till I was fairly forced. By the end of '72 I was obviously ill and incapacitated, and when I asked for leave of absence for a couple of terms it was readily granted —my own object in asking (so I put it to myself) being to get quite away and for long enough to be able to estimate my position and future action fairly and deliberately.

The year '73 was an important one for me. Feeling shattered and exhausted, and with a big holiday before me, I determined to go to Italy. It was a new life and I may almost say inspiration. I spent two months in Rome, a month in the Bay of Naples, and a month at Florence. I was alone, still alone; but the healing influences of the air and the sunshine were upon me. Amid the bright external life of the day, and the rich records and suggestions of the past, all the questions which had been tormenting me faded away. I *thought* about them no more; but new elements came into my life which decided them for me.

The Greek sculpture had a deep effect. The other things, pictures, architecture, etc., interested me much from an historical or æsthetic point of view; but this had something more, a germinative influence on my mind, which adding itself to and corroborating the effect of Whitman's poetry, left with me as it were the seed of new conceptions of life. The marvellous beauty and cleanliness of the human body as presented by the Greek mind, the way in which the noblest passions of the soul—the tender pitying love of Diana for Endymion, the haughty inspiration of Juno, the heroic endurance of the fallen warrior, the childlike gladness of the faun—were united and blended with the corporeal form—or rather scarcely conceived of as separated from it ; the emotional atmosphere which went with this, the Greek ideal of the free and gracious life of man at one with nature and the cosmos—so remote from the current ideals of commercialism and Christianity !—to become aware of all this in the midst of that " delicate air " and delightful landscape and climate of Italy, was indeed a new departure for me.

There are magnificent fragments of Greek sculpture in the British Museum, not forgetting the priceless frieze of the Parthenon—things which to a skilled artistic eye are as suggestive as any that can be found—but to me the great range and completeness of the Italian galleries, the almost perfect Cupids, fauns, Venuses, athletes, warriors, youths, maidens, sages, gods, in unending procession under that southern sky, gave a poetic impulse which I could not, at any rate at that time, have surmised from a broken marble seen in a London fog !

Nor must I omit, as part of the Greek impression, a visit to the Temples of Pæstum—which helped to give a habitation in the mind's eye to those strings of sculptured figures, exiles in alien Rome, and to intensify the sense of harmonious life and divine proportion which they had excited.

I stayed in Italy long enough to see, at Florence, the fireflies skim and flicker over the blossoming wheat-fields of May and June, and then returned home, to find that without worrying about it a change had taken place in my mental attitude which would make my return to the Cambridge life impossible.

And here I must not omit to mention another influence which played a large part in the shaping of my life at this time. Most men own a deep debt to women's influence in the ordering and guidance of their lives. I cannot say that I have felt this. With the exception of my mother and one other person, I cannot remember a single case in which a woman came to me as a strong motive-force or inspiration, or as a help or a guide in doubt or difficulty. Perhaps on the emotional side women did not supply what I needed; while on the intellectual side a woman with decisive, originative, authentic mind is certainly not often to be met with. Such a woman, however, of the latter type, was the person to whom I allude, and whom I may call Olivia (which indeed was one of her Christian names).

She was a connection by marriage with one of my sisters, a woman about fifty, still retaining traces of an exceedingly handsome youth. Married, but separated from her husband; artistic to the finger-tips; brought up in Italy, and loving the South; hating everything British and Philistine and commercial; detesting the Bible and religion; she had fought her way through social odium and disability, and then through severe illness and suffering, till she was but the wreck (she used to say) of her former self. Nevertheless a remarkable fire and enthusiasm still survived in her, and though one of those natures who see everything rather violently black or white, yet the decisive artistic quality of her mind was most refreshing and inspiring. I have given some general account founded on her life and character in a separate sketch.[1] Sufficient to say here that her conversations on literature and art, her criticisms of art work (and of my own efforts), her views on marriage, on religion —though we disagreed a thousand times and often saw things from opposite points—were most helpful to me. They served to liberate my mind, corrected in many respects the native vagueness of my thought,

[1] "Francesca," in *Sketches from Life.*

and certainly helped me greatly on the road to choose my own way in life. I find a scrap of a letter from her, written during this period of my suffering and doubt as to my continuance at Cambridge and in the Church: "I ought not to write this morning, *caro mio*, I am too depressed. It is terrible to me to know how you suffer. Your letter last night made me cold to the finger-ends. One thing is clear anyhow, your present life is intolerable, *change it you must*. . . . When you get away from the depressing influence of your present life with all its worries you will breathe and clap your hands and thank God!" It is needless to say that my move to Italy and my preparations for abandoning Orders were things truly after her own heart.

And now for the first time I seriously entertained the idea of taking to literature as a profession. I saw that my Cambridge career was at an end, and that I must do something else; and for a time (though only for a short time) it appeared to me that I might make a living by writing.

I believe I felt that I really had something to write, that I must write, though certainly my mind and purpose was only vague as yet; and as to the professional side of the question, though I realized, I only partly realized, how difficult it would be to make writing of any kind 'pay.' There were plenty of 'candid friends' however to impress *that* upon me, and I well remember the derisive chorus of the other Fellows which greeted (at some College meeting or other) the announcement of my intention! I stayed at home, at Brighton, during the summer and autumn and gathered my verses—those more careful and academic productions which I had perpetrated in the late years—together in a volume for publication. Of course no publisher would take the volume at

MY SISTER LIZZIE.

his risk, and I was content, after a few efforts, to pay the piper myself for the pleasure of seeing the work in print, and on the chance of its leaping to a world-wide success! The book, under the title *Narcissus, and other Poems,* was published in November 1873, and needless to say fell practically dead—a few notices, mostly depreciatory, in the papers, a few copies bought by friends, and then it ceased to stir.

Nor was there any reason why it should stir. There was nothing of any moment in the book; only a vague sentiment of Nature and humanity running through, not definite enough at any point to carry weight; and really not so much of the author's own self in it, as of his effort to reach a certain literary standard. Perhaps one of the best of the pieces, both in form and intention, was "The Artist to his Lady": which I remember expressed in its indefinite way the dominant feeling which I had those last years, of being drawn away from my surroundings by another ideal than that which I could realize at Cambridge. Of the other pieces, "The Carpenter and the King"—an extract from an unfinished revolutionary drama of which the scene was laid in Austria and Italy in 1848—indicates a certain advance in political ideas and the germ of future developments; while "The Angel of Death and Life" contains in embryo some of the dominant conceptions of *Towards Democracy.*

It so happened that at the time of publication of *Narcissus,* in November '73, I was at Cannes, in the South of France, whither I had gone with my sister Lizzie (to whom I was much attached) on account of her illness. I stayed two or three weeks, and then it became necessary for me to return home, in order to make preparations for and be present at our College Fellows' meeting at Christmas. It had of course become quite imperative that I should make some distinct announcement of my intentions with regard to the future ; and for my part I had now quite decided that I would relinquish my Orders, and go through the legal formalities of unfrocking myself. Sincerely I hoped that this would lead to my disappearance from Cambridge. If, before, I had recoiled from such a thought, the torpor and misery I had experienced since then had quite altered my point of view.

And in all this matter it was not by any means only the clerical difficulty that troubled me. As I have hinted before I had come to feel that the so-called intellectual life of the University was (to me at any rate) a fraud and a weariness. These everlasting discussions of theories which never came anywhere near actual life, this cheap philosophizing and ornamental cleverness, this endless book-learning, and the queer cynicism and boredom underlying—all impressed me with a sense of utter emptiness. The prospect of spending the rest of my life in that atmosphere terrified me ; and as I had seemed to see already the vacuity and falsity of society life at Brighton, so in another form I seemed to see the same thing here.

And now it dawned upon me that my abandonment of Orders, instead of being a thing to be dreaded, would be my veritable deliverance, and would provide just that valid excuse for breaking with my old life, which otherwise might prove hard to find. When friends, relations, Fellows of the College, and others, were all urging upon me the folly of committing professional suicide, I felt that the argument of *conscience*—though not really to myself the final and convincing thing (since that was Necessity)—

was one which I could make use of, and which I should *have* to make use of, since every one, whether I liked it or not, would credit me with it !

I therefore, to avoid all possible lapses or failures that might ensue if I left the matter over to a personal explanation at the College meeting, *wrote* beforehand to the Master of Trinity Hall, explaining that I had entirely made up my mind to formally relinquish my Orders, and placing my Fellowship in his hands, in accordance with what I supposed would be necessary under the circumstances. Then two or three weeks afterwards I followed in person to join in the Christmas festivities.

At that time, every year at the Christmas season, not only did all the Fellows assemble for the transaction of College business at our meetings, but there was a week of dinner-parties, with often fifty or sixty guests each evening (no women) and very serious junketings ! This was, of course, in Commemoration of the Founder of the College—and with money partly left for the purpose. We sat down to dinner, a most extensive one, at six o'clock, which lasted, with the passing of the loving-cup and the serving of wine and dessert, till about eight ; then we adjourned to the combination-room to take coffee and to chat for an hour ; after which the elder men generally resolved themselves into whist parties, while the younger would retire in batches to college rooms in order to smoke and drink brandies and soda. Soon after ten *supper* was served ; and returning to the combination-room one found a table spread with the traditional boar's head, supplemented by oysters, game-pie, and other little delicacies. In order to stimulate the exhausted powers, bottled stout was found useful at this period. Some of the old hands did no scant justice to the supper ; others remained at the whist tables. Finally, and as the *coup de grâce*, about 11.30 hot milk punch and roast apples appeared!

It was generally the duty of the younger Fellows to look after the ceremonies a little, to arrange the whist parties, invite the guests to supper, and ply them with meat and drink. I remember one evening, somewhat past midnight, finding the Mayor of Cambridge (who had been invited) by himself in a remote corner discussing a roast apple. I went and got a good big glass of milk-punch, and brought it him, saying, "Now, Mr. Mayor, I'm sure this will do you good"—but he waived it away, with a comical gesture, replying: "No, no more—I *can't* drink any more, thank you; but this apple is delicious!" Shortly afterwards, leaning on my arm, he was to be seen carefully descending the stairs to his carriage.

My feelings at this particular Christmas were of rather a mixed kind. As to the Fellows they were berating me of one accord for my madness in writing to the Master and practically resigning my Fellowship before it was proved needful to do so; also for my supposed Quixotism in troubling about my Orders. As to the Dean, being of course in Orders himself he made short work of the difficulty: "It is all such tomfoolery," he said, "that it doesn't matter whether you say you believe in it, or whether you say you don't. Look at my sermons in chapel now—are they not models of unaffected piety! You let the matter drop, and it will all blow over."

Among the Fellows and members of my own and other colleges with whom at that time I was often in contact were Henry Fawcett (afterwards Postmaster-General), Henry Latham (Tutor of Trinity Hall), Charles Wentworth Dilke, W. K. Clifford, George Darwin, Robert Romer (afterwards Lord Justice), Lumley Smith, Henry Fielding Dickens,

Augustine Birrell, Edward Beck (present Master of Trinity Hall), and others of course. Most of these—though not all—did their best from their different points of view to dissuade me from the course I had embarked on ; but I was not going to be dissuaded. It was obvious to me that half-measures would be no good, and that if I wanted to make my escape from Cambridge I must throw the whole thing overboard ; so underneath all the unpleasantness there was the secret satisfaction of feeling that unknown to everybody I was really going to gain a point instead of lose one !

What kind of debates they had in College meeting over my case I don't know, for of course I was not present, but it was conveyed to me that though there was a general wish that I should stay on as before, yet if I persisted in relinquishing my Orders, it would be doubtful if I could be asked to remain in the College—owing to the scandal of the thing ! As to the question whether my relinquishment of Orders should involve the loss of my fellowship, that was adjourned for the present.

So again next term I did not rejoin ; but remained at home, at Brighton, occupied with another important literary project ! *Moses* : a drama. Early one morning I had woken from sleep in the midst of a heavy thunderstorm, with an extraordinarily vivid conception (I don't know how it came to be there) of Moses on the top of Sinai. Then and there I wrote out a long soliloquy (Act II. Sc. 1), which now insisted on expanding itself into a considerable poem in dramatic form—the ruling idea being to take the Bible story, treat it in a rationalistic way, as an obscure tradition of an actual event, and to show Moses as a noble but entirely human reformer, embarrassed in his great enterprise more by the apathy, stupidity and superstition of the people he desired to save than by anything else.[1]

Meanwhile through solicitors I set the ecclesiastical law in operation with a view to my unfrockment. The process takes six months for its completion. It was not necessary for me to see my Bishop again ; but I had one or two gravely regretful letters from him. I spent the 'Long' at Cambridge—July and August—the last 'Long' that I spent there ; and during that time received the legal document which rendered me once again a layman.

These summer vacations spent at Cambridge were the part of my university life that—even from my undergraduate days—I had most enjoyed. Chapels and lectures were in abeyance, the monotonous tyranny of boating-practice and training was unknown ; a few students only were up, perhaps twenty or so at our College—but these would be the more intelligent and congenial spirits. During the long morning from nine to two one got through a lot of reading unhindered by lectures and other interruptions ; then came afternoons canoeing up the river, two or three together, in the dreamy sheen of the water and the overhanging willows, or through beds of iris ; or bathing ; or playing fives or rackets ; or walking the country lanes, or sitting long on some turfy bank with a friend. Sometimes we would make quite a party and go, a fleet of canoes, with provisions, far up the river and not return till dark. Then as a rule there were two or three hours more work in the evening, though sometimes this was broken through by some little entertainment.

[1] The drama is now [1911] republished under the title *The Promised Land*, and the soliloquy in question is given in the first part of Act II. Sc. 1. As a reflection of the thoughts which were, I suppose, occupying my mind at that time, it may have some slight interest.

What a curious romance ran through all that life—and yet on the whole, with few exceptions, how strangely unspoken it was and unexpressed! This succession of athletic and even beautiful faces and figures, what a strange magnetism they had for me, and yet all the while how insurmountable for the most part was the barrier between! It was as if a magic flame dwelt within one, burning, burning, which one could not put out, and yet whose existence one might on no account reveal.[1] How the walks under the avenues of trees at night, and by the riversides, were haunted full of visionary forms for which in the actual daylight world there seemed no place!

Yet as time went on I think it must have become clearer to me that Cambridge never would afford in this direction the actual that I wanted. Expectation grew dry at the fount, and torpor and distress in the last year or two took the place of the romance of the years before. Somehow I think I must have dimly understood that the trouble arose partly from a deep want of sympathy between myself and the whole mental attitude, mode of life, and ideals of the university, and of the gilded or silvered youth who lived and moved within it; for I remember that on the memorable journey from Cannes homewards, when I was revolving the whole situation—the abandonment of my Orders and Fellowship, the failure (as it already appeared) of my first literary venture, and the doubt of what I should or *could* do in the future, it suddenly flashed upon me, with a vibration through my whole body, that I would and must somehow go and make my life with the mass of the people and the manual workers.

It was in pursuance of this last idea that shortly

[1] This of course would all be very different now [1915].

after the eventful College meeting above mentioned I went to see James Stuart at Trinity, who was just then organizing the first outlines of the University Extension Lecturing Scheme, and asked him if he could find me a place on it. He agreed to do so; and suggested that I should take the subject of Astronomy. I consented, and shortly after was appointed to begin a course of Lectures (in October 1874) at Leeds, Halifax and Skipton.

SELF, IN ABOUT 1875.

IV

UNIVERSITY EXTENSION AND NORTHERN TOWNS

I SOMETIMES think myself singularly fortunate in the way in which my dreams of life (the wildest and most unlikely) have from time to time been realized ; but in this connection I have noticed two things that have generally happened—one is that the new life-purpose would come, to begin with, with great force, making me believe it was going to be realized at once, and that then it would seem to fail and almost be abandoned, and then again, some years after, it *would* be realized. The second thing is (and this is in accordance with the general law of the " cussedness of things ") that just in the moment of the realization of the first endeavour, *another* ideal would make itself felt, which would in some degree supersede the former.

It had come on me with great force that I would go and throw in my lot with the mass-people and the manual workers. I took up the University Extension work perhaps chiefly because it seemed to promise this result. As a matter of fact it merely brought me into the life of the commercial classes ; and for seven years I served—instead of the Rachel of my heart's desire—a Leah to whom I was not greatly attached. Nevertheless this period was of interest and useful to me. I had never been in the

Northern Towns. I was profoundly ignorant of commercial life. The manners, customs, ideas, ideals, the types of people, the trades, manufactures, the dominance of Dissent, the comparative weakness of the Established Church, the absence of art, literature and science, the dirt of the towns, the rough heartiness and hospitality—all formed a strange contrast to Cambridge and Brighton.

I spent the two winters '74-'75 and '75-'76 at Leeds—lecturing there, and at Halifax and Skipton—living in Leeds, in lodgings—and seeing a good deal of the people (mostly ladies) who were actively engaged in promoting the Extension lectures. My subject was Astronomy. It was a curious subject for these towns where seldom a star could be seen. As far as the heavens were witness I might have told any fables. My own knowledge was derived almost entirely from books, and my pupils' knowledge was practically limited to books. Occasionally I used to drag an evening class onto Woodhouse Moor, at Leeds, to look at the actual subjects of our discussions, but the latter generally withdrew themselves from observation! I don't know whether this kind of learning was of much use; but it was on the same lines as most modern learning. I think the study of books educates the constructive imagination—and teaches people to figure to themselves things and situations they have never seen. That is perhaps the chief use of it. The bulk of the pupils at this time and during my later connection with the University Extension were of the "young lady" class. These were the main support of the movement, and they might be said to fall into three groups—namely, the best scholars from girls' schools, especially some very intelligent ones from the Friends' Schools; girls living at home and having nothing particular to do;

and elder women in the same plight. These formed the great majority of the afternoon classes, and a considerable fraction of the evening classes; the remainder being elderly clerks and a few extra-intelligent young men, and a very small sprinkling of manual workers.

Though for the most part incapable of any mathematical processes, I found my students open to simple geometrical reasoning and consequently able to follow a great deal of formal Astronomy. They took a real interest in the work, which carried them on and which made the teaching a pleasure—a great pleasure in comparison with my experience of the tuition of "poll" men at Cambridge, whose dulness and distaste for their work were crushing.

The modern Women's Movement was just beginning to take shape at that time. And there was at Leeds three women—all remarkable characters in their way—who were very much in evidence in connection with the University Extension. They were Miss Lucy Wilson, Miss Heaton, and Miss Theodosia Marshall. Miss Wilson was Local Secretary to the University Extension; Miss Heaton and Miss Marshall both aspired after the dignity and influence of the position. As may be imagined there was no love lost between the three, and the cabals and conflicts were unending and most amusing. At one time there were two other lecturers from Cambridge living in Leeds besides myself, namely H. S. Foxwell (of St. John's, Cambridge) and E. S. Thompson (of Christ's). We used to meet every day for dinner at each other's lodgings and had no end of fun comparing notes of local scandal. Coming from a distance and being in the position in which we were, we were naturally the recipients of confidences from all sides. The three ladies were constantly asking one or other of us out to *tête-à-tête* breakfasts, lunches, or afternoon teas—pouring out their grievances against one another, and drawing us into deadly plots. These we duly compared—not without hatching comical counterplots of our own.

But Miss Wilson was not to be dislodged; she was firm in her seat. Extremely good-looking and capable, and a good organizer, she yet had two defects. Like many "advanced" women she was very *doctrinaire*; and having swallowed a principle (like a poker) would remain absolutely unbending and unyielding; and, in the second place, she hated men. On one occasion she got up a "Women's Rights" Meeting in Leeds. It was one of the first of these meetings—certainly the first I had been to. It was well attended—by women; Miss Wilson made a clever speech, full of keen thrusts at the male portion of mankind. I dare say it was well deserved. It was very slashing. There were a few of us "lower animals" huddled near the door. At some final witticism there was a yell of applause. We shut our eyes, assured that our last hour had come—but were ultimately spared for another day.

On another occasion a rather amusing thing happened. One of the lecturers—not either of those already mentioned, but one living at Halifax though also lecturing in Leeds—got himself engaged to be married. This in itself was perhaps an offence to Miss Wilson. But what was worse—and certainly foolish of the young man—he went and fixed his wedding (in the South of England) for a date in the middle of the term, and then asked leave to miss a lecture in order to attend it! Of course Miss Wilson refused. Then in a day or two he wrote again. The affair was very pressing, he said, and he must go. Miss Wilson called her committee together.

They were inclined to yield to the over-hasty marriage arrangement—foreseeing no doubt that it was inevitable. But Miss Wilson was absolute. *She* would not yield—a great principle was at stake. "What if all lecturers," etc. Of course her word prevailed, and a refusal was sent. Then the inevitable happened. The fellow went off without leave, only leaving *me*, poor unfortunate! to *read* his lecture to his gently smiling class. After that there was a scene between me and Miss Wilson on which the curtain had better be drawn! "What business had I to give my services and help to the rebellious lecturer?" etc. Sufficient to say that we both survived it, and were quite good friends afterwards.

On the whole it was an interesting time. It was at Leeds that I came to know the three sisters Ford of Adel Grange, whose friendship I have valued ever since; and it was at Leeds that I resumed acquaintance, to deepen into intimacy, with C. G. Oates, of Meanwood Side—a companion of Cambridge days. But my health was not of the best—a certain overstrain and tension of the nerves, dating from Cambridge worries, and carried on and increased by other causes, was continually pulling me down, and rendering my life at times quite painful. It was at this time too that my brother Charlie died in India (March 1876) quite suddenly, as I have already explained, through a fall from his horse. He was just, as it happened, on his way home on furlough after a long absence, and the shock to my mother and those at home was very great. And even I—though I had seen comparatively little of him—felt it a good deal.

In September 1876 my lecturing beat was changed from the Leeds district to Nottingham, York and Hull. I lodged at Nottingham (with a fatuous landlady) for that term and rather enjoyed the brighter air of Nottingham and brighter spirits of the people, after Leeds. The Casey family with their simple rather foreign habits (Mrs. Casey half-English, half-German, Mr. Casey half-Irish, half-French) were my chief refuge during that and later visits to Nottingham. To my Astronomy course, I added Light and Sound. The limelight lantern became my companion, and experiments—though they increased the labour of preparation—made the lectures easier and more successful. By nature an abominably bad speaker, I had at first found lecturing extremely difficult and a great strain. My nervous disorganization increased the difficulty. Words would not come. I suffered; and if possible my audiences suffered more! But by degrees, by very slow degrees, I improved; practice and hard work over my notes in preparation made a vocabulary more ready to my tongue; and at last, by about the end of my seven years, I could get through an hour's talk without absolutely disgracing myself!

In this connection I may tell a story. One term (a little later on, I think) I was lecturing at Barnsley. The place was a little local theatre, unused at the time; but about the middle of the term it was taken by a traveling company, and we had to move into another building. The last evening of our occupation, some scenery was already up, and I, having affixed my star diagrams to the shifts and side-scenes, was lecturing from the stage when a belated stranger, a rough navvy or collier—no doubt attracted by the theatrical bills already out—came stumping down the middle gangway and ultimately dropped into a seat. He remained quiet for a good time; and then—his patience fairly giving out—he rose up and spoke. "Look 'ere," he said, "I've been sittin' 'ere 'alf an hour—and I haven't understood a *word* of what you've been saying, *and I don't believe you do neither.*"

I felt for the poor man—I deeply sympathized He had come in no doubt on the expectation of a theatrical treat—got in too without paying at the door, which was *nuts*, as they say—and now—what had he come to?

There was a scene. Everybody jumped round on their seats. The local Secretary—a tiny little man, a Frenchman, a dentist—approached the bold stranger.

"You must sit down," he said.

"*Shan't* sit down!"

"Den you must go out of de room."

"*Shan't* go out of the room."

"Den I shall have to *make* you."

The situation was too ludicrous—this tiny Gallic David and this huge and beery Goliath! What might have happened we know not. Fortunately the stranger took the better part, and said—

"I'm sure I don't want to stay 'ere any longer"—and left us with contempt to our Astronomy.

In the Spring term, January to April, 1877, I lodged at York—again an improvement in climate. The lectures there were largely supported by Unitarian, Quaker, and other dissenting groups flourishing in the very shadow of the Cathedral. There were the Spences, the Smithsons, the Wilkinsons, and the excellent 'Mount' school ('Friends') managed by Miss Rous—whose girls were good pupils and great chums of mine.

In the end of April that year I went out to America. This was the accomplishment of a long-slumbering intention. Ever since, in my rooms at

Cambridge, I had read that little blue book of Whitman, his writings had been my companions, and had been working a revolution within me—at first an intellectual revolution merely—but by degrees the wonderful personality behind them, glowing through here and there, became more and more real and living, and suffusing itself throughout rendered them transparent to my understanding.

I began in fact to realize that, above all else, I had come in contact with a great Man ; not great thoughts, theories, views of life, but a great Individuality, a great Life. I began to see and realize correspondingly that 'views' and intellectual furniture generally were not the important thing I had before imagined ; that character and the statement of Self, persistently, under diverse conditions were all-important ; that the body in Man (and this the Greek statuary had helped me to realize), and the quality corresponding to body in all art and behaviour, was radiant in meaning and beautiful beyond words ; and that the production of splendid men and women was the aim and only true aim of State-policy. By day and night the presence of this Friend, exhaled from his own book, had been with me—thus working, transforming, drawing me wonderfully to seek him. America too, the United States, began of necessity to compel my interest, and to form an additional attraction across the Atlantic. I wrote to Whitman more than once, and in 1876 obtained from him the complete (Centennial) Edition of his works published in that year. Indeed I made every preparation to go out to the States that summer, but circumstances rendered the voyage impossible.

This year, however, 1877, gave me the long-desired opportunity. I have recorded in another place [1] the

[1] *Days with Walt Whitman* (George Allen and Unwin, 1906).

main outlines of my visit to Whitman on this occasion, so on that subject I need not say anything further here, except that Whitman as a concrete personality entirely filled out and corroborated the conception of him which one had derived from reading *Leaves of Grass*. The Rev. W. H. Channing, who was then acting as Unitarian Minister at Leeds, insisted on giving me letters of introduction to various friends of his on that side—Emerson, O. W. Holmes, Russell Lowell, Charles Norton of Harvard and others—of which I made use. Emerson was very charming and friendly. I stayed one night at his house and dined with him and his wife and his daughter Ellen. His failure of memory for names was considerable, and at times painful, and there was the fixed look of age often in his eye; but otherwise he was active in body and full of fun and enjoyment of intellectual life. His eyes greyish-blue, the corners of his lips often drawn upward—altogether a wonderful bird-like look about his face, enhanced by his way of jerking his head forward—the look sometimes very straight and intense, then followed by a charming placid smile like moonlight on the sea. His domestic life seemed admirable. I took a turn in the garden with him in the afternoon and a drive afterwards—saw the 'Minute Man' and the 'old Manse' where his grandfather lived. Then in his library he talked much about books and authors—handling his books in a caressing loving way—and showed me his Upanishad translations, and his verses "If the red slayer thinks he slays," etc. He expressed his admiration for Carlyle and Tennyson; his want of the same for Matthew Arnold; and his plain contempt of Lewes' Life of Goethe. His conversation generally seemed very *literary* in character and I could not get him to express any views or ideas about America's place and progress. When I spoke of Walt Whitman he made an odd whinnying sound: "Well, I thought he had some merit at one time: there was a good deal of promise in the first edition —*burt* he is a wayward fanciful man. I saw him in New York and asked him to dine at my Hotel. He shouted for a 'tin mug' for his beer. Then he had a *noisy* fire engine society. And he took me there and was like a boy over it, as if there had never been such a thing before." Emerson also took exception to Whitman's metre.

O. W. Holmes did not please me so well—a good-natured little spiteful creature, one might say, with shovel underlip and bright grey-blue eyes under a low brow, a dapper active man of seventy—his vanity qualified by geniality and humour. No ideas whatever about America. "As to Whitman, well, Lord Napier said *He* was the one thing that interested him in the States. And then Lord Houghton at dinner one day came plump out in his favour—but Willie Everett made such a fierce attack in reply that conversation was silenced." And he knew that Rossetti and others in England thought much of him; but he could only say that in America he was not known. Then he told the story about him and Lowell and Longfellow sitting in judgment on Walt Whitman![1]

One of the men who interested me most in Boston neighborhood was Professor Benjamin Pierce—Astronomical Professor at Harvard—a fine capable man. We had a long talk on Astronomy, very helpful, and he gave me a fine set of drawings published by the Observatory.

One day at New York I met Bryant the poet. It was at his editorial office. Though eighty-four years

[1] See *Days with Walt Whitman*, by E. Carpenter, p. 30.

old he was walking down there daily and getting through much work. He was infirm and aged-looking of course, but still wonderfully active; forehead narrowing above, and high like a sort of promontory, straight brow, and eyes sunken but opening out on you occasionally, straight nose inclining to a hook, and high bridge, white hair like a thin fall of spray over neck, ears and mouth. A very literary person—and manners extremely undemonstrative, even unsympathetic.

But it was Whitman I came out to see, and he in interest and grandeur of personality out-towered them all.

The other thing that fascinated me in America was Niagara. I stayed there four days all alone, looking at the Falls all the time, *feeling* their earth-shaking roar under my feet by day and in bed at night, and watching that strange calm sentinel, that column of white spray which, like a great spirit, exhales itself into the immense height of the sky over the roaring gulf, and which, rainbow-tinted in the sun, or glistening mysterious in the moon by night, seems to overlook the land for far and wide around. It was the only thing I saw which seemed quite to match Whitman in spirit.

For the rest the broad, free life—Washington, New York, Philadelphia, Boston, Albany, and the rivers and steamboats—the rough freedom and ease and independence—rougher and better a good deal than exists now—the hearty welcomes and general friendliness were pleasant and inspiring.

On my way down the Hudson I stopped at Esopus and stayed with John Burroughs a night or two. We took a long walk in the primitive woods back of his house, while he talked of Whitman and bird-lore—a tough reserved farmer-like exterior, some old root out of the woods one might say—obdurate to wind and weather—but a keen quick observer close to Nature and the human heart, and worth a good many Holmes and Lowells.

I was alone all this time, and felt lonely, among all these people ; but as it was the same in England there was nothing remarkable about it ! I returned in July to my life of lodgings and lectures ; and in September was put on another lecturing round—to Sheffield, Chesterfield, and part of the time York and Barnsley.

This itinerant life in lodgings was a little dull and unfruitful it must be confessed ; the only relief from the importunities of lodging-landladies being the futile hospitalities of commercial villa-dom. Both experiences however had their comic side. At Nottingham my landlady—a widow of course—used to aggravate me much, when I first came downstairs of a morning, by jumping out upon me from a side-door with " What'll you have for dinner to-day? " This query, unannounced by any morning greeting or salutation, and flung at me *every day* even before I had had breakfast, was a complete poser. If I suggested anything, the suggestion was met by insuperable difficulties. *She* made no suggestions. And there we used to stand staring at each other in a kind of dismay which at that early hour in the morning was sadly demoralizing ! On one occasion I wanted a box made—for some of my books—and I asked this foolish widow to recommend me a joiner for the purpose. She mentioned some man's name ; and I, to make sure, queried : " Is he a good workman? would he make a strong and serviceable article? " " He made my husband's coffin, Sir," she replied with an air of triumph ! And once more I was completely silenced—for I really could not ask whether it had lasted well or otherwise.

My first experiences of lodging in Sheffield were about equally bad. I took a lodging at the top end of Glossop Road. It was a good part of the town ; but the weather was awful. For three successive days it rained blacks mingled with water ! The sky was dark. Lamps had to be lighted indoors. Then my lodging-place people were most doleful—three timid little old maids, like bunnie-rabbits. No. 1, the youngest and most presentable, waited on me ; No. 3 I never saw, she lived in the kitchen below ; No. 2 haunted in the passage or on the stairs half-way between. No. 1 would come in and ask me what I would have for dinner. "Chop and potatoes," I would say. Then she would put her head out of the door and say to the one in the passage "The gentleman says he will have chop and potatoes." Then I could hear the one in the passage say to No. 3 in the kitchen "The gentleman says he will have chop and potatoes." Then a sort of echo came up from below in a deep tone "Chop and potatoes." Then No. 1 would begin again with the second course. "Rice pudding." "The gentleman says he will have rice pudding." And so it went on, also for three days, everything that I said was circulated round the house and echoed back again from below ! It was too much. If this was Sheffield I could stand it no longer—and I fled away and took rooms at Chesterfield—dullest alas ! of earthly places, but with a rather better climate.

Perhaps I rather liked the quietude of Chesterfield—where it was hardly necessary to know anybody. There were good country walks out towards the moors, and once or twice I got as far as Barlow, half-way to Millthorpe—of which place, needless to say, I had then never heard. I penetrated, during my stay in Chesterfield, into the cottage of a plasterer, a dear old man, S. Ashmore, and became familiar in his household—the only permanent alliance I made in Chesterfield.

The next winter—1878-9—I really did manage to settle in Sheffield, in Holland Terrace, Highfields—three old maids again for landladies!—but rather better conditions generally. I lectured at Nottingham and Hull and Chesterfield, so had a good deal of traveling, and added a new course of lectures—"Pioneers of Science"—which was popular on account of its more discursive character: a brief history of scientific progress illustrated by biographies of the great men. The courses on "Sound" and "Light" went on as well; also that on "Astronomy"—which last was a popular subject in Sheffield. *Omne ignotum pro magnifico.* The evening students were very enthusiastic. Many of them bought telescopes, and we had outdoor meetings at night, with all sorts of optical gear, for the purpose of observing the heavenly bodies. One elderly enthusiast was quite sure he had discovered a comet, and was not satisfied till he had written to Greenwich Observatory, and even then (seeing that they could not find it) he was not satisfied. The Sheffield students too formed a Students' Association, and discussed subjects among themselves, organized excursions, and hunted up fresh pupils—all very good. From the first I was taken with the Sheffield people. Rough in the extreme, twenty or thirty years in date behind other towns, and very uneducated, there was yet a heartiness about them, not without shrewdness, which attracted me. I felt more inclined to take root here than in any of the Northern towns where I had been.

But during all this lecturing period my health had been bad, and getting worse instead of better; and now I was approaching a crisis in regard to it. The state of my nerves was awful; they were really in a quite shattered condition. My eyes, which even in Cambridge days had been weak, kept getting worse. There was no disease or defect—I had been to three first-rate oculists and they all agreed about that. It was simply extreme sensitiveness—probably the optic nerve itself. A strong light from a lamp or candle was quite painful. I could hardly read more than an hour a day—certainly not two hours. It caused a pain in the nerve, which seemed to mount to and disorganize the brain. I was conscious that the refusal of my eyes to read was in all probability a kindly indication that I would be much better without reading—but this would mean giving up the lectures—so here I was again!

As long as the lectures went on I was in perpetual suffering with my eyes, and anxiety—sometimes being really unable to prepare the work before me. Then on this came the strain of lecturing—traveling to a place with a great box of apparatus, arriving there three or four hours before the time of the meeting, getting all one's apparatus and experiments ready (in some wretched schoolroom with *no* assistance), having often in those days to make my oxygen gas myself for the lantern; to rush out when all was ready for a cup of tea, to return in time to take an hour's preliminary *class*, and then to give the lecture; all this was terribly exhausting. But it by no means ended there. After the lecture some local manufacturer and patron would carry one off to his residence for the night, there to meet a few friends at supper, and to talk and be talked to till the small hours of the morning. When one got to bed—a vibrating mass of nerves—sleep was out of the question. There were all the pupils and their faces, and their needs and their personalities ; there were the tiresome patrons and committee people, in endless dance on my brain. Often and often I never slept a wink—only to get up the next day and go through a similar round. Often and often when I got back to my lodgings I had to lie on my back on the sofa for hours—not even then to sleep—but simply to rest and soothe the nerve-pain throughout my body. I felt my life was becoming wrecked and I remember at last swearing a great oath to myself that somehow or other I would get out of it and find my health again.

And behind it all there was that other need—which I have already mentioned more than once—that of my affectional nature, that hunger which had indeed hunted me down since I was a child. I can hardly bear even now to think of my early life, and of the idiotic social reserve and Britannic pretence which prevailed over all that period, and still indeed to a large extent prevails—especially among the so-called well-to-do classes of this country—the denial and systematic ignoring of the obvious facts of the heart and of sex, and the consequent desolation and nerve-ruin of thousands and thousands of women, and even of a considerable number of men. I came home in the summer to Brighton to find my sisters, for the most part unmarried, wearing out their lives and their affectional capacities with nothing to do, and nothing to care for : a little music, a little painting, a walk up and down the Promenade ; but the primal needs of life unspoken and unallowed ; suffering (as one can now see all this commercial age has been doomed to suffer) from a state of society which has set up gold and gain in the high place of the human heart, and to make more room for these has disowned and dishonoured love. It is curious—and interesting in its queer way—to think that almost the central figure of the drawing-room in that later Victorian age (and one may see it illustrated in the pages of *Punch* of that period) was a young or middle-aged woman lying supine on a couch—while round her, amiably conveying or consuming tea and coffee, stood a group of quasi-artistic or intellectual men. The conversation ranged, of course, over artistic and literary topics, and the lady did her best to rise to it ; but the effort probably did her no good. For the real trouble lay far away. It was of the nature of *hysteria*—and its meaning is best understood by considering the derivation of that word. I had two sisters—who each of them for some twenty years led that supine, and one may say tragic, life ; so I had good occasion—beside what may have lain within my own experience—to understand it pretty thoroughly. Certainly the disparity of the sexes and the absolute non-recognition of sexual needs—non-recognition either in life or in thought—weighed terribly hard upon the women of that period.[1]

Another cause, increasing the hardship of disparity, was the growing disinclination of men (of the upper classes) to get married. Partly this arose, no doubt, from their growing realization of the perils and complications of matrimony ; but partly also it arose from an increase in the number of men of what may be called an intermediate type, whose temperament did not lead them very decisively in the direction of marriage—or even led them away from it ; men

[1] This is a subject which through the Freudian psycho-analysis has come now [1915] to be much better understood.

who did not feel the romance in that direction which alone can make marriage attractive, and perhaps justifiable. There have of course been, in all ages, thousands and thousands of women who have not felt that particular sort of romance and attraction towards men, but only to their own kind; and in all ages there have been thousands and thousands of men similarly constituted in the reverse way; but they have been, by the majority, little understood and recognized. Now however it is coming to be seen that they also—both classes—have their part to play in the world.

For my part I have always had excellent and enduring alliances among women, and life would indeed be sadly wanting and impoverished without their friendship and society; but since the days when I sat a boy of nine or ten under the table, apparently playing with my marbles, while my elder sisters and their girl friends were talking freely and unconsciously with each other about some ball of the night before, and their partners in the dances, and their conversations—the workings of the feminine mind and nature have always been perfectly open and clear to me. By a sort of intuition (partly no doubt inborn) I never had any difficulty in following these workings. They enshrined no mystery for me. This fact has always caused me to find women's society interesting; but naturally it did not conduce to headlong adorations and marriage! The romance of my life went elsewhere.

Whether such a state of affairs may be desirable or undesirable, whether it may indicate a high moral nature or a low moral nature, and so forth, are questions which (in a land where *everything* is either moral or immoral) are sure to be asked. But in a sense they are quite beside the mark. They do not alter the fact; and that has always been the same since my earliest days.[1] But it will be evident enough—to any one who takes the trouble to think what these things mean—that to a person of my emotional nature the conditions which brought about—to a comparatively late age—the absence of marriage, or its equivalent, were a fruitful source of trouble and nervous prostration. I realized in my own person some of the sufferings which are endured by an immense number of modern women, especially of the well-to-do classes, as well as by that large class of men of whom I have just spoken, and to whom the name of Uranians is often given.

Certainly my isolation was in a sense my own fault—due partly to reserve and partly to ignorance. When at a later time I broke through this double veil, I soon discovered that others of like temperament to myself were abundant in all directions, and to be found in every class of society; and I need not say that from that time forward life was changed for me. I found sympathy, understanding, love, in a hundred unexpected forms, and my world of the heart became as rich in that which it needed as before it had seemed fruitless and barren.

The Uranian temperament in Man closely re-

[1] Many examples of this kind of temperament are given in Vol. II of Dr. Havelock Ellis' classical work *Studies in the Psychology of Sex*—Philadelphia, 1901 and 1915. (See history VII, beginning "My parentage is very sound", history XVII, etc.) And I will say that in my case the temperament has always been quite natural and associated with perfect healthiness of habit and general freedom from morbidity; and that it has been absolutely inborn, and not induced by any outside example or teaching. It is therefore a part of my nature, and a most intimate and organic part. And I have to thank Mr. Edward Lewis that in his *Exposition and Appreciation of E. C.* (Methuen, 1915, pp. 200, 299, etc.) he has so clearly and firmly indicated this.

sembles the normal temperament of Women in this respect, that in both Love—in some form or other—is the main object of life. In the normal Man, ambition, moneymaking, business, adventure, etc., play their part—love is as a rule a secondary matter. The majority of men (for whom the physical side of sex, if needed, is easily accessible) do not for a moment realize the griefs endured by thousands of girls and women—in the drying up of the well-springs of affection as well as in the crucifixion of their physical needs. But as these sufferings of women, of one kind or another, have been the great inspiring cause and impetus of the Women's Movement—a movement which is already having a great influence in the reorganization of society ; so I do not practically doubt that the similar sufferings of the Uranian class of men are destined in their turn to lead to another wide-reaching social organization and forward movement in the direction of Art and Human Compassion.

VI

BRADWAY AND *TOWARDS DEMOCRACY*

EVERYTHING, one sometimes thinks, has its Compensation. The soul of man is so vast, so endless, that no matter on what side or sides it be hemmed in or thwarted, it will find its outlet in some fresh direction—all the more powerfully perhaps for its temporary and local obstruction. This is true of bodies of people, and it is true also of individuals.

The sufferings of these years, the emotional distress and tension which I had experienced, poured themselves out in poetical effusions, outbursts, ejaculations—I know not what to call them. Sometimes lying full length in the train coming home at midnight from some lecture engagement, hardly able to move; sometimes in the morning with a sense of restoration, flying over the fields in the sunlight; sometimes in my little lodging; sometimes on a long country walk—I wrote just what the necessity of my feelings compelled—formless scraps, cries, prophetic assurances—in no available metre, or shape, just as they came. In no shape that they could be given to the world; but they were a relief to me, and a consolation.

Afterwards, when I found as it were the keynote which harmonized these disjointed utterances, I made use of them; and they were mostly embodied and embedded and adapted into the structure of *Towards Democracy*.

I say my nerves had come to such a pass of dislocation, that I was nearly breaking down; and I had sworn a great oath to myself to mend matters somehow. The year 1879 was in many ways the dim dawn or beginning of a new life to me.

Early in that year I made my first valid essays in the direction of a reform in diet. I may have tentatively experimented in vegetarianism before that, but ineffectually and in ignorance. Once I remember boldly dining off nothing but a vegetable marrow. Of course, disastrous defeat and dismay immediately followed! Practically I had always lived along the usual régime, of plentiful meat, washed down with beer or wine; and probably the sick headaches and nervous tension of my early years were to a considerable extent due to this excess of stimulation. Now, the vegetarian ideal, for many reasons, began to commend itself to me; and though I did not abandon meat at once, I gradually pushed along this line—slowly as my way is, but steadily—so that after four or five years, that is, by '83 or '84, I practically was able to dispense with meat (and alcoholics) altogether—and did so dispense, often for months at a time.

A word here about my vegetarian practice generally. I find now [1899] that though I have lived, as said, for months at a time without meat or fish of *any kind*, and have enjoyed in so doing infinitely better health than ever before—and though I feel as if I could continue in this diet indefinitely and much prefer it—I have yet never made any absolute rule against flesh-eating, and have as a matter of fact eaten a very little every now and then—just, as it were, to see how it tasted, or to avoid giving trouble in Philistine households, and so forth. Having a strong (perhaps a too strong) objection to *prin-*

ciples generally, I have disliked the idea of making any absolute rule in the matter. Briefly I find the vegetarian diet—fruit and grains and vegetables, nuts, eggs, and milk—pleasant, clean, healthful in every way, and grateful to one's sense of decency and humanity. It is a real pleasure to live among those who adopt it. But having spent my time for the most part embedded among folk who favour meat, I have not always kept to my own choice, but have given in at times to a supposed convenience or necessity. Perhaps I should have done better, for myself and others, if I had been more resolute, but such are the facts.

In the year 1879 also the absolute necessity for a more open-air life began to make itself felt. I had always lived in towns, and though fond of the country I looked on the town as my natural home. Now I began to long for a country home. I took long walks round Sheffield, and bitterly regretted having to come *back* in the evening, instead of staying permanently outside. I began to revolve how a change might be possible. Manual work, too, in contradistinction to the mere 'exercise' (riding or cricket or athletics) which takes the place of work among the well-to-do classes, began to have a fascination for me. I think it was in this summer [1879] that being at Brighton, I worked for a couple of months in a joiner's shop, regularly, from 6.30 to 8.30 every morning; I used to make panel doors, and got a good experience, so far, of the trade.

Also as I continued to make Sheffield the headquarters of my lectures, I was taking definite root there, and reaching down partly through my classes, partly through explorations of my own, into the actual society of the manual workers; and beginning to knit up alliances more satisfactory to me than any I had before known. Railway men, porters, clerks, signalmen, ironworkers, coach-builders, Sheffield cutlers, and others came within my ken, and from the first I got on excellently and felt fully at home with them—and I believe, in most cases, they with me. I felt I had come into, or at least in sight of, the world to which I belonged, and to my natural *habitat*.

It was about this time that I made the acquaintance of a man who for some years after was a good deal associated with me—Albert Fearnehough. He came up one evening after a lecture, and gave me his name (I remember thinking how strange it was) and address; and asked me if I would come and see him some time. Later, meeting me in the street, he renewed the request, telling me that his friend who came with him to the lectures was a young farmer who was well up in 'book-learning' (which he himself was not)—that they both lived in the country, he in a cottage on the farm of which Fox, his friend, was owner; and that they would both gladly entertain me any time that I cared for a country walk. Here was exactly my opportunity. I accepted the invitation, and not long afterwards went to visit the two friends at the little hamlet of Bradway, four or five miles from Sheffield, on the charming outskirts of Beauchief Abbey.

Fearnehough was a scythe-maker, a riveter, a muscular, powerful man of about my age, quite 'uneducated' in the ordinary sense (since indeed at the age of nine he had pushed a handcart about the streets of Sheffield) but well-grown and finely built, with a good practical capacity though slow brain, and something of the latent fire and indomitableness of the iron-worker—a man whose ideal was the rude life of the backwoods, and who hated the shams of

ALBERT FEARNEHOUGH AND "BRUNO."

commercialism. Indeed he was always getting into coils with his employers because he would not scamp and hurry over his work, as occasion demanded; and with his workmates because he would not countenance their doing so. In many ways he was delightful to me, as the one 'powerful uneducated' and natural person I had as yet, in all my life, met with. Moreover there was a touch of pathos in his inarticulate ways and in his own sense of inability to compete with the cheapjack commercialism of the day. He lived in a tiny little cottage, on Fox's farm as I have said, with his wife, a good patient worker, and two children. And many a Saturday or Sunday afternoon I came up there and had tea with them, or roamed about the fields.

Charles Fox was a very singular character—a bachelor, with a good brain, curiously fond of mathematics in his boyhood, quite an original thinker in his way—yet to look at, a mere clodhopping farmer with inexpressive face, humped shoulders, and beetle-like gait. He was not ill-looking, but decidedly quaint, with his florid, shaven face, and only the sharp gleam of his eye to show you his shrewdness. Most of the country-folk thought him a little touched in the head, for his odd Socratic humour; and never fathomed in the least his real ability. He lived on the farm left him by his father, with an unmarried cousin of his, Miss Fox, for housekeeper, and with *her* son Teddie for his farm-lad and helper; and with a brother, Owen, who certainly *was* weak in the head and feeble, and of no practical use in the establishment. Between Teddie and his uncle quite an affection existed; but of the household, and especially of Charles Fox I have given some account in a separate paper, under the title of *Martin*

Turner[1]; and what I have there said I need not repeat.

My acquaintance with these two men had its inevitable effect on me. I saw at last my way of escape out of that dingy wilderness, that *selva oscura*, in which I had wandered lost, from childhood even down to the very middle of life's journey. They represented at any rate for me a deliverance from the idiotic fatuous life I had been submerged in all my boyhood at Brighton, and more or less ever since. They represented, if nothing more, a life close to Nature and actual materials, shrewd, strong, manly, independent, not the least polite or proper, thoroughly human and kindly, and spent for the most part in the fields and under the open sky.

My visits to little Bradway and the farm became more and more frequent. I was accepted cordially by both households. I joined in the farm work, and spent long evenings with the boy and his uncle in the cowhouse or with the two families round their kitchen fire—quaint scenes of fun and merriment which are graven on my mind, but which it would take too long to recount here. I soon formed a plan of coming to live if possible with these good people, and carrying on my lectures even from this distance out in the country.

It took a little time to arrange anything, but after some months it was agreed that Fearnehough should move into another cottage a little distance off (since the one he occupied was so small) and that I should lodge with him for a time. Accordingly (in May 1880) he migrated with his family to the neighboring parish of Totley, and I joined them there; but in March of the following year, the adjacent

[1] See *Sketches from Life in Town and Country* (George Allen and Unwin), by E. Carpenter.

cottage to the old one on Fox's land having become vacant, and Fox having thrown the two into one, we returned to Bradway and resumed our old relations on the farm.

I had managed to carry on my lectures from Totley —indeed I had added a new course, on the "History of Music," and one that interested me much, to my former ones ; but it was certainly inconvenient, carrying on the work from such a distance in the country ; and new interests and forces were growing within me.

The life, especially since our return to Bradway, was so different from anything to which I had before been accustomed, it was so congenial in many respects, so native, so unrestrained, it seemed to liberate the pent-up emotionality of years. All the feelings which had sought, in suffering and in distress, their stifled expression within me during the last seven or eight years, gathered themselves together to a new and more joyous utterance. My physical health was every day becoming better. There was a new beauty over the world. Everywhere I paused, in the lanes or the fields, or on my way to or from the station, to catch some magic sound, some intimation of a perpetual freedom and gladness such as earth and its inhabitants (it seemed to me) had hardly yet dreamed of. I remember that, all that time, I was haunted by an image, a vision within me, of something like the bulb and bud, with short green blades, of a huge hyacinth just appearing above the ground. I knew that it represented vigour and abounding life. But now I seem to see that, in the strange emblematic way in which the soul sometimes speaks, this image may have been a sign of the fact that my life had really at last taken root, and was beginning rapidly to grow.

Another thing happened about this time. On the

25th January 1881 my mother died. Her death affected me profoundly. Though there had been (as I have explained elsewhere) so little in the way of spoken confidences between us, we were united by a strong invisible tie. For months, even years, after her death, I seemed to feel her, even see her, close to me—always figuring as a semi-luminous presence, very real, but faint in outline, larger than mortal. It was an inexpressibly tender and consoling relation. Gradually, in the course of years, the presence, or the sense of it, faded away, becoming less and less objective, into the background of my mind, where it remains now, more as it were an actual part of myself than it was then.

Her death at this moment exercised perhaps a great etherealizing influence on my mind, exhaling the great mass of feelings, intuitions, conceptions, and views of life and the world which had formed within me, into another sphere. The *Bhagavat Gita* about the same time falling into my hands gave me a keynote. And all at once I found myself in touch with a mood of exaltation and inspiration—a kind of super-consciousness—which passed all that I had experienced before, and which immediately harmonized all these other feelings, giving to them their place, their meaning and their outlet in expression.

And so it was that *Towards Democracy* came to birth. I was in fact completely taken captive by this new growth within me, and could hardly finish my course of lectures for the preoccupation. Already I was speculating how I could cut myself free. No sooner were the lectures over (about the end of April 1881) than I began writing *Towards Democracy.* It seemed all ready there. I never hesitated for a moment. Day by day it came along from point to point. I did not hurry; I expressed everything with slow care and to my best; I utilized former material which I had by me; but the one illuminating mood remained and everything fell into place under it; and rarely did I find it necessary to remodel, or rearrange to any great extent, anything that I had once written.

I soon saw that the whole utterance would take a long time. I decided to give up my lecturing work so as to be quite unhampered. And I did so. What with my savings from Cambridge days, and a small income of fifty or sixty pounds a year springing from them, I knew I could live well enough for a few years—and so I felt supremely happy. It became necessary also to have some place in which to sit many hours a day writing—and so I knocked together a kind of wooden sentinel-box, placed it in a quiet corner of the garden, overlooking far fields, and thither resorted all through the summer, and into the autumn, and far away through the winter.

What sweet times were those! all the summer to the hum of the bees in the leafage, the robins and chaffinches hopping around, an occasional large bird flying by, the men away at work in the fields, the consuming pressure of the work within me, the wonderment how it would turn out; the days there in the rain, or in the snow; nights sometimes, with moonlight or a little lamp to write by; far far away from anything polite or respectable, or any sign or symbol of my hated old life. Then the afternoons at work with my friends in the fields, hoeing and singling turnips or getting potatoes, or down in Sheffield on into the evenings with new companions among new modes of life and work—everything turning and shaping itself into material for my poem. There was a sense to me of inevitableness in it all, and of being borne along, which gave me good courage, notwithstanding occasional natural doubts; and a sense too of unspeakable relief and deliverance, after all those long years of gestation, as of a woman with her child.

In about a year, that is, by early in 1882, *Towards Democracy*—that is the long first poem which bears that name—was completed except for some technical revisions. The child, conceived and carried in pain and anguish, was at last brought into the world.

Some further details with regard to the genesis of *Towards Democracy* were given in a short paper in the *Labour Prophet* for May 1894, and are now reprinted as a Note to the editions of *Towards Democracy*; and the history of its publication is given in Chapter XI below.

E. C. (1887), AGE 43.

VI

MANUAL WORK AND MARKET-GARDENING

IN April 1882 my father died; and I was at once whirled out of my land of dreams into a very different sphere. It became necessary for me to return home, to Brighton, and handle, as executor, a considerable estate—divisible among ten children. The investments were chiefly in American securities—and they gave a lot of trouble! I stayed at Brighton four or five months, dealing with solicitors, brokers, officials, relatives—selling, negotiating, dividing, transferring without end—doing the work of a lawyer's clerk in fact. Indeed our solicitor remarked one day, perhaps rather plaintively, that it was lucky I had had the time to spare, as it had saved the family no doubt some hundreds of pounds! Of course the work was not really finished for three or four years, but the thick of it was got through that summer, and after that I returned to my beloved Bradway.

My forced stay at Brighton brought out into strong relief the contrast between the old life and the new. I felt more than ever the futility and irksomeness of the old order. I missed my companions of the North, I grieved more than ever over the wasted lives around me in the South—but it was with a new sense, the knowledge that there was something better. I employed my spare time in writing shorter pieces in the style of *Towards Democracy* and revising what I had already written, using my new surroundings again as a point of view under the great light of my main inspiration. My unmarried sisters remained on for a few years at Brighton after my father's death, keeping the house together much as of old. Then they removed to London, and at last (in 1886) the old house and furniture were sold and its doors closed on the family who had occupied it for forty years.

At the end of the summer of which I am speaking—about September 1882—I returned to my home at Bradway. My father's death had left me (more or less prospectively) possessor of about £6,000—which with my little savings of earlier years, seemed quite a large fortune—too large indeed—it rather weighed on my mind ![1] My lectures were over and done with ; some years of literary work were before me, but obviously not of a paying sort, either in the way of wages or fame. The question was What should I do?

I might have simply settled down into an arm-chair literary life. I really don't know exactly why I didn't. But the fancy for manual work had seized me, and for some reason or other, nothing but a life of that kind would satisfy me—only it must be in the open air. No sooner had my father died than I made up my mind to buy a piece of land and work on it as a market-gardener.

No doubt it was a healthy instinct. The motive was in the main a purely personal one. I felt (and rightly) the need of physical work, of open-air life and labour—something primitive to restore my over-worn constitution. I felt the need directly and instinctively, not as a thing argued out and intellectu-

[1] However, I happily managed in the next few years to get rid of a good portion of this !

ally concluded. I have sometimes been credited with making this move onto the land in pursuance of some great theory or scheme of social salvation! But it was not so. There was no idea of this kind in it, or if there was, it was of a very secondary character. My thought was my own need. But I may have had some feeling that a life of this kind was more honest than the alternative, and I think also that I felt it would bring me more decisively into touch with the great body of the people (a strong motive at the time)—and so far I believe these two motives had some secondary play.

At any rate I never felt much doubt about the move. I persuaded Fearnehough, after a little time, to join me if I should settle anywhere; and then I set looking out for a bit of land. But that was not easy to find. At intervals for many months I scoured the country in the neighborhood of Sheffield, but could find nothing there except the small holding at Millthorpe, which though good land and in a lovely situation, with water, etc., seemed too far from town to be available for market purposes. Then I went down into Worcestershire; but in truth the difficulty of finding a small freehold anywhere in England—especially with good soil and near a market—is great; and being no more successful in Worcestershire I returned to Sheffield. Ultimately and being (as usual in such things) more compelled by necessity than of my own choice, I fell back on the seven acres at Millthorpe which I now occupy. Of course I could not help rejoicing in the lovely necessity of living in such a place—the charming brook running at the foot of my three fields, the beautiful wooded valley, and the close proximity, a mile or so off, of the open moors. But I had some misgiving, not only about the market side of the question, but about living so completely gulfed in the country—eight or nine miles from a town centre—for I had never tried anything of the kind before.

I spent the winter of '82 and '83 mostly at Bradway, continuing my writing and other life there, in the intervals of the search for land. About Easter '83 I came to terms for the purchase of the three fields at Millthorpe, and soon after that I set to house-building. The house was finished by the end of the summer, and in October '83 the Fearnehoughs and I moved in. About the same time I published through John Heywood of Manchester, my first poem *Towards Democracy*.

It was a small thin volume of 110 pages, meant for the pocket. It was sent out to the Press, but excited very little comment, except as the ravings of some anonymous author. Yet after a time, faithful to its charge, it came back to me, bringing dear and true friends from all sorts of unlikely places and distant parts of the world; and has not ceased to do so since. Not long after its publication Havelock Ellis picked it up on a second-hand bookstall in London, and wrote to me; and he again brought me into communication with Olive Schreiner, whose *African Farm* was then beginning to attract attention.

That winter, of '83-'84, was spent in hard work, getting the house and the yard and out-buildings in order, laying out the garden ground, digging up the grass-land, planting fruit and other trees, etc. And so were the summers and winters following, for four or five years.

That strange œstrum of hard manual work, and digging down to the very roots of things, spurred me on. I hardly know how to account for it. It possessed me. Every habit, every custom or practice of daily life—house-arrangement, diet, dress, medicine, etc., was overhauled and rigorously scrutinized. I worked for hours and for whole days together out in the open field, or garden, or digging drains with pick and shovel, or carting along the roads ; going into Chesterfield and loading and fetching manure, or to the coalpit for coal, grooming and bedding down the horse, or getting off to market at 6 a.m. with vegetables and fruit, and standing in the market behind a stall till 1 or 2 p.m. ; I was not satisfied but I must do everything that was necessary to be done, myself.

It was a considerable strain. With my somewhat vague aspiring mind, to be imprisoned in the rude details of a most material life was often irksome. Yet a consuming passion drove me on—a desire to know, to do something real, an evil conscience perhaps of the past unreality of my existence. I was compelled to eat it all out.

I carried on, for those first three or four years, the superintendence (of course with the help of my friend and his wife) of house and garden, with their manifold points of detail. I went on with my writing—adding essays on social subjects ("England's Ideal" and others) to my poems ; and I started lecturing on similar topics.

It was too much. I remember that period as a time of great strain. I felt indeed the isolation of the country—gulfed as I was among a perfectly illiterate unprogressive country population (much more so than at Bradway), with my friend and his family, who though good and true people were also quite limited to material interests. There was no one to whom I could talk, who could give me any help. My Sheffield friends were far away, only to be seen once a week or so, and (in the early years at any rate) visitors at Millthorpe were rare. It was too much, and my health suffered a little ; and yet (as I have said) I was driven to it. It is strange how unaccounted impulses and instincts underlie the evolution of one's life. Certainly during those years I (in some ways the most unlikely person to do so) bottomed out the whole of the material and mechanical ways of life—from the details of household life to the processes of agriculture and of a great number of other trades and industries. It was a training such as no university could give. And if my health suffered now and then from the strain, *on the whole* it improved immensely during this period ; so that after five or six years I threw off completely my nerve troubles, and became stronger than I had ever been before in my life.

Two other things happened in 1883 besides my migration to Millthorpe, and publication of *Towards Democracy*—namely, my first acquaintance with the Socialist movement, and my reading of Thoreau's *Walden*.

Of course, in a vague form, my ideas had been taking a socialistic shape for many years ; but they were lacking in definite outline—that definition which is so necessary for all action. That outline as regards the industrial situation was given me by reading Hyndman's *England for All*. However open to criticism the Marxian theory of surplus-value may be (and *every* theory must ultimately succumb to criticism), it certainly fulfilled a want for the time by giving a definite text for the social argument. The instant I read that chapter in *England for All*—the mass of floating impressions, sentiments, ideals, etc., in my mind fell into shape—and I had a clear line of social reconstruction before me.

I gave my first semi-socialistic lecture (though I

think this was before reading the above book)—on "Co-operative Production"—in that year; and later on in the same year I one evening looked in at a committee meeting of the Social Democratic Federation in Westminster Bridge Road. It was in the basement of one of those big buildings facing the Houses of Parliament that I found a group of conspirators sitting. There was Hyndman, occupying the chair, and with him round the table, William Morris, John Burns, H. H. Champion, J. L. Joynes, Herbert Burrows (I think) and others. After that, though I did not actually join the S.D.F., I kept in touch with them, and was able at a later time to render material help in the establishment of *Justice* as their organ.

From that time forward I worked definitely along the Socialist line: with a drift, as was natural, towards Anarchism. I do not know that at any time I looked upon the Socialist programme or doctrines as final, and it is certain that I never anticipated a cast-iron regulation of industry, but I saw that the current Socialism afforded an excellent text for an attack upon the existing competitive system, and a good means of rousing the slumbering consciences—especially of the rich; and in that view I have worked for it and the Anarchist ideal consistently.

The other thing that happened in 1883 was my reading of Thoreau's *Walden*. Just about the very day that I got into my new house and onto my plot of land—the realization of the plotting and scheming of some years—that book fell into my hands, which took the bottom completely out of my little bucket! Having just committed myself to all the exasperations of carrying on a house and market-garden and the petty but innumerable bothers of 'trade,' the charming ideal of a simplification of life below the level of all such things was opened out before me—and for the time I felt almost paralyzed.

Whatever the practical value of the Walden experiment may be, there is no question that the book is one of the most vital and pithy ever written. Its ideal of life spent with Nature on the very ground-plane of simplicity (though probably only permanently realizable by a highly cultured humanity, having access to all the results of art and science, as Thoreau had at Concord) has yet shattered the conventional views of thousands of people. It helped, I must confess, to make me uncomfortable for some years. I felt that I had aimed at a natural life and completely failed—that I might somehow have escaped from this blessed civilization altogether—and now I was tied up worse than ever, on its commercial side.

What sort of line my life would have taken if Thoreau had come to me a year earlier, I cannot tell. It is certain that there would have been a considerable difference. Perhaps it is lucky I was not drifted away by him and stranded, too far from the currents of ordinary life. At any rate I do not regret now that things happened as they did. Instead of escaping into solitude and the wilds of nature—which would have satisfied one side—but perhaps not the most persistent—of my character, I was tied to the traffic of ordinary life, and thrown inevitably into touch with all sorts of people.

Early in 1883, as I have said, I gave my first lecture on social questions, and from that time forward I spoke on these subjects. In the summer of '84 I went again to the United States, my chief object again being to see Whitman—though I had also friends to visit. I crossed the Atlantic as a steerage passenger—in a big Inman boat, the *City of Berlin*—with seven or eight hundred other steerage passengers. It was a great experience. I have described it in my poem "On an Atlantic Steamship." The fact of my venturing it shows the determination with which I was working down into a knowledge of the life of the people. Besides, I had crossed as a *saloon* passenger before, and I felt that *that* was intolerable! The experience was not nearly so rude as I had expected. We had good weather, which of course is everything, and were on deck all day; the nationalities, Swedes, German, Irish, English, etc., were kept apart from each other below; I secured a cabin with a very decent set of young English fellows, and we got on first-rate. The food was quite clean and good. So well satisfied was I that I actually *returned* (from Quebec) in the steerage section!

I spent three or four days in Philadelphia and saw Whitman each day (of which I have given an account elsewhere [1]); and then went on to Massachusetts. The visit to Whitman did not help me so much as the first time. He was very friendly; he gave me introductions to Dr. Bucke in Canada, and to W. Sloane Kennedy, and was generally kind; but his self-centredness (arising no doubt largely from physical causes) had increased, and seemed difficult to overcome.

In Massachusetts I stayed with my friends the Rileys, who had at one time been on St. George's farm (Ruskin's) near Sheffield. They were now on a farm near Townsend Centre, and I remained with them about three weeks, joining in the life, doing a bit on the farm with them, and seeing

[1] See *Days with Walt Whitman* (George Allen and Unwin, 1906), by E. Carpenter.

something of the neighbours. George Riley, the son, and I were chums, and spent some of the time walking together—on one occasion a two days 'out' to Wachusett, mountain and lake, a charming neighborhood. During the time I also visited Sloane Kennedy, at Belmont, and together we went to Walden pond, bathed in it, and added a stone to Thoreau's cairn. Thence to Pennsylvania, beyond Pittsburg, to stay with Mrs. Hardy and her three daughters—also people I had known in Sheffield—who together were 'running' a big farm and making it pay well, an excellent example of female management. Thence, after a pleasant stay of four or five days, across Lake Erie to Toronto and so to London, to see Dr. Bucke. Dr. Bucke was acting as head and superintendent of a large Asylum for Insane folk—over a thousand patients—which he managed excellently. I found him very interesting. We had long talks about Whitman; he showed me his Whitman books, pictures, etc., and then after another four or five days I got the steamer at Toronto, and went down the St. Lawrence to Quebec. The Lake itself, the passages of the thousand islands and of the successive rapids, were a great delight. I had only an hour or two at Quebec, unfortunately—not time to see much of the town; and then I embarked on the *Parisian* for home. Here again the lower reaches of this magnificent river, the coast of Gaspé, and of Labrador, the hundreds of icebergs we saw that day, becalmed in a glassy blue sea, and in blazing sunlight, were most interesting. We slipped through the straits of Belle-Isle and had an enjoyable passage to Liverpool.

It was, I think, some little time before the events recorded in the first part of this chapter—though

I cannot be quite sure about the date—that I had the signal experience of meeting with Edward J. Trelawny, the devoted friend of Shelley and the companion of Byron. For years and years—until indeed the star of Whitman rose in the West—Shelley had been my own ideal. To grasp Trelawny's hand was to gain an unexpected link with a far remote past.

Trelawny's life had been one of extraordinary adventure. To understand even a part of it one must read his *Adventures of a Younger Son* (largely his own story), and his book *Records of Shelley, Byron, and the Author* (1858 and 1878). Born in 1792 of a well-known Cornish family he joined the Navy as a mere boy, and then at an early age *deserted* and took up, according to his own account, with a pirate gang among the seas of Java and Borneo. After some amazing adventures, he returned in about 1813 to Europe ; and soon after married an English lady. Of this period however, between 1813 and 1820, very little seems to be known, except that he himself says : "I became a shackled, careworn and spirit-broken married man of the civilized West!" It was in 1820 at Lausanne that a German bookseller chanced to show him *Queen Mab*; and a little later, at Geneva, that he met Thomas Medwin, Shelley's cousin. The reading of the book and the conversations with Medwin convinced Trelawny that here was a man worth knowing ; and he did not rest till a year or two later he went to Pisa and actually made Shelley's acquaintance (early in 1822). The two were about the same age ; and it shows something of what manner of man Trelawny was, that he so quickly recognized the quality of Shelley ; and something of what Shelley was that he so soon commanded the admiration of this buccaneer and man of adventure. After Shelley's death Trelawny was with Byron a great deal, both as Captain of Byron's yacht and companion in his expedition to Greece; but he never expressed a great regard for Byron—perhaps indeed he hardly did the latter justice. Byron died at Missolonghi in 1824; but Trelawny stayed on in Greece, joined the Greek cause against the Turks, took to wife the sister of Ulysses, or Odysseus, a Greek chieftain, lived for some time with him and his guerilla band in a cave on Mount Parnassus, and was nearly killed there by a bullet from a spy. These and many other things are written in the *Records* above mentioned.

Later, after his return to England, and somewhere about 1840, Trelawny fell in love with a certain Lady Goring, and finally induced her to leave her husband and live with him. And it was this, curiously enough, which at a later period led to my acquaintance with him. Lady Goring's son, by the old Sir Harry, married a cousin of mine, and when a boy of sixteen or seventeen I used occasionally to go and stay with the young pair at Highden near Worthing where they lived, and where I was initiated in the mysteries of coursing, ferreting, etc., which were very much in the order of the day there. Charles Goring, my cousin's husband, was the very type of the "bold bad baronet" of the shilling novels—a type fairly common then, though almost extinct now—a rather handsome man with fierce twirlable moustache, and thoroughly bearish manners, given to swearing and drinking, and devoted to his dogs and guns. Whatever induced my cousin—who was the sweetest and gentlest of girls—to marry him I do not know. But that is always the way: the mild and forgiving women marry the wicked men, and of course make the latter all the wickeder by doing so! In course of time he grew a little tired of his wife (there were no children) and behaved badly towards her. Then his mother died—whom he had not seen since she ran away with Trelawny, some twenty-five or more years before ; and so, seized with some sort of compunction after all this time, Charles Goring went on a pilgrimage to his mother's adopted home ; found there Trelawny *and* his mother's daughter by Trelawny—his own stepsister, by that time a rather beautiful girl or young woman.

From all this complications arose, which I need not go into, but which ultimately in an indirect way led to a somewhat celebrated affair in the Divorce Courts—the Goring Case of the year 1878. Suffice it to say that soon after these unfortunate squabbles were over, Charles Goring had the grace to die, and my cousin (who had obtained a separation order) was left quite free. It was then that I asked her one day to give me an introduction to Edward Trelawny, which she willingly did.

I found him at the house which he was then occupying in Pelham Crescent, S.W.—No. 7, I think —a quite old man of about eighty-seven or eighty-eight, rugged to a degree, with sunken eyes and projecting cheek-bones, but with a strange gleam of fire about him even at that age—not unlike some semi-extinct volcano—and the appearance of what had once been a rather massive and powerful frame. He was sitting in a high chair near the fire with a pile of books on the floor beside him. "You are interested in Shelley," he said. And then without waiting for a reply : "He was our greatest poet since Shakespeare." And then : "He couldn't have been the poet he was if he had not been an Atheist." That was a pretty good beginning ; he rolled out the "Atheist" with evident satisfaction. He went on to express his contempt for the contemporary poets, like Tennyson and Browning; then returned to Shelley: "I am not sure he wasn't the greatest man we have ever had: all these others just tinker with the surface; Shelley goes down to the roots." We talked a little about individual poems, but I forget what. Then he took up one of the books beside him—a Godwin's *Political Justice*, and read extracts from it—always with a choice which showed his hatred of modern Civilization. (And this was interesting from one who had seen so much of the world outside the bounds of our civilization.) Indeed there was something astonishing in this old man's intensity of rebelliousness, which extreme age had apparently done nothing to reduce. He directed my attention to an oil-portrait over the mantelpiece: "Do you know who that is?" I guessed. It was a portrait—apparently not a very good one—of Mary, Percy Shelley's wife[1]: the face rather milk-and-watery in expression. "She did him no good," he said—"was always a drag on him—shackling him with jealousies and the conventions of social life." [Trelawny was never quite fair to any one he did not like, and it was evident he did not like Mary—though in the earlier days of their acquaintance he had certainly been fond of her.] "Poets," he continued, "ought never to marry. It's the greatest mistake. A poet ought to be free as air—free to say and do what he pleases—and he cannot be free if he is married." This was pretty good from a man who had been so very *much* married as Trelawny!

He had had four wives at least—no one knew how many more. His first wife (as appears also from *The Younger Son*) was a girl of Borneo. The second was the lady who filled somehow the gap between 1813 and 1820. The third, as we have seen, was a

[1] Perhaps the portrait by Edward Williams, but I cannot say.

Greek, the sister of Odysseus; the fourth was the former Lady Goring. There were many stories about him in the family, mostly no doubt somewhat embellished. His second wife, it was said, was only a small woman, and when she was "naughty" he would dangle her by the scruff of her neck *out of the window*, until she was good again. He had various dried heads, of pirates and others, among his treasures; and swords and daggers stained with the blood of enemies! Our conversation rambled on, but at this distance of time I forget details. As I say, it gave me a strange thrill on leaving (and he died soon after) to grasp the hand of one who had been so near to Shelley, and whose character undoubtedly had a great fascination for the poet. In Shelley's *Fragments of an Unfinished Drama* (in which the Pirate on the Enchanted Isle is generally supposed to represent Trelawny), the poet says—

> He was as is the sun in his fierce youth,
> As terrible and lovely as a tempest.

On the other hand Trelawny in the Preface to his *Records* says of Shelley: "After glancing one day at an old Italian romance, in which a knight of Malta throws down the gauntlet defying all infidels, Shelley remarked: '*I* should have picked it up. All our knowledge is derived from infidels.'" These two quotations give a good idea of the relation between the two men.

VII

SHEFFIELD AND SOCIALISM

DURING my absence in the United States, my friend Harold Cox, who had just left Cambridge, came down to Millthorpe and spent a good part of the summer there—remaining a bit after my return home. He wanted to get manual and farm and garden experience, and that same autumn he plunged into farming—took a farm at Tilford in Surrey, and inducted a little colony into it. But the land was mere sand, and the experience of one winter and spring was enough! In less than a year he gave the place up, and went out, by way of a change, to India, to the Anglo-Mohammedan College at Futtehgur. While in India he went in '85 or '86 for a tour in Cashmere, and from Cashmere he sent me a pair of Indian sandals. I had asked him, before he went out, to send some likely pattern of sandals, as I felt anxious to try some myself. I soon found the joy of wearing them. And after a little time I set about making them. I got two or three lessons from W. Lill, a bootmaker friend in Sheffield, and soon succeeded in making a good many pairs for myself and various friends. Since then the trade has grown into quite a substantial one. G. Adams took it up at Millthorpe in 1889; making, I suppose, about a hundred or more pairs a year; and since his death it has been carried on at the Garden City, Letchworth.

In 1885 I published the second edition of *Towards Democracy*—still through John Heywood; and early in '86 quite an important local event occurred in the establishment of our Sheffield Socialist Society. One or two of us beat round the town and got together a few Socialists and advanced Radicals; we persuaded William Morris to come down (early in March)—and the result of that was the formation of the Society.

At that time, William Morris, having with a few others parted from Hyndman and the S.D.F., had founded the Socialist League—branches of which were springing up merrily all over the country. And it was William Morris's great hope, often expressed in the *Commonweal* and elsewhere, that these branches growing and spreading, would before long "reach hands" to each other and form a network over the land—would constitute in fact "the New Society" within the framework of the old, and destined ere long to replace the old. No doubt the forces of reaction—the immense apathy of the masses, the immense resistance of the official and privileged classes, entrenched behind the Law and the State, and the immense and growing power of Money—were things not then fully realized and understood. There seemed a good hope for the realization of Morris' dream—and we most of us shared in it. But History is a difficult horse to drive. In this matter of the Socialist movement, as in other matters, it has always been liable to take the most unexpected turns; and the little League societies after flourishing gaily for a few years—suddenly began to wane and die out; I believe indeed that at this moment there is not one of them left. Morris saw with some sadness that his hope was not going to be fulfilled—and though I do not think that he altogether lost heart he was fain in his last years to bury his disappointment in a return to his art work, and even to favour as a forlorn hope the Parliamentary side in revolutionary politics! It is curious indeed in this matter to see how, of all the innumerable little societies—of the S.D.F., the League, the Fabians, the Christian Socialists, the Anarchists, the Freedom groups, the I.L.P., the Clarion societies, and local groups of various names—all supporting one side or another of the general Socialist movement—not one of them has grown to any great volume, or to commanding and permanent influence; and how yet, and at the same time, the general teaching and ideals of the movement have permeated society in the most remarkable way, and have deeply infected the views of all classes, as well as general literature and even municipal and imperial politics. Perhaps it is a matter for much congratulation that things have turned out so. If the movement had been pocketed by any one man or section it would have been inevitably narrowed down. As it is, it has taken on something of an oceanic character; and if by its very lack of narrowness it has lost a little in immediate results, its ultimate success we may think is all the more assured.

The real value of the modern Socialist movement—it has always seemed to me—has not lain so much in its actual constructive programme as (1) in the fact that it has provided a text for a searching criticism of the old society and of the lives of the rich, and (2) the fact that it has enshrined a most glowing and vital enthusiasm towards the realization of a new society. It is these two points which have always drawn and attached me to it. The constructive details of the future are things about which there may and indeed must be different opinions.

The necessity of organization in society, and of united action, the avoidance of officialism and bureaucracy, the handling of the land so as to afford the most general access to it, the barring of monopolies and of all industrial parasitism, the liberation of labour to dignity and self-reliance, the conduct of public ownership, the questions of taxation, representation, education, etc.—these are all most complex affairs whose united and detailed solution can only proceed step by step, by slow trial and experience. We must expect mistakes and differences of opinion here. Nevertheless I think we may say that in the broad lines of its constructive policy Socialism has taken the right course and the one which time will justify. It has laid down in fact once for all the principles that parasitism and monopoly must cease, and it has set before itself the ideal of a society which while it accords to every individual as full scope as possible for the exercise of his faculties and enjoyment of the fruits of his own labour, will in return expect from the individual his hearty contribution to the general well-being, and at least to claim nothing for his own which (or the value of which) he has not by his own effort produced. Towards the fulfilment of these aims Socialism has proposed a guarded public ownership of land and of some of the more important industries (guarded, that is, against the dangers of officialism), and it seems likely that this general programme is the one along which western society will work in the near future; that is, till such time as the State, quâ State, and all efficient Government, are superseded by the voluntary and instinctive consent and mutual helpfulness of the people—when of course the more especially Anarchist ideal would be realized.

As I say, while there is practically no dissent

about the future form of society as one which shall embody to the fullest extent the two opposite poles of Communism and Individualism in one vital unity, there may and naturally must be differences on the question of the detailed working out of the problem, and indeed it may well be that the solution will take somewhat different forms in different places and among different peoples.

It has not been, I repeat, the belief in special constructive details as panaceas which has led me into the Socialist camp, so much as the fact that the movement has been a distinct challenge to the old order and a call to the rich and those in power to remodel society and their own lives ; and that other fact that within the Socialist camp has burned that wonderful enthusiasm and belief in a new ideal of fraternity—which however crude and inexperienced it may at times appear is surely destined to conquer and rule the world at last.

It is this latter side of the movement which by the outsider is so little known and understood. Those who stand outside a revolutionary agitation, or who look down on it from above, necessarily only see the defiant subversive elements of it, they do not guess the glowing heart within. To me, passing from time to time from one stratum of life to quite another, it was a strange experience and not without its comic side, to see the wildly different features which one and the same movement wore to those within and those without ; to hear Socialism spoken of from above, as nothing but an envious shriek and a threat, a gospel of bread and butter, a grab, a " divide up all round "—the work of unscrupulous demagogues and tinsel politicians ; and then the next moment to pass into the heart of the thing and to find oneself in an atmosphere of the most simple fraternity and idealism, where the coming of the kingdom of Heaven, a kingdom of social order and decency, was entertained with a childlike faith that might almost make one smile; where it seemed only necessary to go out into the streets and preach the better ideals for crowds to flock to the standard; and where, if a betterment of conditions was the main thing sought for, it was a betterment of social life and a satisfaction of the needs of the heart fully as much as an increased allowance of bread and butter. It was a strange experience to pass from cold to hot, and from hot to cold, as it were, and to realize how little those in the one current could understand what was going on in the other.

Certainly from what experience I have had of a movement at one time thought very revolutionary, I am inclined to think that most revolutions must have been pretty well justified before they took place. One hears of dangerous mobs led by demagogues and fed on fancied wrongs; and of course there are such things in every movement as self-seeking blusterers, or designing misleaders; there is ignorance and non-reasoning exasperation; but my experience of the (British) masses is that instead of being too inflammable, they are surely only too *slow* to move, too slow to perceive the burdens which they bear, or to point out the cause of their own suffering; and—in the Socialist agitation—the number and influence of the blusterers and self-seekers compared with the genuine leaders has always been very small. No, revolutions do not take place without cause; and I doubt whether in any case the excesses accompanying a rising have exceeded the cruelties and injuries of the preceding tyranny. There is such a heart of tenderness and patient common sense in the mass of the people—everywhere I believe—as to convince one that, notwithstanding the slanders that have been heaped up by the arm-chair historian, they are really more inclined to endure than to accuse, more ready to forgive than retaliate. No—the general Socialist movement (including therein the Anarchist) has done and is still doing a great and necessary work—and I am proud to have belonged to it. It has defined a dream and an ideal, that of the common life conjoined to the free individuality, which somewhere and somewhen must be realized, because it springs from and is the expression of the very root-nature of Man.

Our "Sheffield Socialists," though common working men and women, understood well enough the broad outlines of this ideal. They hailed William Morris and his work with the most sincere appreciation. I found among them the most interesting personalities, saturated for the most part, as I have said, with the thought of fraternity and fellowship; and I made one or two lifelong friends.

We organized lectures, addresses, pamphlets, with a street-corner propaganda which soon brought us in amusing and exciting incidents in the way of wrangles with the police and the town-crowds. At first an atmosphere of considerable suspicion rested upon the movement, and dynamite and daggers were assumed by outsiders to be indispensable parts of our equipment; but as time went on, and after a few years, this died away—and where there had been only jeers or taunts at first, crowds came to listen with serious and sympathetic mien. A dozen or twenty at most formed the moving and active element of our society—though its membership may have been a hundred or more; and these disposed themselves

G. E. H.

(One of the first "Sheffield Socialists.")

to their various functions. Mrs. Usher, large-bosomed and large-hearted, would move on the outskirts of our open-air meetings, armed with a bundle of literature. She was an excellent saleswoman and few could resist her hearty appeal "Buy this pamphlet, love, it will do you good!" Even in the streets or the tramcars the most solemn and substantial old gentlemen fell a prey to her. Her brothers, the two Binghams, were among our two speakers, and both of them pretty effective, the one in a logical, the other in a more oratorical way. They were provision merchants in the town; and their business suffered at first, but afterwards gained, by the connection. Then there was Shortland, handsome, fiery and athletic, an engine fitter, always ready for a row and to act as 'chucker out' if required. Or J. M. Brown, who took quite an opposite part. He (tailor by trade) the very picture of kindness and broad good-nature would move among the crowd as if he hardly belonged to us, and engaging persuasively in conversation, first with one and then with another, would draw many a doubter into the fold; or George E. Hukin, with his Dutch-featured face and Dutch build—no speaker, nor prominent in public—but though young an excellent help at our committee meetings, where his shrewd strong brain and tactful nature gave his counsels much weight; and always from the beginning a special ally of mine; or George Adams, afterwards associated with me at Millthorpe, with his amusing quips and sallies, and plucky antagonisms, a good friend and a good hater, and always ready for an adventurous bout; or Raymond Unwin, who would come over from Chesterfield to help us, a young man of cultured antecedents, of first-rate ability and good sense, healthy, democratic, vegetarian, and now I need not say a well-known architect and promoter of Garden Cities.

Then at one time there was Fred Charles—who was afterwards accused of an anarchist plot and sentenced, most unfairly, to ten years' hard labour. He was already leaning to the Anarchist side of the movement, but was ready to work with us ; and certainly was one of the most devoted of workers. No surrender or sacrifice for the 'cause' was too great for him ; and as to his own earnings (as clerk) or possessions, he practically gave them all away to tramps or the unemployed. The case was tried at Stafford in March '92 by Justice Hawkins, and though the incriminating evidence was quite slender yet, there being a panic on at the time with regard to Anarchism, there was an obvious determination to convict. I appeared in the box to testify to Charles' excellent character and public spirit, but needless to say without success. Or there was Burton, engine-tenter, rather a type of the stout, somewhat self-satisfied and ignorant street-speaker, who would get us into trouble shouting "The land for the people!" or other cant phrases of the period, with really no clear idea of what they meant, and would have to be rescued when attacked or challenged by some keener critic among the audience; or again, Jonathan Taylor, the very opposite in type to these, tall, lean, logical and conclusive to the last degree; who with a kind of homely unconquerable humour, compelled his hearers from finger to finger, and from point to point, of his argument, and somehow always succeeded in holding the most restive crowd, and for any period. He had been on the school-board at one time, and was useful to us also by his knowledge of local and municipal expediencies. Or again, John Furniss: he was a remarkable man, and perhaps the very first to preach the modern Socialism in the streets of Sheffield. A quarryman by trade, keen and wiry both in body and in mind, a thorough-going *Christian* Socialist, and originally I believe a bit of a local preacher; he had somehow at an early date got hold of the main ideas of the movement; and in the early 'eighties used to stride in—he and his companion George Pearson—five or six miles over the Moors, to Sheffield in order to speak at the Pump or the Monolith; and then stride out again in the middle of the night. And this he kept up for years and years, and when later he migrated to another quarry about the same distance from Chesterfield did exactly the same thing there; for perhaps twenty years, with marvellous energy and perseverance, he must have kept up this propaganda; and the amount of effective influence he must have exercised would be hard to reckon.

Such were some of the characters with whom I found myself associated, and for five or six years we carried on the Society with the utmost friendliness, accord and enthusiasm. It was a most interesting time. I knew all those mentioned and many others, very intimately, was familiar in their houses, stayed with them, knew all their goings-out and comings-in, and something of the details of their various trades.

In 1887 we took a large house and shop in Scotland Street, a poor district of the town; and opened a café, using the large room above for a meeting and lecture room, and the house for a joint residence for some of us who were more immediately concerned in carrying on the business. We had all sorts of social gatherings, lectures, teas, entertainments in the Hall—the wives and sisters of the "comrades" helping, especially in the social work; we had Annie Besant, Charlotte Wilson, Kropotkin, Hyndman, and other notables down to speak for us; we gave teas to the slum-children who dwelt in the neighboring crofts and alleys (but these had at first to be given up on account of the poor little things tearing themselves and each other to pieces, perfect mobs of them, in their frantic attempts to gain admittance—a difficulty which no arrangement of tickets or of personal supervision seemed to obviate); and we organized excursions into municipal politics; and country propaganda. This last was often amusing as well as interesting. While, in the towns, as time went on, audiences grew in numbers and attentiveness, it still remained very difficult to capture the country districts. The miners would really not be uninterested, but in their sullen combative way they would take care not to show it. Many a time we have gone down to some mining village and taken up our stand on some heap of slag or broken wall, and the miners would come round and stand about or sit down deliberately *with their backs to the speaker*, and spit, and converse, as if quite heedless of the oration going on. But after a time, and as speaker succeeded speaker, one by one they would turn round—their lower jaws dropping—fairly captivated by the argument. It was much the same with the country rustics—but as a rule less successful. I remember on one occasion seven or eight of us, armed with literature, going for a long country walk to Hathersage in the Derbyshire dales. We had Tom Maguire with us, from Leeds, an excellent speaker, full of Irish wit and persuasiveness. We set him upon a stoneheap in the middle of the village and standing round him ourselves while he spoke, acted as decoy ducks to bring the villagers together. The latter full of curiosity came, in moderate numbers, but not one of them would approach nearer than a distance of twenty or thirty yards—just far enough to make the speaker despair of really reaching them. In vain we separated and going round tried to coax them to come nearer. In vain the speaker shouted himself hoarse and fired off his best jokes. Not a bit of it—they weren't going to be fooled by us! and at last red in the face and out of breath and with a string of curses, Tom descended from his cairn, and we all, shaking the dust of the village off our feet, departed!

I meanwhile and during these years, not only took part in our local work, but spoke and lectured in the Socialist connection all round the country—at Bradford, Halifax, Leeds, Glasgow, Dundee, Edinburgh, Hull, Liverpool, Nottingham and other places—my subjects the failures of the present Commercial system, and the possible reorganization of the future. As to the Café, we were only able to hold to it for a year. Though quite a success from the propagandist point of view, financially it was a failure. The refreshment department was not patronized nearly enough to make it pay. The neighborhood was an exceedingly poor one. And so we were obliged to surrender the place, and retire to smaller quarters. During that year however I really lived most of the time at the Scotland Street place. I occupied a large attic at the top of the house, *almost* high enough to escape the smells of the street below, but exposed to showers of blacks which fell from the innumerable chimneys around. In the early morning at 5 a.m. there was the strident sound of the 'hummers' and the clattering of innumerable clogs of men and girls going to their work, and on till late at night there were drunken cries and shouting. Far around stretched nothing but factory chimneys and foul courts inhabited by the wretched workers. It was, I must say, frightfully depressing; and all the more so because of tragic elements in my personal life at the time. Only the enthusiasm of our social work, and the abiding thoughts which had inspired *Towards Democracy* kept me going. I spent my spare time during the year in arranging and editing the collection of songs and music called *Chants of Labour*—a thing which might have been much better done by some one else, but I could find no one to do it. And it was a queer experience, collecting these songs of hope and enthusiasm, and composing such answering tunes and harmonies as I could, in the midst of these gloomy and discordant conditions.

As I say, we only stayed a year here, and as far as my health was concerned I don't think I could have endured it much longer. I realized the terrible drawback to health and vitality consequent on living in these slums of manufacturing towns, and the way these conditions are inevitably sapping the strength of our populations.

VIII

TRADE AND PHILOSOPHY

IN 1887 or 1888 I turned over the organization and commercial side of the garden at Millthorpe to my friend Albert Fearnehough. During the first four years or so I had taken the responsibility, and by many mistakes bought some valuable experience—but now I found that my literary and social work demanded so much time that I wanted my brain free from agricultural cares. So after this, while still contributing a fair amount of manual labour I left the organization alone.

I cannot say that, adopting the commercial standard, the experiment at Millthorpe could at any time be called *paying*. At the same time it was never (to me) disheartening. Taking strawberries as our main crop, we found, with several years' experience, that £40 per acre was a fair estimate of the gross produce. (And I do not think that this is excessive since I know that £60 or £70 is a not uncommon estimate.) If we had put, say, 5 acres out of our 7½ under strawberries, this would have yielded £200 a year, which, allowing for extra labour, manure, etc., would still have maintained a man and his family; 100 fowls would probably have paid the rent (if it had not been a freehold); and the 2½ acres would have gone far to keep a horse or pony. But I had not the time to give to a complete organization, nor perhaps felt the necessary interest in it; and my friend had hardly the required energy; so we just paddled along, keeping two or three acres only under spade cultivation, and making a small sum, but not sufficient to meet expenses. I think, as I say, that the thing might have been made to pay in the commercial sense—but there is no doubt that under prevailing conditions and prices in England, agriculture of any kind requires pretty hard work and long hours to make it fairly successful. One of the reasons of this is the want of a prosperous country population and the local markets which this would afford. With industrial villages scattered over the land, eggs, fruits, vegetables would be in great demand—even in country districts—prices would be fair, the middleman would be dispensed with; even the horse and cart might not be needed. But it is quite a different matter when the stuff has to be sent to a distant market, there to be bought by hucksters, and to feed middlemen and railway shareholders, before it feeds either the producer or consumer. This trouble is really one of the great troubles of modern civilization—and while there is no doubt a certain advantage gained by division of labour among nations and provinces, and by the raising of products in the most suitable localities, it is a matter quite open to question whether the enormous expenses of the present world-wide exchange and the maintenance of these swarms of merchants, traders, shipping and railroad companies, with their innumerable shareholders and employees, does not quite obliterate or absorb the advantage so gained. Indeed when one thinks of the immense numbers of people in this way withdrawn from any direct service in production and made systematically dependent on the others, one may question whether the gain does not at times come very near a loss; and one ceases to wonder that the condition of the actual producers, agricultural and others, remains so poor and unimproved.

In '86 and '87 I prepared for the Press and published the volume called *England's Ideal.* The papers composing it had been written at different times during the two or three years preceding—some of them at Brighton, during intervals when family affairs had taken me back there for a time. Especially I remember writing *Desirable Mansions* in this way in an interval when I was tangled in family business and the idiotic life of the place—and with a kind of savage glee as I sought to tear the whole sickly web to pieces. Descended from the transcendental generative thought of *Towards Democracy* on the one hand, and my new-found acquaintance with intensely practical life on the other, these papers, though crude in some respects, bear I believe a certain impetus about them. Once or twice, by the violent opposition they have excited (always a reassuring thing for an author), I have had evidence of this. When *Desirable Mansions* was first issued, as a separate pamphlet, I received a copy, anonymously sent and written all over with the most furious and scurrilous denials, challenges, abuse, etc.; and after the publication of *England's Ideal* as a volume, a friend of mine had a letter from a lady, in which she said that her husband had been reading the book, and that she had got hold of it and "poked it into the fire, as she found it was unsettling him so!" I have always regretted that I did not get hold of that letter, with leave to publish it. It would have made such a splendid advertisement.

The influences of Ruskin, in style and moral bias,

and of Marx in economics, are very apparent in the volume; and though I do not think that I ever gave myself 'hand and foot' to Marx in his views; yet I was very willing to adopt his theory of surplus value as a working hypothesis. The truth is that though no exact measure of 'surplus value' or of the amount of which the workman is 'defrauded' by the capitalist, is possible—and though any theory which attempts to exactly define this amount is sure to be open to criticism [1]; yet, the general fact of surplus value, namely that the workman does *not* get the full value of his labours, and that he is taken advantage of by the capitalist is obvious—and serious—enough. And it is on this general position that *England's Ideal*—like the whole Socialist movement—is founded. The seriousness of the matter may be seen from the fact that from this original falsity (of the appropriation of other folks' labour) are flowing to-day by a perfectly logical evolution two other great falsities or failures—Commercial Crises and shop-keeping Imperialism—which are now threatening ruin to all the Western Civilizations.

Commercial Crises, as has been often explained (see *England's Ideal*, pp. 42, 43) flow primarily from the fact that the working masses for their wages only receive a fraction of the value of the goods produced, and therefore can only *buy back* a fractional part of the same, while the capitalist classes (though with their share of the swag they *could* buy back the remainder) do not want more than a part of the remainder. Consequently there occurs every year on the one hand an accumulation of goods unused and on the other an accumulation of capital waiting for reinvestment; and these two

[1] See "The Value of the Value-theory," an article by myself in the little magazine *To-day* for June 1889 (published by W. Reeves).

things from time to time clog the Commercial Machine so as to render it hardly workable, and will probably in the end bring it to a standstill. As to modern Imperialism it is a logical outcome of the last-mentioned item, the accumulation of capital waiting for reinvestment. For all the openings for capital in the mother country having been filled up there remains nothing but to invest it in manufactures abroad. And since other Western countries are similarly filled up, there further remains nothing but to go to savage and outlying nations and force *them* to become our employees and our customers. But to do this with safety requires military occupation and the country's flag. Hence in a nutshell the flag-waving and Imperialism of the day.

In 1889 I got off *Civilization: Its Cause and Cure*—another series of reprints. And here too the philosophical position, though often crudely expressed, and with more attempt at *suggestion* than finish, is I think in the main well-founded and valuable. The attacks on Civilization and on Modern Science were both wrung from me, as it were by some inner evolution or conviction and against my will; but in both cases the position once taken became to me fully justified. In neither case did I take any great precautions to guard against misunderstanding, and in consequence I have been freely accused of blinding myself—in respect of Civilization—to modern progress, and of desiring to return to the state of primitive man; and in respect to Science—of preferring ignorance to intelligence. But no careful reader would make these mistakes. The monumental, patient, one may almost say heroic, work which has been done by Science during the nineteenth century, in the way of exact observation, classification, and detailed practical application, can never be ignored and can hardly be over-estimated. None the less the very decided criticism in *Civilization: Its Cause and Cure,* of the limits of scientific theorizing and authority has been quite necessary; as well as the forcible insistence on the fact that Science only deals with the surface of life and not with its substance. As to Civilization the advances of Humanity during the Civilization period have been largely bound up with the advance of Science and have chiefly consisted perhaps in increase of technical mastery over Nature and materials. Like every increase of power this has led to greater opportunity of good and greater opportunity of evil. On the moral side however, we may believe that men's sympathies *have* broadened and widened during the civilization period—so that there is a larger and more general sense of Humanity. On the other hand during this period something of the intensity of the old tribal kinship and community of life has been lost, as well as something of the instinctive kinship of each individual to Nature. It is obvious enough that there can be no *return* to pre-scientific or pre-civilization conditions—though it may be hoped that a later age may combine some of the virtues of the more primitive man with the powers that have been gained during civilization.

In the year following [1890] something happened which in a curious vague way I had been expecting to happen for some time. It almost amounted to my making the acquaintance of a pre-civilization man of a very high type. I have mentioned how the *Bhagavat Gita* falling into my hands at a certain date, gave the clue to and precipitated the crystallization of *Towards Democracy.* From that time of course I was intensely interested in the wise men of the East, and that germinal thought which in various ages of the world has become the nucleus and impulse of new movements. During the years '80 to '90 there was a great deal of Theosophy and Oriental philosophy of various sorts current in England, and much talk and speculation, sometimes very ill-founded, about 'adepts,' 'mahatmas,' and 'gurus.' I too felt a great desire to see for myself one of these representatives of the ancient wisdom. But it did not seem very clear how the thing would come about. However at last there came a very pressing letter from my friend Arunáchalam in Ceylon (the very friend who had given me the *Bhagavat Gita* at an earlier date), asking me to come out and meet a certain Gñani to whose discourses and teaching he was himself already deeply indebted, and who was willing to give some time to me if I should come. So the way was made plain, and I immediately made arrangements to go.

I have given a careful account of this Gñani, his personality and teaching, in my book *Adam's Peak to Elephanta*—and I need not repeat the material here. As I say, he was in some respects a high type of pre-civilization man. For, like most men of this class in India, he identified himself so closely with the ancient religious tradition that one could almost feel him to be one of the old Vedic race of two thousand or three thousand years back. His modes of thought, appearance, personality, all suggested this. And here in this man it was of absorbing interest to feel one came in contact with the root-thought of all existence—the intense *consciousness* (not conviction merely) of the oneness of all life—the germinal idea which in one form or another has spread from nation to nation, and become the soul and impulse of religion after religion. However one might differ from him in points of detail, in matters of modern science or of politics, one felt that he, and his predecessors three thousand years ago, had seized the central stronghold, and were possessors of an outlook and of intuitions which the modern might truly envy. After seeing Whitman, the amazing representative of the same spirit in all its voluminous modern unfoldment—seven years before—this visit to the Eastern sage was like going back to the pure lucid intensely transparent source of some mighty and turbulent stream. It was a returning from West to East, and a completing of the circle of the Earth.

It is curious that *his* teacher (Tilleinathan Swamy) seems to have told this Gñani many years before that an Englishman or Englishmen would come to him. Probably he foresaw, from the growth of the English mind, that the time was not very far distant when the English would rise to an understanding of the great Indian tradition and would come over to study it.

Looking back now [1901] after ten years, on my personal experiences of the Eastern teachings, I seem to realize more and more that the true line is that (first adequately pointed out by Whitman) which consists in combining and harmonizing *both* body and soul, the outer and the inner. They are the eternal and needful complements of each other. The Eastern teaching has or has had a tendency to err on one side, the Western on the other. The Indian methods and attitude cause an ingathering and quiescence of the mind, accompanied often by great illumination; but if carried to excess they result in over-quiescence, and even torpor. The Western habits tend towards an over-activity and external distraction of the mind, which may result in disintegration. The true line (as in other cases) is not in mediocrity, but in a bold and sane acceptance of both sides, so as to make them offset and balance each other, and indeed so that each shall make the extension of the other more and more possible. Growth is the method and the solution. The soul goes out and returns, goes out and returns; and this is its daily, almost hourly, action—just as it is an epitome of the æonian life-history of every individual.

This visit to the East in some sense completed the circle of my experiences. It took two or three years for its results to soak and settle into my mind; but by that time I felt that my general attitude towards the world was not likely to change much, and that it only remained to secure and define what I had got hold of, and to get it decently built out if possible into actual life and utterance.

With regard to this process of "building out" into the actual world I should feel very ungrateful if I did not acknowledge my indebtedness to the Nature-conditions around me. For any sustained and more or less original work it seems almost necessary that one should have the quietude and strength of Nature at hand, like a great reservoir from which to draw. The open air, and the physical and mental health that goes with it, the sense of space and freedom in the Sky, the vitality and amplitude of the Earth—these are real things from which one can only cut oneself off at serious peril and risk to one's immortal soul. And there is somewhat of the same potency and vitality in the very life of the mass-peoples who are in touch with these foundation-facts and outdoor occupations. It was a true instinct or a gracious Fate—and I realized this more and more—which had compelled me to locate myself in the midst of such surroundings.

I should feel ungrateful too if I did not express my indebtedness to the lovely little stream which like a live thing ran night and day, winter and summer, full of grace and music at the foot of my garden. It entered into my life and became part of it.[1] The hut, which I had built at Bradway to write the earlier part of *Towards Democracy* in, I transported with me to Millthorpe, and planked it down on the edge of the brook, facing the sun and the south; and thenceforth it served a double purpose—that of a study in which, a hundred yards away from the house, I could write in comparative safety from interruption; and that of a bathing shelter with its feet almost in the water. Here through uncounted hours I continued the production of *Towards Democracy* and my other books, avoiding always the act of writing within the house except when absolutely forced to retire by stress of weather or other causes, and rejoicing always to get the sentiment of the open free world into my pages; and here I came, either alone or with friends, to rest from labour in the garden, or to bathe and be refreshed after the heat of the day.

[1] See the last poem but one in *Towards Democracy*, p. 502.

THE HUT AND THE BROOK.

IX

MILLTHORPE AND HOUSEHOLD LIFE

IT must be admitted, however, that the acclimatization to the new and somewhat limited and strenuous life at Millthorpe did not take place all at once ; and perhaps the fact of my having burnt my boats, as it were, and committed myself as I had done, was after all a good thing. For some little time I felt restive and unsettled at the enchainment—partly, as I have said, because the Thoreau ideal, opening out *underneath,* took the bottom out of the commercial and rather materialistic life in the way of Trade in which I was embarking ; and partly because anyhow the latter sort of life—though valuable as an experience—was not by its nature likely to hold my interest for long. The rustics too and farmfolk around me were on my first arrival a little strange, and inclined, as often happens in such cases, to hold off and be suspicious of a newcomer ; my reputation as a Socialist alarmed them ; there was none of the cordiality of little Bradway ; the climate was damp and the winters were long ; and I had occasional relapses of feeling about it all.

Yet if I *had* cut the painter and floated my little boat away onto the great deep I doubt whether the result would have been favorable. After all, all life means a denial of *part* of oneself. It is obviously impossible to find a situation or conditions which will satisfy *all the demands* of one's nature —millionfold complex as they are. Some must be sacrificed. To moan over that necessity or to pose as a martyr is absurd. All one can reasonably do is to find a situation which will satisfy the *root*-demands, and the *rooting* demands—those that have the power of growth in them. Then the seed, though it seem to die in its prison-house, will assuredly find its outlet and quicken into a new life.

I could not complain in this case that the root-needs of my temperament were unsatisfied. Quite the contrary. I was plunged in the very heart of Nature—that Nature which for many years I had felt the need of—in a singularly beautiful Derbyshire valley with plentiful woods, streams and moors; I had already become familiar with the mass-folk of Sheffield, and found friends among the workers in many trades; and was beginning to know the rustics of my own neighborhood. I was leading an outdoor life, and my health was every day becoming firmer and more consolidated. I had escaped from the domination of Civilization in its two most fatal and much-detested forms, respectability and cheap intellectualism. In my happy valley there was no resident squire of any kind, nor even a single "villa," while the church, more than a mile distant, was quite amiably remote! We were just a little population of manual workers, sincerely engrossed in our several occupations. And finally, and perhaps more than all, I had found a firm basis and secure vantage-ground for my literary and productive work.

People have often asked me if I did not miss the life I had left behind. I cannot truly say that I ever did. At Brighton and at Cambridge and partly in London I had had my fill of balls and dinner-parties and the usual entertainments, and when at the close of those two dispensations (somewhere in the early 'eighties) *I gave my dress clothes away,* I did so without any misgiving and without any fear that I should need them again. The fact is that though it is perfectly true that by steadily and persistently going to evening parties and social functions one may come into touch with interesting or remarkable people of sorts, yet the game is hardly worth the candle. Through leagues of boredom, platitudes and general futility one occasionally has the satisfaction of exchanging a wink of recognition, so to speak, with some really congenial and original woman or man; but at all such functions the severe flow of amiable nonsense soon cuts any real conversation short, and if one wants to continue the latter the only way is to arrange a meeting quite outside and apart—which after all one might have done in other and simpler ways. As to the matter of dress, the adoption of a pleasant yet not strictly conventional evening garb of one's own has the useful effect of automatically closing doors which are not "worth while" and opening those that *are*—so in that way it is much to be recommended!

On the whole, though just the first few years at Millthorpe were somewhat isolated I believe my independent life there has really enabled me to see more of the great world than I should otherwise have done. Visitors from a distance have often many and intimate things to tell one, and questions can be discussed in a more leisurely way than in a great centre where every one stands watch in hand, counting the minutes. And on the other hand, by going myself to London for a fortnight or so three or four times a year, I found I could get into touch with all sorts of cliques and circles—such as I perhaps should not have cared to be involved in if I had been permanently living there! The country became a splendid basis for literary work, with the opportunity it afforded (so priceless to me) of writing in the open air and in close contact with the ordinary realities of life; it supplied a good basis for my lecturing and other excursions into the Northern Towns; and with its market-gardening and sandal trades kept my hands busy when my head required a rest.

Of the many years mainly spent here at Millthorpe, the first fifteen—from 1883 to 1898—were somewhat handicapped for me by the presence of a small working-family in the house; first, for ten years, the Fearnehoughs of whom I have already spoken; and afterwards, for five years, the Adams'. No other arrangement was at that time possible. Both families were charming and interesting in their different ways; but necessarily they hampered my freedom a good deal. With children in the house (in both cases) the domestic arrangements had largely to be suited to their necessities and convenience, and my interests had to come very decidedly second. This did not so much matter at the beginning of the time, but later with the expansion of my own sphere of operations a different household arrangement became imperative.

Fearnehough, as I have said, was of a "powerful uneducated" type—a good specimen of the British worker—a bit slow in brain, but exceedingly thorough and downright in all his dealings. His wife possessed the infinite patience and kindliness of the household guardian—going always about her work with untiring forethought and industry—even when, as often happened, she was silently suffering from bad headaches. There was a certain native grace about her, and dignity about him, which well became them. The two children, boy and girl of about nine and ten when they first arrived, were sensible and natural too. To have this family living with me—though it may have been hampering in some ways—was for some years very helpful. Whether at meals, or working in the fields, or sitting round the fire of an evening, to be in close touch with so sane and simple an outlook on life, and one so entirely different from that to which I had generally been accustomed, was in itself an education. The very downrightness of daily existence among those who live close upon absolute necessity is a thing hardly realized even by the most well-meaning of the well-to-do, unless they positively share that existence. Of course it cuts away a vast deal of sentimentalism, æstheticism, and all that. But on the whole it is rather healthy.

I remember one day—in later years when Annie, the daughter, had gone away to work in Sheffield—speaking to her mother about the girl (whose absence I knew she felt) and saying rather sentimentally, "I expect you miss Annie a good deal nowadays." The answer was characteristic, and in its way quite lovely: "*Yes, I do miss her—especially on washing days!*" It was not that Mrs. Fearnehough cared one whit less for her daughter than many a very cultured mother might, but simply that her answer allowed the bed-rock of human nature to be seen. At any rate it took the wind out of my sentimentality! Not long ago I was asking a neighboring farmer—whose son had just got married and migrated on to a little farm of his own—how the son "liked his new place." "Like it?" said the old man with a dryish sort of laugh—"well, I guess he'll like it if he can any way make a living out of it—and if he can't he won't; he'll be better able to say in a year or two." It is from answers like these that one perceives how close on the rocks the lives of the mass peoples are thrust—too close indeed to allow much scope for expression of their real life or liking.

Fearnehough and I stumbled away at our market-gardening for a good many years. Being both to begin with quite ignorant of the trade we made our full complement of mistakes and purchased our experience sometimes dearly. Yet by degrees we got the land into good order. We dug it over, made drains to carry off the water, planted a hundred or two of fruit and forest trees, built bits of walls and fences, kept a horse, and fowls, and grew our crops, and took our produce into market—a strenuous time, but greatly interesting in its way. My commercial instinct was weak, but Albert's was perhaps even weaker! With his real love of good work he would spend as much time preparing an onion-bed as could only be paid for by ten times the value of the crop; and at one period he insisted on rooting every bit of rock and stone out of the subsoil so persistently that I began to think the garden would be turned into a quarry! It was characteristic of him when I remonstrated, to say: "I can't help it—if I didn't do my work thorough when I'm at it, I should only keep awake at night thinking about it." I have already given some of the general results and conclusions of our labours of that time. When the period of our experiment came to an end, Fearnehough returned again to his scythe-making trade in Sheffield, which he still carries on, hale and hearty, down to this day [1915].

I cannot pass this period by without dwelling for

a moment on another friend at that time a member of the household. I mean my dog Bruno [1]—so called not from his colour, for he was a very handsome black spaniel, but from some fanciful association with Giordano Bruno the Italian. That dog—like so many black animals, black horses, black cats, black poodles, black-plumaged birds, rooks, jackdaws, starlings, and so forth—had something *demonic* about him. The tenderness and gentleness of his spirit, combined with a penetrative vision which searched one's very soul, was almost superhuman. I came first to know him when he was merely a puppy at a friend's house. We almost fell in love with each other then and there, and I was not altogether surprised when a few weeks afterwards he arrived at my door, sent on as a present from the said friends. He never doubted for a moment that he had come to his true home, and he settled down at once, a most loving member of the household. The Fearnehoughs took to him right cordially, and Albert himself a year or so later had the great satisfaction of saving him from a horrible death.

I had been out somewhere on foot with Bruno and arriving back within a couple of hundred yards of my gate I perceived the local pack of foxhounds (the pests of this as of all countrysides !) scattered about the road between me and home—the huntsmen having gone into the public-house for a moment to have a drink. But that moment was more than sufficient—for hounds are dangerous things unless under severe control. Something occurred—I know not what. A hound gave cry ; the others joined in ; and in an instant, to my horror and despair, the whole pack was yelling in pursuit, and Bruno flying for his life—in the only direction he *could* at the moment

[1] Shown in the illustration facing page 103.

fly, away from home"! The dog was swift and active, but what chance had he? I gave him up for lost. With extraordinary agility however and much presence of mind he doubled and, clearing ever so many garden walls and gates, dashed through the little hamlet back again, finally racing across one of my fields with the whole pack close behind and of course gaining on him. Most luckily Albert was in our yard at the moment, and hearing the hullabaloo rushed out with a pitchfork in his hand, just in time to check the ravening horde while Bruno rushed past him to safety. A moment more and the dog would have been torn to fragments.

Bruno showed in high degree that curious quality resembling *conscience* in man, by which dogs, having contracted and adopted a new standard of life from their masters, betray an emotional conflict going on within them. Sometimes—as is often the case where fowls are kept—we would have a nest of newly-hatched chicks being kept warm and dry in a basket on the hearth. On such occasions Bruno was torn by conflicting passions. The very sight and smell of the chicks roused the old primitive hunting instinct, and he would creep nearer and nearer to the basket in a very ecstasy of excitement—his limbs trembling and his nose quivering as he sniffed the prey. Yet he knew perfectly well that he must not touch ; and his fidelity was so absolute that I firmly believe he harboured no intention of doing so. But who can tell? We felt that possibly a sudden frenzy of the animal nature might overtake him ; and we could not do otherwise than keep on the watch. As a matter of fact he never did do anything rash ; but the tension on him, poor dog, was so great that sometimes for two or three days he would hardly touch his food, and he positively grew quite thin under the strain. It was really a relief for all of us when the hatching days were over.

There is something strangely touching in the fact that dogs not only thus develop a conscience and a morality foreign to their canine nature, but that also from their intense devotion to their so-called 'masters' they are severed and alienated to some degree from the natural loves of their race—at any rate on the affectional side. I think Bruno nourished in his heart a strange susceptibility to beauty. His amours with other dogs were only of the ordinary kind; but he cherished for a certain white kitten a positive adoration. The kitten was certainly beautiful—snow-white and graceful to a degree—and to Bruno obviously a goddess; but alas! like other goddesses only too fickle and even cruel. When Bruno arrived on the scene, the kitten would skip on to the vantage-ground of a chair-seat; and from thence torment the pathetic and pleading nose of the dog with naughty scratches. Again and again would Bruno—wounded in his heart as well as in his head—return to his ineffectual suit, only to have his advances rejected as before. At last he had to abandon this quest, but it was curious that a year or two later he fell in love with *another* white kitten in much the same way and with much the same result.

"Everything however comes to him who waits"; and the most curious and pathetic part of this story is its ending. For, a good many years afterwards when Bruno had become quite an old dog and had lost much of his activity, a *cat* came and fell in love with him! This cat used to come from a neighboring farm and spend much of its time with the dog, and frequently at night would stay with him in the little outhouse which he used as a kennel, sleeping between the dog's paws. Ultimately the cat was there when Bruno died.

Fearnehough's place, when he returned to Sheffield, was taken by George Adams, who (also with wife and two children) came to share the Millthorpe Cottage with me. Adams was in most ways the very reverse of Albert Fearnehough. Town bred, rather slight and thin, with a forward stoop and a shock of black hair, he was of an impetuous humorous and rather artistic temperament—not too exact or precise about details, but one who could cover a good deal of ground in a day. Born in the poorest slums of Sheffield he told me more than once how, after his mother died, he was left alone a mere urchin in a tiny lodging with his father. His father was a cobbler by trade rather given to drink, and in the habit of going out early of a morning to work as a wage-slave in some shop, and returning late. When he went out he left a *halfpenny* on the table for the boy to find his food with during the day! Not a very good start in life. The boy roamed about, half-starved, cadging or 'snaking' what he could—but developed, perhaps in consequence, a singular resourcefulness. When about thirteen his father died, and he was left absolutely alone in the world. The neighbours may have been kind in their way, but he was alone and without refuge to flee to. Then something pathetic happened. An orphanage for little *girls* had lately been opened in the neighborhood, and the boy knew one or two of these girls. One evening, at closing time, the matron discovered among her little flock this large-eyed, thin-legged almost rickety ragamuffin sitting! Asked what he was doing there he replied that he wanted to be taken in. "But the orphanage is for girls only," said the matron, "and you are not a girl." It was no use, he would not go; tears ran down his face; he told his plight; and they were fain to find him a bed in an attic for the night. Needless to say he remained a second and a third night. The pale mobile face made friends; and the end of it was that a boys' *side* was created in the orphanage and added to that of the girls!

After remaining in the orphanage for a year or two a place was found for George Adams in the villa-residence of a Sheffield manufacturer, where he went first as knife and boot boy and afterwards as under-gardener. The good people of the villa discovered his taste for drawing and painting, and sent him to a School of Art for lessons; and so when at the age of twenty or so he left 'service' and started for himself as an insurance-collector (most depressing of occupations) he had a fair knowledge of gardening and a fair artistic ability at his command. He married, and joining the Socialist movement became one of our most lively and adventurous spirits. The departure of the Fearnehoughs gave me the opportunity of offering their place at Millthorpe to him (and his family)—which he accepted as a joyful exchange from the dismal trade of eternally dunning the needy denizens of mean streets for their funeral and coffin monies.

With his arrival at Millthorpe things took on a more lively air there. His knowledge of gardening was a decided help, and the financial side of the venture—if not exactly a success from the purely commercial point of view—did certainly under the circumstances (absence of any rent, etc.) yield a small profit to the good. He took up cordially with the sandal-making, which I had at first carried on alone, and which came in useful in winter when the outdoor work was slack; and he added bee-keeping to our activities. My literary work and connections were increasing, and the place became more social, and more especially socialistic, than it had been before—so much so indeed that the country folk (or some of them at any rate) became a little alarmed!

A year or two after George Adams' arrival the Parish Councils Act came into operation, and the first election was the cause of much excitement in the villages. Adams and I—though knowing perfectly well that we had no chance of success—decided—chiefly for the fun of the thing—to come forward as candidates; and almost a panic ensued among the larger farmers and the parson as to what we might possibly do or propose. Strange stories were circulated of the Socialist programme, and of the expenses into which the community would certainly be plunged if it were adopted. But the finishing touch to our chances was given by an election address printed and circulated by one candidate of decidedly Conservative type, in which he did not hesitate to say that "it is reported publicly in Holmesfield that one of our opponents advocates the burning of the Bible, and also working on the Sabbath Day." After that we had no prospect of success! *Which* of us two was really pointed at in this accusation we never quite knew, though we entered into a sort of friendly rivalry for the honour. But the printed card containing the address I retain to this day, and it is a treasured possession.

Adams was certainly not mealy-mouthed, and I am afraid he made very blasphemous remarks at times, but his intense sense of fun and his twinkling delight over 'good stories' quite redeemed any such deficiencies. His courageous humour was all the more remarkable because, poor thing, he was always suffering from ill-health. Dating from the early life which I have described, his internal arrangements, as can easily be imagined, never worked really properly; and at times he would suffer a lot of pain, and become seriously emaciated. How he managed to keep up his gardening and other activities in spite of frequent illness was always a wonder; but his vivid imagination carried him on, and if he were downcast at times, new plans and enterprises were sure to come in and disperse the pessimistic mood.

The gardening work however at Millthorpe *was* too much for his slight frame; and after some five years' stay there he elected to retire with his family into a cottage not far off in the same parish and devote himself to the sandal-trade and to the occasional sale of his water-colour drawings. This he did; and after remaining for four or five years moved on to the Letchworth Garden City where his labours and his personality were much appreciated, and where he occupied a little home of his own until his death in 1910.

The Adams' left Millthorpe early in February '98; and the next day—trundling with the help of two boys all his worldly goods in a handcart over the hills, and through a disheartening blizzard of snow —George Merrill arrived. This extraordinary being, in many ways so kindred a spirit to my own, had now been known to me for some years. I had met him first on the outskirts of Sheffield immediately after my return from India, and had recognized at once a peculiar intimacy and mutual understanding. Bred in the slums quite below civilization, but of healthy parentage of comparatively rustic origin, he had grown so to speak entirely out of his own roots; and a singularly affectionate, humorous, and swiftly intuitive nature had expanded along its own lines—subject of course to some of the surrounding conditions, but utterly untouched by the prevailing conventions and proprieties of the upper world. Always—even in utmost poverty—clean and sweet in person and neat in attire, he was attractive to most people; and children (of whom he was especially fond) would congregate round him. Yet being by temperament loving and even passionate—to a degree indeed which sometimes scandalized the "unco' guid"—he was, it may safely be said, never 'respectable.' Fortunately he was either too careless or too unconscious of public opinion to trouble much about that; and despite the shafts of occasional criticism he remained always fairly assured of himself—with the same sort of unconscious assurance that a plant or an animal may have in its own nature. What struck me most, however, on my first meeting with him, was the pathetic look of wistfulness in his face. Whatever his experiences up to then may have been, it assured me that the desire of his *heart* was still unsatisfied.

To George Merrill the arrival at Millthorpe was the fulfilment of a dream; and a blizzard ten times as bad as the actual one would not I believe have daunted him. The departure of the Adams' had left the house largely denuded of furniture, and for some days we bivouacked with a trestle table for meals and a sanded floor. By degrees we got things into order, acquired the necessaries of life and comfort; and started housekeeping on a new footing. For seven years the possibility of this arrangement had I believe wavered before George's eyes, and it had certainly been considered by me. But we had hardly spoken about it. It was too remote. On my side other arrangements and engagements precluded the plan; on his, the various situa-

GEORGE MERRILL.

(*Photo: Lena Connell.*)

tions he had found—once in a newspaper office, once in an hotel, and lastly in an ironworks—were not to be lightly thrown aside. It was only now, when the Adams' were leaving and George at the same time was out of work, that the Fates pointed favorably and the thing was done.

If the Fates pointed favorably I need hardly say that my friends (with a few exceptions) pointed the other way! I knew of course that George had an instinctive genius for housework, and that in all probability he would keep house better than most women would. But most of my friends thought otherwise. They drew sad pictures of the walls of my cottage hanging with cobwebs, and of the master unfed and neglected while his assistant amused himself elsewhere. They neither knew nor understood the facts of the case. Moreover they had sad misgivings about the moral situation. A youth who had spent much of his early time in the purlieus of public-houses and in society not too reputable would do me no credit, and would only by my adoption be confirmed in his own errant ways. Such was their verdict. For myself if I entertained any of these misgivings it was but very faintly. Of the fellow's essential goodness I felt no doubt. What rather troubled me was the question whether *he* would be able to endure the dulness and quiet of a country life.

With a remarkably good ear for music, and a sympathetic baritone voice, he had a ready talent which would have taken him far on the music-hall stage. In fact I hardly know how it was that he did not find a vocation on that stage. Anyhow he was known in not a few circles for his musical quips and his comic or sentimental songs; and was pretty familiar with the doings and *personnel* of the theatres. To take such an one away into the depths of rustic life might have been a great mistake. Probably if this had been the prevailing side of his character it *would* have been a mistake. As it was the move proved a complete success. In a few months or a year my friend was quite acclimatized, and while enjoying (like myself) a day or two in town was always genuinely glad to get back again to our little home in Cordwell Valley.

As I have said, the families I had with me before were both kindly and good sorts, and in their different ways helpful and useful. But a time had come with the growing expansion of my work when it became quite impossible to continue running things on the old footing, and quite necessary for me to have the house really at my own command. The arrival of George Merrill rendered this possible. And immediately a new order of things began. Merrill from the first developed quite a talent for housework. He soon picked up the necessary elements of cookery, vegetarian or otherwise ; he carried on the arts of washing, baking and so forth with address and dispatch ; he took pride in making the place look neat and clean, and insisted on decorating every room that was in use with flowers. I, for my part, finally gave up the market garden business and contracted the garden ground into merely sufficient to supply the needs of the house. This I cultivated partly myself and partly with the occasional help of an outsider ; and in addition I made it a rule to dust my own study and light the fire in it every morning. These little garden and household works —if not amounting to much—I have still always found very helpful and rather pleasant—as giving the bodily side of life some decent expression, and at the same time rendering the mental perspective more just.

Thus we settled down, two bachelors: keeping the mornings intact for pretty close and rigorous work; and the afternoons and evenings for more social recreation. As a rule I find the housekeeper who is a little particular and 'house-proud' is inclined, not unnaturally, to be somewhat set against visitors—especially those who may bring some amount of dirt and dishevelment with them. But George—though occasionally disposed that way—was so genuinely sociable and affectionate by nature that the latter tendency overcame the former. The only people he could not put up with were those whom he suspected (sometimes unjustly) of being pious or puritanical. For these he had as keen a *flair* as the orthodox witch-finder used to have for heretics; and I am afraid he was sometimes rude to them. On one occasion he was standing at the door of our cottage, looking down the garden brilliant in the sun, when a missionary sort of man arrived with a tract and wanted to put it in his hand. "Keep your tract," said George. "I don't want it." "But don't you wish to know the way to heaven?" said the man. "No, I don't," was the reply, "can't you see that *we're in heaven here*—we don't *want* any better than this, so go away!" And the man turned and fled. Like the archdeacon in Eden Phillpotts' *Human Boy* "he flew and was never heard of again."

No doubt his objection to the pious and puritanical was returned with interest by their objection to him. Whatever faults or indiscretions he may have been guilty of, they were occasionally (in true provincial style) fastened on and magnified and circulated about as grave scandals. It was on such occasions however that the real affection of the country people for us showed itself, and they breathed slaughter against our assailants. George in fact was accepted and one may say beloved by both my manual worker friends and my more aristocratic friends. It was only the middling people who stumbled over him; and they did not so much matter! Anyhow our lives had become necessary to each other, so that what any one said was of little importance.

It thus became possible to realize in some degree a dream which I had had in mind for some time—that of making Millthorpe a *rendezvous* for all classes and conditions of society. I had by this time made acquaintances and friends among all the tribes and trades of manual workers, as well as among learned and warlike professions. Architects, railway clerks, engine-drivers, signalmen, naval and military officers, Cambridge and Oxford dons, students, advanced women, suffragettes, professors and provision-merchants, came into touch in my little house and garden; parsons and positivists, printers and authors, scythesmiths and surgeons, bank managers and quarrymen, met with each other. Young colliers from the neighboring mines put on the boxing-gloves with sprigs of aristocracy; learned professors sat down to table with farm-lads. Not, thank heaven! that this happened all in the lump; but little by little and year by year my friends of various degrees and shades got to know each other—and this was a real satisfaction to me. Many lady friends also came to stay with us—some of them unmarried (which may, who knows? have been a cause for scandal); and not a few married couples who liked our way of life and enjoyed talking over questions of household arrangement and simplification.

Of course, after reading Thoreau's *Walden*, whatever simplifications I may have effected in my own household management seemed very negligible and unimportant. Still I felt that some move in that direction, and some propaganda on the subject, was really needed. I tried hard to get some lady friend or other—who would probably understand household affairs much better than I—to write about the subject; but tried in vain. None would take it up. And so ultimately I was reduced to writing on the question myself—in *England's Ideal* and elsewhere.

To-day I feel the importance of the subject as much as—perhaps more than—I did then. I certainly often wish that our household life, plain as it is, was even more plain. But I find that Time—mere Time—has a sinister effect in complicating life. Things arrive, and cannot so easily be got rid of again. Presents are made by well-meaning people, and cannot very well be returned to the donors; new habitudes of life are grafted on the old ones without actually displacing the latter; the wheel of life turns one way, like a ratchet, but will not turn back again; and so the complications grow and the embarrassments multiply—often to such a degree that they become almost unendurable; and one realizes at last why Death came into the world, and how necessary as a Deliverer of souls and a loosener of mortal knots he is. For myself I can truly say that the Waste Paper Basket stands as a signal of one of my greatest pleasures; and that when I feel depressed (which is not very often) I go about the house and hunt up things to destroy or give away—after which ritual act I feel ever so much better and happier.

Simplicity and plainness of life are necessary, on account of the frightful waste of time and strength which the opposite policy entails—a waste which is obviously becoming daily worse and worse. Nor is it necessary to point out that if you employ *servants* to keep all these beggarly elements of life in order for you, instead of looking after them yourself, you still only waste your time and strength in securing (or appropriating in some way) the money with which you pay those servants, as well as in the extra labour and anxiety of looking after the said servants—a state of affairs probably worse than the first.

Plainness again is necessary from foundation considerations of humanity and democracy. To live in opulent and luxurious surroundings is to erect a fence between yourself and the mass-world which no self-respecting manual worker will pass. It is consequently to stultify yourself and to lose some of the best that the world can give.

Thirdly, from mere considerations of health the thing is necessary. My Japanese friend, Sanshiro Ishikawa, calls our houses *prisons*. Plain food, the open air, the hardiness of sun and wind, are things practically unobtainable in a complex ménage.

And lastly, and most important, the complexity of material possessions and demands all around one almost inevitably has the effect of stifling the life of the heart and of the spirit. "The thorns sprang up and choked them." The endless distraction of material cares, the endless temptation of material pleasures, inevitably has the effect of paralysing the great free life of the affections and of the soul. One loses the most precious thing the world can give—the great freedom and romance of finding expression and utterance for one's most intimate self in the glorious presence of Nature and one's fellows.

X

MILLTHORPIANA

WHAT I have just said might seem to suggest a sort of perpetual garden-party going on at Millthorpe. But this of course was by no means the case, and for weeks at a time we would often be quiet enough. A distance of four miles from the nearest railway-station is a good defence; especially in winter with snow on the ground; also the general rule of not seeing visitors till the afternoon. Still we were liable to incursions. To Job are ascribed the pregnant words (xxxi. 35) "O that mine adversary had written a book!" And I am afraid that I had in some such way laid myself open to attack. The ubiquitous American who (to adopt the style of Bernard Shaw) only stayed in England to visit Millthorpe and Stratford-on-Avon, was much in evidence. And faddists of all sorts and kinds considered me their special prey. I don't know what I had done to deserve this—but so it was. Vegetarians, dress reformers, temperance orators, spiritualists, secularists, anti-vivisectionists, socialists, anarchists—and others of very serious mien and character—would call and insist in the most determined way on my joining their crusades—so that sometimes I had almost to barricade myself against them. A friend suggested (and the idea was not a bad one) that I should put up at the gate a board bearing the legend "To the Asylum" on it. Then the real lunatics would probably avoid the neighborhood.

Nevertheless on the whole we got a good deal of fun out of these incursions, and occasionally some real and solid advance.

On one occasion—it was when the Fearnehoughs were living with me—we were sitting quietly at our humble dinner of carrots or what-not, in the middle of the day, when I saw two young ladies pass the window. There came a knock at the door, and I opened it. There stood a very good-looking elegantly dressed girl of twenty-three or twenty-four, with terracotta frock and gainsborough hat, rather Londony in style; with a less showy companion beside her. Said number one: "Does Mr. Carp——" and then breaking off, "Oh! I see you are Mr. Carpenter. You know, I heard you once speak at the Fabian Society. I belong to the Fabian Society. And my cousin and I were near here, and thought perhaps we might call."

"Very glad to see you, I'm sure."

"And is this *really* where you carry on your Simplification of Life? Oh! Madge! isn't it interesting" (this last thrown in as an interjection).

"I don't know about that; but won't you come in and sit down?"

"Thank you so much, I should be glad of a rest."

"Will you have a bit of cake and a glass of milk?"

"Oh no! but I *should* like a piece of dry bread."

"Well, you need not 'simplify' so much as that."

"Oh! but I am so *fond* of dry bread!"

Then it came out that the Uncle and Aunt were waiting outside, so they had to be got in, and ultimately the party were all safely landed in my study—where after the simplification trouble had been

MILLTHORPE COTTAGE AND ORCHARD.

(Holmesfield on the hill above.)

got over, we made a reasonable acquaintance with each other.

But I never afterwards quite forgot that expression "Is this where you *carry on* your?" etc.—as if one hung a flag out of the window.

On another occasion, it being summer-time, a party of forty Spiritualists came over from Manchester to spend Sunday at a neighboring farmhouse, and with the intention of digging me out in the course of the afternoon. Providence however interposed and sent *pelting* rain all day, and the poor things having to walk several miles from the station arrived at their farmhouse simply drenched; and when they had had their dinner, and partially dried their clothes, were naturally in no mood or condition to turn out again—with the exception of ten or twelve of the more heroic, who came on and called on me. What I had done to merit this honour I do not know, as I had had very little experience of Spiritualism; but they sat round and told me all sorts of wonderful stories. In the middle of it all, a plashing was heard outside in the rain, a knock at the door, and a young lady *sandal*-enthusiast arrived. She was a neat-looking well-made girl, in sandals, with bare, unstockinged feet, and she wore a simple navy blue serge dress; but of course she was wringing wet. We had not seen her before; her name was Swanhilda Something (somehow it sounded appropriate); she had set out to walk all the way from Sheffield (nine miles). On the way the rain had come on, and the sandals had nearly come off. She had no umbrella or waterproof; and she was decidedly more than damp. Mrs. Adams, who was then in charge of our ménage, took her upstairs and gave her a change, and she presently joined the Spiritualist party, looking it must be confessed somewhat like a ghost ; but full of spirit and pluck. Her pluck (as I found afterwards) as a dress-reformer was really splendid. On this occasion, after tea, she refused all offers of a bed for the night, donned her still damp clothes and her sandals, and joining the forty Spiritualists, they all splashed back across the hills to the station.

One of the pathetic things of the Socialist movement is the way in which it has caused not a few people of upper class birth and training to try and leave their own ranks and join those of the workers, when—by their very birth and training being unable to bridge the gulf—the result has been that they, belonging neither to one class nor the other, outcasts from one, and more or less pitied or ridiculed by the other, have fallen into a kind of limbo between. I have known several cases of young men of this kind. One of them I may describe under the name of 'Bryan.' His father, being a country squire, wanted Bryan to go into the army. The boy had ideas of his own about the matter, and simply refused. Differences ensued, and ultimately the father offered him £100 a year for three years, and told him to find his *own* way into life. The youth drifted to London, fell in with the Socialists at a street corner, became inspired with their 'cause,' and sought to identify himself thenceforth with the working class. He came and spent a year or more in our neighborhood at Millthorpe. He was a good fellow—his heart, as they say, in the right place ; but whether owing to the wretched character of his training, or to native want of skill or perseverance, he never could or would shape himself to do any solid work. He would dabble a little at the joiner's bench, or in the garden, or with the woodmen in the woods—but only a little. When we urged him to learn some one trade

thoroughly—if only cobbling or cabinet-making—he would always say "Ah! but things will be different when the Revolution comes—we shall all go barefoot, or these things will be done by machinery";
and so one got no nearer any practical result. On one occasion being in the neighborhood of his family home, I went and called on his father, thinking I might be of some use, but found him in a state of despair.

"Oh, Bryan," he said, "I don't know what has taken the boy. Why the other day he came to see us in our London house, and the first thing he said was 'Father, all these houses ought to be burnt down.'

"'Burnt down,' I replied; 'are you mad?'

"'Well, they *ought* to be,' he said, 'and the people made to do some honest work instead of idling their lives away on other folk's labour.'

"'And pray what sort of work would you set them to, young man?'

"'Oh, anything,' he said, 'any straightforward work like mending the roads or breaking stones.'

"'Then I suppose you Socialists would take an old man like me, seventy years of age, and turn me out of house and home, and set me to break stones on the roads—nice "saviours of society" you are!'

"'Well,' he replied, 'of course there would be exceptions—I daresay we should allow you a pension, say £100 a year, on account of your age and infirmity!'

"Think of that, Mr. Carpenter, think of your own son offering you £100 a year, and in the name of these rascally Socialists!"

Needless to say I deeply sympathized—(I don't think in fact he suspected me of being a Socialist)—

but I saw that nothing useful could be done, and at an early opportunity I retired.

Bryan drifted out to Topolobampo, a socialist colony on the Gulf of California; and when that broke up he floated about the borders of Mexico and California, living on chance luck and occasional remittances until family changes brought him finally home.

Another case of a somewhat similar kind was that of a young R.E. captain, Captain Peterson, let us call him, who had read Tolstoy and convinced himself that a military life was wrong, and that he must leave the Army. Being at the time Adjutant of Volunteers in a neighboring town, he used to come up to Millthorpe to discuss these questions and as to how he should ordain his life when once free. I admired his enthusiasm, but felt obliged to warn him not to be in too great a hurry; for it was easy to see that in practical matters he was a mere babe. Certainly the Army was not the place for him. Anything but 'correct' in dress, with generally a large gap between his waistcoat and his trousers, and again another between his trousers and his boots, with projecting schoolboy ears and red nose, he was just the man who would be unmercifully chaffed or even 'ragged' by his fellow-officers. But on the other hand his capacity for battling his way in the world, or for earning his own living, was evidently of the smallest; and his schemes for the future were of the most wild-cat kind. He was going to build a house —but as he would have no money to pay for it, he should get together a little group of workmen (who desired to improve their minds) on the condition that he should teach them elementary mathematics, surveying, etc., during one half of the day, while they should set bricks and mortar for him during the other half! (A charming scheme! but I think I see the British workman agreeing to it!) His house, according to the plan which he drew out of his pocket, was more like a greenhouse than anything else—with walls and roof largely glass; and when I suggested that it might prove rather hot in summer (!) he seemed to have no difficulty in imagining plentiful vines trailing overhead, with foliage and hanging bunches of grapes, to ward off the sun's rays. For the floor of his room he had a device of which he was quite proud. "It is often convenient," he said, "to have *two* carpets—a rough one for ordinary use, and a better one for special occasions."

I assented to this rather dubious premise, for the sake of seeing what would follow!

"Well" he continued "my idea is to sew these two carpets together like a roller towel, and have them passing over rollers at the two opposite ends of the room, so that one carpet should be *on* the floor, and the other *underneath*. Then, you know, when you saw visitors coming, all you would have to do would be to turn the crank (suiting the action to the word), and you would have your best carpet on in a jiffey!"

Too amazed and speechless to make any objection, I could only see with my mind's eye, a cottage piano and a table and an armchair or two gaily sailing across the room, as the crank was being turned.

"Meanwhile" he went on "as carpets are always wanting brushing I intend to have brushes *fixed* underneath the floor, so that every time the carpet is changed it will be automatically brushed. Nothing could be simpler."

It would have been cruel to make further objections to schemes so indeed transparently simple. But they will give the reader an idea of the difficulties and dangers attending the metamorphosis from the condition of an army officer to that of a private in the peaceful regiments of humanity. What has become now of our friend Peterson I cannot certainly say. That he nobly and consistently abandoned his life in the army I know; but whether he succeeded in getting a house built on the Principles of Euclid is doubtful.

Peterson was also connected with an occurrence which at the time was rather mysterious, and caused us some puzzlement. My friend George Merrill had come to live with me, and we two were occupying the house alone. One evening, late in the summer, we had just returned from Sheffield, and tired had thrown ourselves for a moment into chairs, when almost at once a knock came at the door—so soon indeed that we wondered how the visitor could have been so close behind. George went to the door and then turning to me said " A lady wants to see you." At once a voice from outside said very distinctly, " A *woman*, if you please." Roused to a sense of serious events impending, I went forward, and saw, as well as the falling dusk would allow, what appeared to be a fairly pleasant-looking woman of about thirty-five, but somewhat dishevelled and untidy in dress ; and said—

" Can I do anything for you? "

" You can," she replied, " I'm lost, I'm an outcast from the world, will you befriend me? "

" I will if I can," I said, " but tell me first about yourself—what is your name? do you come from Sheffield? "

" You," she exclaimed, " Mr. Carpenter, the author of *Towards Democracy*—and you won't help me, till you know my name and all about me ! "

I looked at George with a wild surmise. "Certainly," I said, "I can't very well help you till I know what is the matter."

"I tell you," she rejoined with increasing emphasis, "I'm lost, I'm an outcast, I can never go back to the world again. Ah!" (pointing to the garden and the rising moon) "if I could only live here in this beautiful scene, with you, far away from the town and all its belongings. Mr. Carpenter, will you befriend me?"

What an appeal to a lone bachelor! Luckily I resisted the temptation to a too ready sympathy, and leaning forward said again, "But still you have not told me anything about yourself and your troubles."

As I did so I caught a distinct and strong waft of liquor.

"Is it not enough that I am lost?" she replied.

The situation was really embarrassing. At last I said:—

"Well, you know, I and my friend have only just come back from Sheffield, and are very tired; will you come again to-morrow, or any day you like to name, when we shall have more time, and tell me your whole story."

At this she threw up her head with a kind of snort, and said: "And you are Mr. Carpenter! and you say come to-morrow—and to-morrow perhaps I shall be *dead*!" And thus saying she strode off to the gate with the air of a tragedy queen.

Nevertheless for some days we could not help feeling a little uncomfortable. The people at the neighboring inn told us that she had come from the Sheffield direction during the afternoon, and had been hanging about waiting for our return for some hours, doubtless had been in the garden on our arrival—which accounted for her sudden appearance

—but no one knew who she was ; nor did tidings of her, or of any mischance to her, reach us for some weeks—till at last the memory of the incident died out.

Then one afternoon, the said Captain Peterson having turned up and being engaged in expounding his theories over a cup of tea—my attention (which had quite wandered from his conversation) was suddenly caught by the words " and there's that woman, she gets drunk, and then comes to my house, and won't go away—it's very awkward !—and she has read your *Towards Democracy* too."

" That's the woman," I exclaimed, " tell me about her ! " and a few explanations soon disclosed the fact that my mysterious visitor was the wife of Peterson's colour-sergeant—a decent sort of body apparently, and all right except for occasional drinking-bouts, when she became liable to these vespertinal excursions !

During the first year or so after Merrill's arrival, and for a year or two before that, we had a young Russian, or Russian Jew, staying in the house. Invalided with consumption he had somehow taken refuge with us. He went by the name of Max Flint. He was of that fine and delicate type of Jew (somewhat perhaps like Mordecai in George Eliot's *Daniel Deronda*) which one associates with Polish origin—a sensitive face with slender nose (not the Jewish proboscis), arched fine eyebrows and brown pensive eyes, well-formed features on the whole, and hands the same—something refined and almost womanly about him. He was handy in a house, and skilful with a needle ; for indeed he was a tailor by trade. His history is worth relating if only because typical of hundreds and thousands of similar cases.

G. M. FEEDING THE FOWLS.

His father, who was a Jewish butcher by trade, "very religious" according to Max "and always lending money and always losing it," lived at Slobodka across the river from Kovno, and not far from the German frontier. Slobodka was the Jewish quarter and consisted of small wooden houses, two stories at most, but even so not unfrequently each occupied by more than one family. Noah Flynck however and his wife and the eight children were proud to have a house all to themselves. The mother died early but Max remembered her telling stories in which she recalled the subjugation of Poland. How Polish 'gentlemen,' landowners, took refuge in Slobodka, were hunted down by the Russian soldiers and *hanged*, and their lands appropriated—especially one well-known old story of a Polish noble who concealed himself in the interior of a haystack. The troops surrounded and searched his house and farmyard, but could not find him, till at last his little dog (who had smelt him out) was seen scratching and routing on the top of the stack, and he was betrayed!

When Max was about sixteen or seventeen the terror of the Russian conscription came upon him. Few people realize what this nightmare is to the Russian peasantry. Even in the late Japanese war, villages were surrounded at midnight by Cossacks and police, houses if not opened immediately were broken into, men roused from sleep, and all between the ages of twenty-one and forty-three taken away, in most cases never to be heard of again! In Max's time it was as bad, if not worse. The same thing went on. At any moment, at dead of night, the home might be broken into and plundered—the young men snatched away for ever. Bribes might defer your fate for a time—but only for a time. As to passports, you could not move without a passport—even to go from one village to another.

Max determined—even against old Noah's wish—to get away to England; and he managed to effect the escape. There are of course professional smugglers who undertake this business for you; and Max often told the story of how he paid three roubles to one of these for the job. He was instructed to be at a certain village close to the river Memel on a certain evening. He gave his family the slip, and arrived there to time; met the agent all right, and with twenty others bound on the same errand was packed in a stable for the night. Half of the company went off in the small hours of the morning, but Max and the remaining half had to remain there all the next day and night till 2 a.m., when the man came and gave them the signal to follow. They crept through the deserted street and along the road till they came to the bridge which alone divided them from Germany. But how to cross this in face of the Russian sentinel keeping watch at the near end? Needless to say it was a question of bribes. Of the three roubles the soldier was to have one. And Max with a kind of glee used to describe how he saw the man sitting there in his box as they crept by, and pretending to be asleep, yet visibly peeping with one eye through his fingers to see that *only the bargained number got through*. Once on the German side they were all right, and could breathe again freely. They met at an inn, counted up their remaining monies, and went on in parties together.

Max came to Leeds. Of the hundreds of Russian Jews there he knew a little about some. He changed his name from Flynck to Flint, to suit the English ear, and soon settled down into sweated work in a Jewish tailors' den.

One must hope and suppose that the move was for the better; but what a long crucifixion is the life of the people! You escape from the horrors of the Russian army—from being preyed upon by human and insect vermin, as well as becoming food for powder—only to sit cross-legged for the rest of your life in a dirty, evil-smelling workshop, with gas flaring, stoves superheated (for making the irons hot), and windows all tightly shut—and that, in the heart of a sad-eyed smoke-ridden manufacturing town in the North of England. The wages I believe, in Max's case, were not so bad as in some such dens, but the 'drive' and the pressure were incessant, the machine-work was exhausting, and the hours amounted to ten and a half per day. Little wonder that in a few years he developed the seeds of phthisis, and was practically marked down as its victim.

Turning into a rebel and a hater of the present order (or disorder) of things, he joined the Socialist club in Leeds and became a worker in the cause. That led to his abandoning his own religion, lodging with Christians, and doing such outrageous things as poking the fire or preparing his own meals on the Sabbath Day—which in turn led to the Jewish community slandering and persecuting *him*! They threw mud and stones at him in the streets; and he became an outcast among his own people. The Jewish girl he was courting refused to consort with him any more and went off with another man, driving him so mad that (as Max told me himself) he on one occasion nearly killed her.

It was somewhere about this time that, in connection with the said Socialist club, I happened to meet him. It was at the deathbed of another Socialist; and perceiving his distress and evident need of a change I asked him for a short holiday to Millthorpe. After that he came again, and again. There was something so gentle and helpful about him that he was always gratefully received by my friends ; and the stories of his life and times were always interesting. Once or twice I wrote—in my best German—to his father[1] ; and the innocent joy of the old man (in his replies) was touching. But naturally Max did not get stronger—and a time came when after being here a week or two he obviously could not go to work again and had to stay on rather indefinitely. The Adams' and he became great friends, and he even helped a little in the sandal-work. Then later, when this was too laborious for him, he took up basket-making, and turned out quite a number of useful baskets ; and as many of these were "waste-paper baskets," one must feel that in this alone—in the providing receptacles for the printed rubbish of the day—he performed a useful service ! Gradually however he got weaker, and had to give up all work. Then it became necessary for him to go to a convalescent Home at Bournemouth ; and there after some months he died.

It is often the case that invalids and old people feel themselves a burden on the household in which they live, think they are no good in the world, and wish themselves out of the way ; and yet all the time the opposite may be the fact. Often they form a point of real interest in the house, they call out people's sympathy and helpfulness, and their own pluck and sociability under failing health gives courage to others who are stronger. Something of this was true of Max. Though depressed at times his quaint and delicate humour was a joy to his friends and acquaintances. One event, which might

[1] At Kovno or Slobodka, now alas ! ravaged by the German invasion [1915].

have proved prematurely fatal to him, he would frequently recount with pleasure. It was one Christmas ; a time when the Village Band is in the habit of coming round to each house in turn and playing its rather fearsome tunes ! As it happened Max's bedroom, being at one end of the house, was over a more or less open shed. It was evening and he was composing himself to sleep ; when the band arrived. But, snow being on the ground, their footsteps were not heard ; and the bandmen very naturally disposed themselves, for more shelter, inside the shed, quite unconscious of course that they were exactly underneath the bed on which an invalid was sleeping. All of a sudden they struck up with a tremendous blare "Christians, Awake !" or some such tune. It was like St. Jerome hearing the last Trump. Poor Max was nearly lifted out of bed by the shock. For a moment he did not know whether he was in this world or the next. When he concluded in favour of this one he found himself lying there in the old bedroom, but his heart palpitating so violently that, combined with the fit of laughter which also seized him, he was quite a wreck for some days after.

There was something ironical in the idea of a Christian hymn proving so nearly fatal to a Jew ; but a similar irony, curiously enough, pursued him to his end at Bournemouth. At the Home there —in order to avoid unpleasant questionings, and also because to him the matter was of no importance— he had said nothing about his Jewish connection but had declared himself a Christian, and had received in a friendly way the visits of the chaplain. When he died the Home made the usual arrangements for his interment in the Protestant Cemetery. But—and the story shows how the Jewish community hangs together—the Jews at Leeds and Manchester got to know somehow about it all, and telegraphed to the synagogue at Southampton to stop the infamy of Christian burial. A deputation came over from Southampton and arrived at the Bournemouth home only an hour or two before the funeral—to claim the body for removal to Southampton and burial with Jewish rites. I of course was on the spot; and a nice position I was in! The matron of the Home and the Chaplain on the one hand had "always understood" that he was a Christian; the Chief Rabbi and his friends insisted absolutely that he was a Jew; the funeral car was already waiting in the yard; and Max himself lay there in the mortuary chapel with his features in death finer and paler than ever, and wearing such an expression of high calm and indifference as might well represent his own actual feeling in the matter. I, of course, to all the parties concerned was obviously the "guilty" person—guilty of having got them into such a coil—and they looked at me with eyes of blame. But—though really just as indifferent as Max himself—I thought it best to 'play the game'; and insisted that as he had openly declared himself a Christian he *was* a Christian and should be buried as such. The Jewish party on its side brought arguments to show that a mere declaration on such a matter counted for nothing; and soon we plunged into a long discussion which I kept up for some time in order (partly) to hear what they would say. When I perceived however how tremendously seriously the Jews took the whole matter, and reflected also that Max's father would be broken-hearted if he heard that his son had been put in a Christian grave, I thought it best to give way. The Chaplain and the matron agreed, and were indeed quite sensible about it all—and finally poor Max's mortal remains were carried off in triumph by his own people.

In conclusion of this chapter I may relate a curious story which perhaps helps to show how the elements of real inspiration and of mental aberration may sometimes get mixed up in the same person.

I had received a letter from London from a man who described himself as a gold-miner from the Sierra Nevada, saying that he had just arrived in England, and was wishful to see me, as he had a message to deliver, and proposing to come on immediately to Millthorpe. As it happened I was just starting for Glasgow and Edinburgh on a lecturing tour. So I wrote at once telling him to wait a week for my return, and to employ his time meanwhile in sight-seeing. But on my return I found to my surprise that he had already been in the village some days, that he had taken a lodging, and was awaiting my arrival. The next day, November 21, 1910, he walked into my yard—obviously an American of a manual worker type, thin, sandy-haired and tall, with dark clothes and black slouch hat, somewhat horny-handed, but with a certain refinement of figure and physiognomy. Also there was a slightly "fallen in" and tired look about him which puzzled me at the moment, but was soon explained. He began almost immediately—as soon as we were sat down—telling me a long story—of which I can only give the outlines.

It seemed that he had been working for a good many years in a gold-mine (probably as part-owner of it)—a mine up 10,000 feet in the Sierra Nevada. One day—six years before the events which he was about to narrate—a strange vision came to him. He had lost his way on the Nevada sandhills, and was searching about in some anxiety, when a sudden transformation of the landscape occurred, and he was transported into a new world, which he could only describe as 'heaven.' On several succeeding occasions the same vision came to him. Meanwhile, he said, he had been fighting hard against the three great temptations of a miner's life—drink, tobacco, and an irascible temper. Each of these troubles in turn disappeared finally with a sudden deliverance and certain assurance of success. Then, only a couple of months before coming to England, more frequent visions came to him, accompanied by voices; and the affair culminated in his getting hold of Dr. Bucke's book on *Cosmic Consciousness* when he read the chapters about Buddha and Jesus. Then followed what he described as "seven days of ecstasy, agonizing ecstasy—tears of peace and joy streaming down my face—in which I saw *everything, everything*." After that he read one day in the same book the chapter on E. C.

Then one morning—as he was going up the mountain to his work from the camp below (Victor, Colorado), he heard the voices again shouting: "They came surging up close to my ears, and then faded away into the far distance, and then came close again—and two of the voices were God's, and one was my own [!], and they were shouting *Edward Carpenter, Edward Carpenter, go and see E. C., go and see*, etc., etc. And I at the same time was shouting *Brother E. C.—God's beloved Son, I am coming to you*."

[George and I looked at each other again with a wild surmise! Another case for the Asylum !]

"And all this," he continued, "kept being repeated as I walked up the hill, over and over again, till at last it faded away in the distance. And all the morning over my work I was in tears—tears of joy and pain—and had to conceal my face from my mates. But as I turned the crusher I felt enormous strength, and was quite unconscious of effort."

Then followed all sorts of stories about God telling him to do this and that, and the Devil telling him to do this and that, and of temptations and *tests* to which he had been subjected. But in the end, he said, he had been impelled to come and see me, and he had come. One day he just threw down his tools and left them lying there, went and said good-bye to his mother (and she evidently did not want him to go) and set sail for England. And now we two (he and I) were to lead a mission round the world—he had some idea about a new Messiah—and to preach and convert the nations together.

Things were evidently getting serious! Yet I hardly knew what to do. He was such a very decent fellow, quiet and kindly and essentially reasonable, and by no means a fanatic; and most obviously genuine and spontaneous. I hardly knew how to attack him.

Then George Merrill saved the situation. He asked Grogan (C. E. Grogan was his name) to have some tea; and the answer gave the needed clue.

"Tea? No, thank you, I haven't taken tea or any food for three weeks." [Afterwards on inquiry at his village-lodgings I found his landlady had been dreadfully disturbed at his not touching a crumb of anything all the time he was there.]

"But if you won't eat, you'll have a cup of tea, or something to drink?"

"No, nothing—except a glass of water—I haven't eaten anything for three weeks, and I don't think I shall ever eat again."

The cat was out; and the line of action was clear.

"Look here!" I said, "I quite understand you, and sympathize with your experiences—and I think indeed you have had some very real experiences, and some realizations of another kind of consciousness; but you must be careful, and have some idea of what you are doing. There is no doubt that sometimes abstinence from food will help to develop internal faculties. On the other hand to go too far and to weaken the body, perhaps permanently, may be most foolish, and dangerous. The body is there to give expression to the soul, and if you have any important spiritual revelation to express you want all the faculties of your body in good order for the purpose. Starvation, it is well known, engenders visions and voices, often of a very delusive character. You must not give yourself away to all that. How do you know that what you say is of God is not of the Devil; and *vice versâ*? And how do *I* know?"

So I went on at him; making him plainly understand that I was not going to join in his crusade—whatever it was. "Besides," I said, "I still do not see what made you come here. You say you have not read any of my writing—except what was contained in Dr. Bucke's book. *What do you know about me?*"

Then he leaped out again. "Oh, I know all about you. *I know that you will never die!*"

"That is not a very cheerful prospect," said I, gently laughing.

"Oh, well," he replied, "you will at any rate

live four hundred years. It is like this: The earth and all that are in it, are from this day passing gradually into a new and higher plane of existence. That process will complete itself in four hundred years, and at the end of that time the earth will be absorbed into the Sun and the ethereal life. A wonderful period of new life will arrive; and all those who are living then will be transformed without passing through Death."

He spoke earnestly and with conviction. I did not oppose him; but warned him again about going too far with his abstinence, and advised deliberation in his conclusions. He did not seem inclined to give way about food—said he thought he should never require it again, and maintained that the internal breathing (*prana*) came to him with a wonderful sense of fragrance and refreshment.

He was extraordinarily good; for though I had refused, almost rudely, to join in his schemes, he took no offence—simply said that he was satisfied, now that he had given the message he had been told to give, and would return to America "to-morrow."

Having then made my negative attitude quite clear, so that there should be no misunderstanding, I now adopted a positive line; and talked to him for some little time about experiences of the kind he had described. Then I went and fetched some books—the *Bhagavat Gita*, some of the Upanishads, and other works. He had never even heard their names. I opened the *Bhagavat Gita*, almost at random, and pointed him out a passage. He almost clapped his hands for joy. "Oh yes, that is exactly what I feel." He seized the book, and turned over the pages, pouncing on passage after passage with delight. "Yes, yes, that is just it!" There was no doubt about his sincere and instant appreciation. Then I showed him the passage in the *Bhagavat Gita* about moderation in eating and moderation in abstinence ; but he did not seem inclined to agree. " I just do what God tells me."

Finally I *gave* him the *Gita*, and some other books of similar character. And he on his side decided to return to America " to-morrow "—and insisted on my writing at once for a cab. I did not attempt to dissuade him—feeling that perhaps he was right—also that his friends in America would be more satisfied if he returned.

Meanwhile he *looked* ever so much better than when he came into the house—and evidently was so —" glad to have carried out what he had to do," he said. I told him that on board ship his mind would settle itself ; and he went off.

He wrote from Liverpool next day, saying he was very happy ; and a month or so later from Colorado —in which letter he said, " The *unseen force* which caused me to quit eating caused me to begin again (as suddenly as I quit). My fast was merely a part of the *lesson* which is continually before me." Since then I have heard from him from time to time. In one letter he says : " I am feeling fine, and slowly but surely am I (as a child) permitted to learn the *a, b, c* of *real life*. It is my belief that we are all permitted to pierce the veil that conceals *real Life* from our view, only accordingly as our minds are ready to absorb the knowledge gained thereby. From a point of view of Cosmic Consciousness I am beginning my life all over again, and am only beginning in a small way to see and understand some of the simpler truths of the same ; but I have lost much of that feeling of haste, and learning with the idea in mind that I have all eternity to learn in. My folk and relatives all glad that I am home and quit my wanderings for the present. I think I shall engage in mining again in a small way. This mining camp is about 10,000 feet altitude, and the weather is beautiful, plenty sunshine, and not cold winter weather."

In his latest to me he says: "You will remember when I visited you I said you would never die. I still feel same way and see no chance of my dying, personally it is a matter of indifference whether I live or die. If I must die in order to live again, so be it, but may we not be permitted to enjoy eternal life here and now? I think so. I think the Harvest of the world is ripe, but such great changes are slow and almost unnoticeable and I think overlap each other, so that *harvest* or death of one thing is the Birth of another, that is consciousness of Eternal Life becoming more general. Well, I think that I have written enough that you may see the drift of my mind, and I think that is what you want. Love to Mr. Merrill and yourself, yours truly, C. E. GROGAN."

To which words of Grogan's I would only add: "No doubt we *are* permitted to enjoy eternal life here and now—even in this tiniest corner, wherever it may be, of space and time."

XI

THE STORY OF MY BOOKS

THE fate of my books has been interesting—at any rate to myself! Leaving aside *Narcissus and Other Poems*, and *Moses: a Drama*—which were written in early days at Cambridge, and were only, so to speak, exercises in literature and efforts to vie with then-accepted models—*Towards Democracy*, of course, has been the start-point and kernel of all my later work, the centre from which the other books have radiated. Whatever obvious weaknesses and defects it may present, I have still always been aware that it was written from a different *plane* from the other works, from some predominant mood or consciousness superseding the purely intellectual. Indeed, so strong has been this feeling that, though tempted once or twice to make alterations from the latter point of view, I have never really ventured to do so; and now, after more than thirty years since the inception of the book, I am entirely glad to think that I have not.

It is a curious question—and one which literary criticism has never yet tackled—why it is that certain books, or certain passages in books, will bear reading over and over again without becoming stale; that you can return to them after months or years and find entirely new meanings in them which had escaped you on the first occasion; and that this can even go on happening time after time, while other books and passages are exhausted at the first reading and need never be looked at again. How is it possible that the same phrase or concatenation of words should bear within itself meaning behind meaning, horizon after horizon of significance and suggestion? Yet such undoubtedly is the case. Portions of the poetic and religious literature of most countries, and large portions of books like *Leaves of Grass*, the *Bhagavat Gita*, Plato's *Banquet*, Dante's *Divina Commedia*, have this inexhaustible germinative quality. One returns to them again and again, and continually finds fresh interpretations lurking beneath the old and familiar words.

I imagine that the explanation is somewhat on this wise : That in the case of passages that are exhausted at a first reading (like statements say of Church doctrine or political or scientific theory) we are simply being presented with an intellectual ' view ' of some fact ; but that in the other cases in some mysterious way the words succeed in conveying the fact itself. It is like the difference between the actual solid shape of a mountain and the different views of the mountain obtainable from different sides. They are two things of a different order and dimension. It almost seems as if some mountain-facts of our experience *can* be imaged forth by words in such a way that the phrases themselves retain this quality of solidity, and consequently their outlines of meaning vary according to the angle at which the reader approaches them and the variation of the reader's mind. None of the outlines are final, and the solid content of the phrase remains behind and eludes them all. Anyhow the matter is a most mysterious one ; but as a fact it remains, and demands explanation.

I have felt somehow with regard to *Towards Democracy* that—while my other books were merely subsidiary and mainly represented 'views' and 'aspects'—this one (with all its imperfections) had that central quality and kind of other-dimensional solidity to which I have been alluding. And my experiences in writing it have corroborated that feeling.

I have spoken elsewhere about the considerable period of gestation and suffering which preceded the birth of this book; nor were its troubles over when it made its first appearance in the world. The first edition, printed and published by John Heywood of Manchester, at my own expense, fell quite flat. The infant showed hardly any signs of life. The Press ignored the book or jeered at it. I can only find one notice by a London paper of the first year of its publication, and that is by the old sixpenny *Graphic* (of August 11, 1883), saying—not without a sort of pleasant humour—that the phrases are "suggestive of a lunatic Ollendorf, with stage directions," and ending up with the admission that "the book is truly mystic, wonderful—like nothing so much as a nightmare after too earnest a study of the Koran!" The *Saturday Review* got hold of the *second* edition, and devoted a long article (March 27, 1886) to slating it and my socialist pamphlets (*Desirable Mansions*, etc.) as instances of "the kind of teaching which is now commonly set before the more ignorant classes, and which is probably accepted in good faith by not a few among them. A haphazard collection of fallacies, to which the semblance of a basis is given by half a dozen truisms, flavored by a little Carlylese, or by diluted extracts of Walt Whitman . . . such is the compound which 'cultivated' Socialism offers as a new and saving faith to the working classes, and of which the works before us offer a good example." Then follow severe comments on my absurd views about Usury and the manners and customs of the Rich, and finally a long quotation from *Towards Democracy*; of which book the writer says: "And this sort of thing goes on through two hundred and fifty pages, the blank monotony of which is only relieved here and there by a few passages which it would be undesirable to quote, and which it is not wholesome to read."

The London Press—when it did deign to notice my work—followed the same sort of lead; and it was left (as usual) to comparative outsiders to make any real discovery in the matter. Curiously enough, a very young man (George Moore-Smith) in a long article in the *Cambridge Review* of November 14, 1883, led the way in drawing serious attention to the first edition. The *Indian Review* (Wm. Digby) of May 1885 had a remarkably sympathetic and intelligent notice of the second edition, and I owe much to my friend W. P. Byles' introduction of the book to Northern readers through the *Bradford Observer* (of March 19, 1886); also to an article by H. Rowlandson in *The Dublin University Review* for April, 1886.

With the third edition (1892) a certain amount of timid acknowledgment set in. Notices in a few more or less well-known papers were friendly though brief and cautious, as with a scent of danger. The fourth and complete edition did not appear till ten years later (1902), and by that time the book had established itself. It had ceased to demand Press-appreciations, favorable or otherwise; and so the critics—*very luckily for themselves*—escaped, and have escaped, without ever having had to give any sort of full pronouncement or verdict on the book!

To return to the first edition. I had only five

hundred copies printed; but at the end of two years when I had gathered material enough for a second edition, there was still a hundred or so of these on hand. All the same I did not feel any serious misgiving. I caused a thousand copies to be printed of the second edition (260 pp.), sent them round to the Press again, and waited. This was in 1885. If anything the reception accorded was worse than before—in a sense worse—because there was more of it! By 1892—when I needed to print a third edition—only some seven hundred copies of the second edition had gone. Seven hundred in seven years! The prospects were not good, yet I did not feel depressed. I had certainly not expected any great sale; and there were even signs of improvement. My *other* books were beginning to attract a little attention. It was obviously also hard on this book to have it published in Manchester. So I determined to go to London. There was no possible chance of getting a publisher there to take it as his own speculation; so I went to Mr. Fisher Unwin and asked him to print at my expense and sell it on commission—which he naturally was quite willing to do! The book had now grown to 368 pp., and its price had to be raised from 2s. 6d. to 3s. 6d.; but its sales actually improved, and for two or three years ranged at about two hundred copies a year. I began to think it was just possible that my little bark would navigate itself, that it would float out on deeper waters and into the world-current; when something disastrous happened which left it in the shallows for quite a few years longer.

That something was the Oscar Wilde trial or trials, which took place in the spring of 1895; but to understand how they affected *Towards Democracy* I must go back a little. Early in 1894 I started writing a series of pamphlets on sex-questions—those questions which at that time were generally tabooed and practically not discussed at all, though they now have become almost an obsession of the public mind. As pamphlets of that kind would have no chance with the ordinary publishers, I got them printed and issued by the Manchester Labour Press—a little association for the spread of Socialist literature, on the committee of which I was. The pamphlets were *Sex-love*, *Woman*, and *Marriage*; and they sold pretty well—three or four thousand copies each. Encouraged by their success I began early in '95 to put them together, and add fresh matter to them, till I had a book ready for publication—which I afterwards entitled *Love's Coming-of-Age*. This book I offered to Fisher Unwin (as he was already selling *Towards Democracy*) and he accepted it—undertaking to produce the book himself and give me a fair Royalty. His Agreement was signed in June 1895.

Meanwhile, in January 1895 (though dated 1894) I issued from the Labour Press, and in the same connection as the other pamphlets, a fourth one, entitled *Homogenic Love*—which I suppose was among the first attempts in this country to deal at all publicly with the problems of the Intermediate Sex. I placed "printed for private circulation only" on the Title-page, and had only a comparatively small number of copies struck off—which were not sold but sent round pretty freely to those who I thought would be interested in the subject or able to contribute views or information upon it. My object in fact was to get in touch with others and to obtain material for future study or publication. Even in this quiet way the pamphlet created some alarm—and in the dove-cotes of Fleet Street (as I heard) caused no little fluttering and agitation ; but it is quite possible the matter would have ended there, if it had not been for the Oscar Wilde troubles. Wilde was arrested in April 1895 and from that moment a sheer panic prevailed over *all* questions of sex, and especially of course questions of the Intermediate Sex.

I did not include *Homogenic Love* in my proposed new book, nor had I any intention of including it ; but when the mere existence of the thing came to the knowledge of Fisher Unwin he was so perturbed that he actually cancelled his Agreement with me, with regard to the book *Love's Coming-of-Age*, and broke loose from it. It was in vain that I tried to restrain him. He had got his leg over the trace, as it were, and was 'off.' Indeed, he was quite willing to sacrifice the expense he had already incurred (for the book was now partly set up) rather than go on with it. Under the circumstances I could not, of course, very well compel him to publish. Moreover I felt sorry for his perturbation, and quite understood some of its causes. The extent of it was finally shown by his going so far as to turn *Towards Democracy* out of his shop, and refuse to publish *that* any longer !

Thus my two books *Love's Coming-of-Age* and *Towards Democracy*—like two poor little orphans—were both out on the wide world again.

For the moment I will go on with *Love's Coming-of-Age*. Being routed by Fisher Unwin, I went to Sonnenschein, Bertram Dobell, and others—altogether five or six publishers—but they all shook their heads. The Wilde trial had done its work ; and silence must henceforth reign on sex-subjects.[1] There was nothing left for me but to

[1] I may say here that I never happened to meet Oscar Wilde personally.

return to my little Labour Press at Manchester, and get the book printed and published from there—which I did, the first edition being issued in 1896.

It is curious to think that that was not twenty years ago, and what a landslide has occurred since then! In '96 no 'respectable' publisher would touch the volume, and yet to-day [1915] the tide of such literature has flowed so full and fast that my book has already become quite a little old-fashioned and demure! But the severe resistance and rigidity of public opinion at the time made the volume very difficult to write. The readiness, the absolute determination of people to *misunderstand* if they possibly could, rendered it very difficult to guard against misunderstandings, and as a matter of fact nearly every chapter in the book was written four or five times over before I was satisfied with it.

Love's Coming-of-Age ought of course (like some parts of *England's Ideal*) to have been written by a woman; but, though I tried, I could not get any of my women-friends to take the subject up, and so had to deal with it myself. Ellen Key, in Sweden, began—I fancy about the same period—writing that fine series of books on *Love, Marriage, Childhood,* and so forth, which have done so much to illuminate the Western World; but at that time I knew nothing of her and her work.

My book circulated almost immediately to some extent in the Socialistic world, where my name was fairly well known; but some time elapsed before it penetrated into more literary and more 'respectable' circles. One of the first signs of its succeeding in the latter direction took a rather amusing shape. I had, one day, to call upon a well-known London publisher (who was already publishing some of my books, though he had refused this particular one) on business, and having discussed the matters immediately in hand, he presently turned to me and inquired how my *Love's Coming-of-Age* was selling. I of course gave a fairly favorable account. "I think," said he in a somewhat chastened tone "that perhaps we made rather a mistake in refusing some little time back to take it up. A Sunday or two ago I was at church [probably a Congregational or Unitarian Chapel], and the minister quoted a page or two from your book, and spoke very highly of it, and actually gave the published address and price, and all; and I saw quite a lot of people noting the references down." He paused, and then added, "Quite a good advertisement—worth thirty or forty copies I daresay." I could not help smiling. No wonder he was sorry! But the story gave promise of better things to come.

In 1902 the said publishing firm was glad to take the book up and publish it on commission for me—which they (and their successors) have done ever since. And its sale in England (though not phenomenal like that of the German translation) has, I must say, been very good.

To return to *Towards Democracy*. Considering its expulsion from Mr. Fisher Unwin's shop and the generally panicky condition of the book market in London, there seemed nothing to do but to return to Manchester and place it also in the hands of the little Labour Press for publication. The two thousand or so copies remaining in Unwin's hands were my property, and I had only to remove them to Manchester, get a new title-page printed, and have them issued from there. This I accordingly did, and in '96 the Labour Press edition appeared—368 pp., the same as Fisher Unwin's. Naturally the Labour Press connection was not very favorable as regards circulation, and the price (3s. 6d.) was high for Socialist and Labour circles. The spread of the book remained slow—slower of course than it had been with Unwin, and hardly amounted to a hundred copies a year.

This was bad; but worse remained behind. Somewhere early in 1901 the Labour Press—whose financial affairs had never been very satisfactory—went bankrupt.! I knew of course what was pending; and as the stock of *Towards Democracy* belonged to *me*, and I knew that if left at the Press it would be in danger of falling into the creditors' hands, there was nothing left but to smuggle it away as soon as I could into some place of safe keeping. Mr. James Johnston, City Councillor, always a good friend, came to the rescue and offered me storage room in his office. I hired a dray. And so one foggy day, with a good part of a ton of *Towards Democracy* on board—which I helped to load and unload—I jogged with the drayman through the streets of Manchester amid the huge turmoil of the cotton goods and other traffic. A strange load—and I never before realized how heavy the book was!

It lay there for some months, and then about July of the same year I made arrangements with Sonnenschein & Co. for them to sell the book on commission, and the stock was transferred into their hands. From that time its sales slowly went forward —from a hundred or a hundred and fifty per annum in 1902, to eight hundred or nine hundred in 1910, when the Sonnenschein business, and with it my book, passed into the hands of George Allen & Co. In 1902 the fourth part of *Towards Democracy*, i.e. "Who shall command the Heart" was published; and in 1905 this was incorporated with the three former parts in one complete volume. Later in the same year I succeeded (a long cherished project) in producing a pocket edition of the whole on India paper, which has ever since sold alongside and *pari passu* with the Library edition. Thus after twenty-one years (in 1902) these writings (begun in 1881) came to an end; and three years later the book took its definite and permanent form in print and binding, and some sort of rather indefinite place in the world of letters.

Talking about their place in the world of letters, some of my books have, I fear, puzzled the public by their titles. *Ioläus* has been much of an offender in this way. The uncertainty as to who or what Ioläus might be, the difficulty of knowing how to spell the word, and the impossibility of pronouncing it, proved at one time such obstacles that they quite adversely affected the sales. On one occasion I received a telegram from a firm asking me to send at once two hundred Oil-cans. My puzzlement was great, as I had indeed never embarked in the oil trade, nor in my wildest dreams thought of doing so—till suddenly it flashed upon me that the message, having had to pass through a rustic post-office, had been transformed on the way, and that the romantic friend and companion of Hercules had been turned into a paraffin tin! After that I modified the title so as to avoid any such sacrilege in the future.

Coming back to *Towards Democracy* again, I do not know that I have ever seen a very serious estimate or criticism of that book in any well-known literary paper. Like others of my works it has come into the literary sheep-fold not through the accepted gate but "some other way, like a thief or a robber." It has been generally ignored—as already explained—by the guardians of the gate, yet it has quietly and decisively established itself, and the 'sheep' somehow have taken kindly to the 'robber.' And perhaps the matter is best so. A book of that kind is not easy to criticize; it cannot be dispatched by a snap phrase; it does not belong to any distinct class or school; its form is open to question; its message is at once too simple and too intricate for public elucidation—even if really understood by the interpreter. That it should go its own way quietly, neither applauded by the crowd, nor barked at by the dogs, but knocking softly here and there at a door and finding friendly hospitality—is surely its most gracious and satisfying destiny.

But though the ignoring by the critics of *Towards Democracy* has seemed natural and proper, I confess I have been somewhat surprised by their non-recognition or non-discussion of the questions dealt with in the other books; because, as I have said these books are on a different plane from *Towards Democracy*. They deal with theories or views which flow (as I think) perfectly logically from the central idea of *Towards Democracy*—just as the different views or aspects of a mountain flow perfectly logically from the mountain-fact itself. We cannot discuss the central idea, but we can discuss the aspects, because they come within the range of intellectual apprehension and definition. If the world—it seems to me—should ever seize the central fact of such books as *Leaves of Grass* and *Towards Democracy*, it must inevitably formulate new views of life on almost every conceivable subject: the aspects of all life will be changed. And the discussion and definition of these views ought to be extraordinarily interesting. It is therefore surprising I say that no serious discussion of the underlying or implicit assumptions of these two books has yet taken place.

It is true, of course, that to-day the world is witnessing a strange change of attitude on almost all questions, and a vague feeling after the new aspects to which I am alluding ; but it does not concatenate these views on to any central fact, and therefore cannot deal with them adequately or effectively. It is as if people, having taken drawings of a hitherto undiscovered mountain from many different sides, and comparing them together, should not realize that it is the *same* mountain which they have been observing all the time, and that there *is* a unity and a reality there which will explain and concatenate all the outlines. I say it is a little disappointing that this point has not yet been reached, because it would make the discussion and definition of the new views so wonderfully interesting. On the other hand it is obvious that in the midst of the enormous output and rush of modern literature, critics generally have thrown up the sponge, and are content to get through their work perfunctorily or as best they can, without the added labour of tackling, or attempting to tackle, a great new synthesis.

The attempt made a quarter of a century ago—in *Civilization: its Cause and Cure*—to define the characteristics of (modern) civilization, and to show the civilization-period as a distinct stage in social evolution, destined to pass away and to be succeeded by a later stage—of which later stage even now some of the features may be indicated—has never as far as I know been seriously taken up and worked out. The Socialists of course have certain views on the subject, but they are limited to the economic field, and do not by any means cover the whole ground ; and various doctrinaire sets and sects are nibbling at the problem from different sides ; but a real statement and investigation of the whole question, and a linking of it up to deepest spiritual facts, would obviously be absorbingly interesting. I first read the paper which bears the above name at the Fabian Society (? in 1888), and, needless to say, it was jeered at on all sides ; but since then, somehow, a change has come, and even Sidney Webb and Bernard Shaw, who most attacked me at the time, have ceased to use the word 'Civilization' in its old optimistic and mid-Victorian sense. What we want now is a real summing-up and settling of what the word connotes—both from the historical point of veiw, and with regard to the future.

Another paper in the same book, which shocked a good many of my Cambridge friends, was my "Criticism of Modern Science." The Victorian age glorified modern Science—not only in respect of its patient and assiduous observation of facts, which every one allows, but also on account of the supposed Laws of Nature which it had discovered, and which were accounted immutable and everlasting. A light arising from some quite other source convinced me that this infallibility of the scientific "Laws" was an entire illusion. I had been brought up on mathematics and physical science. I had lectured for years on the latter. But now the reaction set in ; and—rather rudely and crudely it must be confessed—I turned on my old teacher to rend her ! I published in 1885, and in Manchester, a shilling pamphlet called *Modern Science: A Criticism,* and sent it round to my mathematical and scientific friends. I think most of them thought I had gone daft ! But, after all, the whirligig of Time has brought its revenge, and the inevitable evolution of human thought has done its work ; and now, one may ask, where *are* the airy fairy laws and theories of the Science of the last century? The great stores of observations and facts are certainly there, and so are the marvellous applications of these things to practical life—but where are the immutable Laws?—where are the clean-cut systems of the families and species of plants and animals? where is Boyle's law of gases? where the stability of the planetary orbits? where the permanence and indestructibility of the atom? where is the theory of gravitation, where the theory of light, the theory of electricity? the law of supply and demand in Political Economy, of Natural Selection in Biology? of the fixity of the Elements in Chemistry, or the succession of the strata in Geology? All gone into the melting-pot—and quickly losing their outlines!

It is true that in the great brew which is being thus formed, rags and chunks of the old "Laws of Nature" are still discernible; but no one supposes they are there for long, and on all sides it is obvious that the scientific world is giving up the search for them, and the expectation (in the face of such things as radium, Hertzian waves, Karyokinesis and so forth) of ever reconstituting Science again on the old Victorian basis. These fixed 'Laws,' it is pretty evident, and their remaining débris, will melt away, till out of the seething brew something entirely different and unexpected emerges. And that will be? . . . Yes, what indeed out of such a Cauldron *might* be expected to emerge—a strange and wonderful Figure, a living Form!

Yet the curious thing is that while this process of the dissolution of scientific theory is going on before our eyes, and on all sides, no one seems to be aware of it—at any rate no one sums it up, gives it outline and definition, or tackles its meaning and result. Tolstoy was pleased with the attacks on Modern

Science contained in *Civilization: its Cause and Cure*, wrote to me about it, and had the chapter printed in Russian, with a preface by himself. But his point of view was that Science being a serious enemy to Religion anything which bombarded and crippled Science would help to free Religion. That was not my point of view. I do not regard Science—or rather Intellectualism—as the foe of Religion, but more as a stage which *has to be passed through* on the way to a higher order of perception or consciousness—which might possibly be termed Religion—only the word religion is too vague to be very applicable here.

Another airy castle which is obviously fading away before our eyes is that of the "Laws" of Morality. The whole structure of civilization-morality is being rapidly undermined. The moral aspects of Property, Commerce, Class-relations, Sex-relations, Marriage, Patriotism, and so forth, are shifting like dissolving views. Nietzsche has scorched up the old Christian altruism; Bernard Shaw has burned the Decalogue. Yet (in this country and according to our custom) we jog along and pretend not to see what is happening. No body of people faces out the situation, or attempts to foretell its future. The Ethical society professes to substitute Ethics for Religion, as a basis of social life; yet never once has it informed us what it means by Ethics! The Law courts go mumbling on over ancient measures of right and wrong which the man in the street has long ago discarded. Much less has any group attempted to foreshadow the new Morality, and concatenate it on to the great root-fact of existence. In my "Defence of Criminals: a Criticism of Morality,"[1] I gave an outline and an indication of what was happening, and of the way

[1] One of the chapters in *Civilization: its Cause and Cure*.

out into the future ; but that paper, as far as I know, has never been seriously discussed.

Nevertheless under the surface new ideas are forming, the lines of the coming life are spreading. The book *Civilization*—first published by Sonnenschein, in 1889—has had a good circulation, and been translated into many languages. Though somewhat hastily and crudely put together, yet owing to a certain *élan* about it, and probably largely owing to the fact that it gives expression to the main issues above-mentioned, it has been well received.

One idea, which runs all through the book—namely, that of there being three great stages of Consciousness : the simple consciousness (of the animal or of primitive man), the self-consciousness (of the civilized or intellectual man), and the mass-consciousness or cosmic consciousness of the coming man, is only roughly sketched there, but is developed more fully in *The Art of Creation.* It is of course deeply germane to *Towards Democracy.* And though we may not yet be in a position to define the conception very exactly, still it is quite evident, I think, that some such evolution into a further order of consciousness is the key to the future, and that many æons to come (of human progress) will be ruled by it. Dr. Richard Bucke, by the publication (in 1901) of his book *Cosmic Consciousness* made a great contribution to the cause of humanity. The book was a bit casual, hurried, doctrinaire, un-literary, and so forth, but it brought together a mass of material, and did the inestimable service of being the first to systematically consider and analyse the subject. Strangely here again we find that his book—though always spreading and circulating about the world, beneath the surface--has elicited no serious recognition or response from the accredited authorities, philosophers, psychologists, and so forth; and the subject with which it deals is in such circles practically ignored—though in comparatively unknown coteries it may be warmly discussed. So the world goes on—the real expanding vital forces being always beneath the surface and hidden, as in a bud, while the accepted forms and conclusions are little more than a vari-coloured husk, waiting to be thrown off.

Relating itself closely and logically with the idea (1) of the three stages of Consciousness is that (2) of the Berkeleyan view of matter—the idea that matter in itself is an illusion, being only a film between soul and soul: *called* matter when the film is opaque to the perceiving soul, but called mind when the latter sees through to the intelligence behind it. And these stages again relate logically to the idea (3) of the Universal or Omnipresent Self. The *Art of Creation* was written to give expression to these three ideas and the natural deductions from them.

The doctrine of the Universal Self is obviously fundamental; and it is clear that once taken hold of and adopted it must inevitably revolutionize all our views of Morality—since current morality is founded on the separation of self from self; and must revolutionize too all our views of Science. Such matters as the Transmutation of Chemical Elements, the variation of biological Species, the unity of Health, the unity of Disease, our views of Political Economy and Psychology; Production for Use instead of for Profit, Communism, Telepathy; the relation between Psychology and Physiology, and so forth, must take on quite a new complexion when the idea which lies at the root of them is seized. This idea must enable us to understand the continuity of Man with the Protozoa, the relation of the physiological centres, on the one hand to the individual Man and on the other to the Race from which he springs, the meaning of Reincarnation, and the physical conditions of its occurrence. It must have eminently practical applications ; as in the bringing of the Races of the world together, the gradual evolution of a Non-governmental form of Society, the Communalization of Land and Capital, the freeing of Woman to equality with Man, the extension of the monogamic Marriage into some kind of group-alliance, the restoration and full recognition of the heroic friendships of Greek and primitive times ; and again in the sturdy Simplification and debarrassment of daily life by the removal of those things which stand between us and Nature, between ourselves and our fellows—by plain living, friendship with the Animals, open-air habits, fruitarian food, and such degree of Nudity as we can reasonably attain to.

These mental and social changes and movements and many others which are all around us waiting for recognition, will clearly, when they ripen, constitute a revolution in human life deeper and more far-reaching than any which we know of belonging to historical times. Even any *one* of them, worked out practically, would be fatal to most of our existing institutions. Together they would form a revolution so great that to call it a mere extension or outgrowth of Civilization would be quite inadequate. Rather we must look upon them as the preparation for a stage entirely different from and beyond Civilization. To tackle these things in advance, to prepare for them, study them, understand them is clearly absolutely necessary. It is a duty which—however burked or ignored for a time—will soon be forced upon us by the march of events. And it is a duty

A. Mattison photographer   Emery Walker Ph. sc.

Self in Porch
1905

which cannot effectively be fulfilled piecemeal, but only by regarding all these separate movements of the human mind, and of society, as part and parcel of one great underlying movement—one great new disclosure of the human Soul.

My little covey of books, dating from *Towards Democracy*, has been hatched mainly for the purpose of giving expression to these and other various questions which—raised in my mind by the writing of *Towards Democracy*—demanded clearer statement than they could find there. *Towards Democracy* came first, as a Vision, so to speak, and a revelation—as a great body of feeling and intuition which I *had* to put into words as best I could. It carried with it—as a flood carries trees and rocks from the mountains where it originates—all sorts of assumptions and conclusions. Afterwards—for my own satisfaction as much as for the sake of others—I had to examine and define these assumptions and conclusions

That was the origin of my prose writings—most of them—of *England's Ideal, Civilization, The Art of Creation, Love's Coming-of-Age, The Intermediate Sex, The Drama of Love and Death, Angels' Wings, Non-governmental Society*,[1] *A Visit to a Gñani*,[2] and so forth. They, like the questions they deal with, have led a curious underground life in the literary world, spreading widely as a matter of fact, yet not on the surface. Like old moles they have worked away unseen and unobserved, yet in such a manner as to throw up heaps here and there and in the most unlikely places, and bring back friends to me on all sides—lovely and beautiful friends for whom I cannot sufficiently thank them.

[1] A chapter in *Prisons, Police, and Punishment*.

[2] In *Adam's Peak to Elephanta*.

XII

PERSONALITIES—I

IT is curious that, with my somewhat antinomian tendencies, I should have gone to Trinity Hall—which was, and is, before all a Law College—and should thus have been thrown into close touch with the *legal* element in life. As an undergraduate, whose days were consumed in boating and mathematics, this was not noticeable; but it was not entirely after my heart when I became a Fellow, to find myself in a society which was almost wholly composed of barristers; and in after life to discover that my friends of early days had nearly all become eminent K.C.'s and Judges!

Just before my entering Trinity Hall, an undergraduate of that College, Robert Romer, had become Senior Wrangler—and I really believe this had something to do with my selecting the College for myself. The 'Hall' men were hugely delighted, as this distinction in the Tripos had never come to the College before—the more so, because Romer was a boating man and rowed in the First Boat; and a myth grew up (possibly encouraged by the subject himself, and in order to show how easily a real boating man can do anything he turns himself to!) that he passed his examinations by the light of nature, and never needed to 'swot' like an ordinary mortal. Others however said—and this was a more likely explanation—that he used to sit at his study table with a pot of beer and a sporting journal before him, while in the open drawer of the table lay his mathematical books and papers. When a knock came at the door it was the simplest thing in the world to close the drawer, and be found consuming his ale! After his degree he remained at Cambridge for a time as mathematical coach, but was by no means a success in that line. He could not sympathize with a learner's difficulties; and when a pupil came to him with a problem which he could not understand, Romer would say "What? You can't understand that? You can't understand that? —then God help you, I can't!" Naturally he soon gave up teaching and took to the Bar. After *my* degree—when we were Fellows of the College together—I saw quite a little of him: a rough, muscular-brained, "damn-your-eyes" type of man, and as may be imagined quite ignorant of art and literature, but good-natured and healthy. Later however the sheer physical force of his mentality took him to the highest reaches of the legal profession (Lord Justice of Appeal) and he passed out of my sphere.

Another Senior Wrangler whom I knew fairly well, as he headed the Tripos in my own year (1868), and who afterwards became Lord Justice (in the Court of Patents) was J. Fletcher Moulton. He was one of those people who without any great depth of intellect or even of character possessed an extraordinary rapidity of mind. His information was encyclopædic, and in examinations he threw off his papers with the airy ease of a tree throwing off its dead leaves in autumn; to the wonderment indeed both of examiners and fellow-students. Yet I am not aware that he ever contributed anything very original in the study of mathematics or law—or in any other department of human thought.

Great success in examinations does naturally not as a rule go with originality of thought. W. K. Clifford who had undoubtedly one of the finest mathematical, scientific, and philosophical minds of the period of which I am speaking was only Second Wrangler; and my friend Robert F. Muirhead who, as Smith's Prizeman and later, has contributed important papers on mathematical subjects, was nowhere to speak of in his Tripos. One could hardly of course expect that originality and the pigeon-hole mind should go together.

To return to our Judges. That men like Romer and Moulton should attain the highest places in their profession is natural; but I confess I have been surprised (having known them so well in boating days) at the kind of men who are commonly made High Court or County Court Judges. I will not mention names (!)—but here is one, for instance, who was Captain of the boat-club in my time—a physically powerful, but mentally quite muddle-headed person; here is another, whose *forte* was *boxing* (no harm in that, but one might have wished that he had other interests besides)—a rather brutish and decidedly illiterate type; a third, whose constitution, both physical and mental, was feeble, but who had powerful relatives in the legal profession. All these were of the kind that have considerable difficulty in passing their elementary examinations. And there were many more of the same kind. Nevertheless, having once got their feet on the ladder, they have slowly and gradually—by family influence or sheer physical health (an important thing)—climbed nearly to the top. No blame to them, certainly; but one cannot help asking—and I put the question especially to Labour M.P.'s: Are these the sort of men we really require for such posts? Let alone their want of bookish culture—which perhaps does not so much matter—we cannot but ask: What do men of this class—who have been brought up at a public school, who have worked hard at boating or cricket at the University, who afterwards have buried themselves in law-chambers and the purlieus of the Courts—and whose acquaintance with manual workers is pretty well confined to 'scouts' and 'gyps' and an occasional gamekeeper in the country—what do they know about the great mass-people on whom they have to sit in judgment, about the habits and temperament and customs of life of the latter? and how on earth are they qualified to bring order and good sense and real sympathy and understanding into that most important branch of public life—the administration of the law? These are indeed questions to which serious answers will have to be given ere long.

I have already mentioned Henry Fawcett (afterwards Postmaster-General) who was a Fellow of Trinity Hall at the time of which I am speaking. The story of his blindness is well known. It was only just after his degree that he was out pheasant-shooting with his father. In a rather thick covert the father fired at a bird, unknowing that his son was standing in the line of fire. Two small shot struck the latter—one entering into each eye—a strange and fatal chance. It was the father, I think, who told me that as soon as Henry knew that he was permanently blinded he said "Well, it shan't make any difference in my plans of life!" And certainly it made very little. As may be guessed from that, Fawcett was a man of astounding pluck and vitality—a vitality which would have been almost overbearing if it had not been tempered by extreme good nature—and his force of character, combined with very democratic sympathies, enabled him despite his blindness to do valuable work in Parliament and in connection with the Post Office. The adoring gratitude of the father at the public success of the son whom he had so badly crippled was most touching, and he would follow his son about the country and attend his public meetings for the mere pleasure of witnessing his success. As Fawcett was member for Brighton—and my father lent his support to his candidature—he, and Mrs. Fawcett, used frequently to dine with us at Brunswick Square, and I saw a good deal of them both at Brighton and at Cambridge. Fawcett's pluck and vitality were however sometimes a trial to his friends. I have a rather *too* vivid recollection of riding with him, over the Brighton Downs or along the green lanes of Cambridgeshire. "Carpenter," he would say, "this is a nice piece of grass, isn't it? Let's have a canter." Then he would set off at an amazing rate, and I would have to keep close alongside of him, with a sharp look-out and warning for unexpected ditches and stoneheaps, and in momentary fear of a headlong fall—which for a man of his weight would have been a terrible thing! Or he would insist on my coming to skate with him, in winter, on the Cam. We would go five or six miles down the river, and back—he holding one end of a stick and I the other. That was all very well if the ice was sound, but every one knows what river ice is; and I have often skated with him when I, being a light weight, passed over easily, while he, holding on to the stick and a pace or two behind, was cracking through at every other step. The prospect of having to fish a public man, weighty in every sense, out of a flowing river was certainly not pleasant. However I am happy to say that I was not present with him at any disaster. Except once. That was at a public meeting when he was speaking, at Brighton. I was on the platform. A stone was thrown by some one at the back of the hall, which struck him on the forehead, causing blood to flow. Great sensation ensued. For the moment he felt a little faint and relapsed into a chair. Ladies rushed up on all sides with smelling salts. However in a few minutes he was all right, and resumed his speech. Afterwards he said to me "I didn't mind the stone; but those scent-bottles made me sick!" So it will be seen that he and I had points in common! Since his death Mrs. Fawcett and I have still met not unfrequently—generally perhaps as joint speakers on some Women's Suffrage platform.

Charles Wentworth Dilke was a 'Hall' man. He had just taken his degree when I arrived as a 'freshman'; but he stayed up in College for a year or so more on account of some law-examination or other. He never became a Fellow, but was an enthusiastic lover of his College; and was always very good to us undergraduates. I remember breakfasting with him at his rooms, and his showing me, pencilled on his door-jamb, the record of his hours of work, day by day, for the last year or so—*seventy hours per week*, as regular as clockwork! He was, then and afterwards, always an amazing worker—his room even in those youthful days pigeon-holed all over with notes and documents. He was also a man with a high sense of chivalry and honour, and I have no doubt that the *contretemps* which threw him for a time out of public life—and which his chivalry forbade him to explain—weighed pretty heavily on him. His love of facts and statistics, so conspicuous throughout his political life, was shared by his brother Assheton; and it used to be said that the two brothers never enjoyed themselves more thoroughly than when sitting knee to knee they spent an hour or so in 'imparting facts to each other'!

Another politician of my time, though a little younger than myself, was Augustine Birrell. Even in those days he was chiefly known for his quaint humours and jokes—though the term 'birrelling' had not then been adopted. But being, as an undergraduate, somewhat interested in politics and not at all interested in rowing, he did not bulk largely in the eyes of his contemporaries, and I fear was a little neglected. In a late letter to me he chaffs me in his own native style on my academic and clerical past, saying "I have the most vivid recollection of you as Junior Tutor. The marvellous neatness of your now discarded *white tie* lives especially in my untidy mind!"

Socialism and Millthorpe, I need hardly say, swept me out of these academic and semi-political surroundings into a different world—the world of a new society which was arising and forming within the structure of the old. William Morris represented this new society more effectively and vitally than any one else of that period; because away and beyond the scientific forecast he gave expression to the emotional presentment and ideal of a sensible free human brotherhood—as in *John Ball*, or *News from Nowhere*. His sturdy, brusque, sea-captain-like figure, with his fine-outlined face and tossing hair, his forcible unpolished speech, yet all so direct, sincere, enthusiastic—brought inspiration and confidence wherever he went; and for a time, as I have already said, there was a widespread belief that the Socialist League was going to knit up all the United Kingdom in one bond of new life.[1] Having set the "Sheffield Socialists" going in '86, he came one day not long after to speak at Chesterfield, and stayed at Millthorpe a night or two. I remember his arriving from the train with Jefferies' book *After London* in his hands—which had just come out. The book delighted him with its prophecy of an utterly ruined and deserted London, gone down in swamps and malaria, with brambles and weeds spreading through slum streets and fashionable squares, and pet dogs reverting to wolfish and carrion-hunting lives. And he read page after page of it to us with glee that evening as we sat round the fire. He hated modern civilization, and London as its representative, with a fierce hatred—its shams, its hypocrisies, its stuffy indoor life, its cheapjack style, its mean and mongrel ideals ; with a hatred indeed which, I cannot but think, thousands and hundreds of thousands following him will one day share. Once he said to me, talking about his own life : "I have spent, I know, a vast amount of time designing furniture and wall-papers, carpets and curtains ; but after all I am inclined to think that sort of thing is mostly rubbish, and I would prefer for my part to live with the plainest whitewashed walls and wooden chairs and tables." He certainly was no drawing-room sort of man. His immense energy did not run to small talk. As a rule in conversation, seized by his subject, and oblivious of the arguments of others, he would jump from his chair and stride up and down the room in ardent monologue—condemning the present or picturing the future or the past. I once asked his daughter, May,

[1] See p. 125, *supra* (Ch. VII).

what he did in the way of recreation. "My father never takes any recreation," she said, "he *merely changes his work*." And so it was. When he had been toiling at Merton Abbey all day, and preaching Socialism at a street corner all the evening, then at night—sick of the ugly life around him—he would come home and dream himself away into the fourteenth century, and for his recreation produce a masterpiece like *John Ball*. Be it said, nevertheless, that he did sometimes relax, and that when in the humour, no one enjoyed a pipe and a glass and the jovial company of friends and the telling of good stories, more than William Morris.

He certainly did not like anything resembling sentimentality. A friend tells me that he used to recite the following stanza, apparently delighting in its quaintness—but whether Morris composed it himself or had found it elsewhere he does not know :—

I sits with my feet in a brook,
 And if any one asks me for why,
I hits him a crack with my crook,
 For it's sentiment kills me, says I.

Among those who came from time to time to speak for our Socialist group in Sheffield or to stay at our "Commonwealth" Café were, besides William Morris, two notable personalities—Peter Kropotkin and Annie Besant. Their work and influence, both worldwide—the one in the Anarchist, and the other in the Theosophist, field—have been really important. Though never myself strictly identified with either of these movements I have been in touch with them, and consequently in more or less friendly relation with their two leading spirits during a long period —now nearly thirty years. Both characters are certainly remarkable for their vigour, their sincerity, their ability and devotion. Kropotkin at the age of seventy and after fifty years of passionate conflict with 'government' and 'authority' still retains his sunny and almost child-like temperament and still believes in the speedy oncoming of an age of perfectly voluntary and harmonious co-operation in the human race. Indeed it is mainly due to him that this magnificent dream has spread so far and wide over the world, and has done so much as it has towards its own realization. The dramatic circumstances too of Kropotkin's own life have greatly helped—his early escapes from prison and from death, his abandonment of a princely inheritance to become the companion and fellow-prisoner of criminals and outcasts, his later life spent in poverty and among obscure circles of enthusiasts—these things combined with encyclopædic knowledge and a high scientific reputation have compelled attention and respect. As in the case of many ardent social reformers, and certainly in the case of most notorious Anarchists, there is a charming naïveté about Kropotkin. It is so easy—if you believe that all human evil is summed up in the one fatal word 'government' (or it may be that the word is 'white-slave-traffic,' or 'war,' or 'drink,' or anything else) —to order your life and your theories accordingly. Everything is explained by its relation to one thing. It is easy, but it is misleading. And Kropotkin's writings, despite their erudition, suffer from this naïveté. Whether it be History (his *French Revolution*), or Natural History (his *Mutual Aid*) or economic theory (his *Paroles d'un Revolté*) the reader finds one solution for everything, and the countervailing facts and principles consistently—though certainly not intentionally—ignored. This detracts from the value of the writings; though in justice it should be said that the principles on which Kropotkin so vigorously insists—i.e. individual liberty and free association—*are* of foundational importance. In a country like Russia—obsessed by authority and officialism—it is not unnatural that its reformers, such as Tolstoy and Kropotkin, should be almost over-conscious of the governmental evil ; and this fact rather encourages the hope that Russia may one day after all be the leader in the great European reaction towards a freer and more voluntary state of society.

The naïveté of the social reformer explains too the common fact that the Anarchist who is in theory " thirsting for the blood of kings " and occasionally perhaps capable of perpetrating a deed of violence himself, is generally (like Kropotkin) the gentlest and mildest of men, who " would not hurt a fly." It is only such men—having the love of humanity in their hearts—who are able to believe in the speedy realization of an era of universal goodwill ; and again it is only such men—being innocent enough to believe that the only impediment to the realization of this era is a certain wicked person in ' authority '—who can spur themselves on to the bloody dispatch of such person.

If the career of Kropotkin has been romantically varied in one way, that of Mrs. Besant has been equally so in another. To begin as a curate's wife, with a vivid strain of religious devotion ; to break away into Broad Churchism and then into boundless disbelief ; to become an ardent Secularist, companion of Bradlaugh and propagandist of anti-population doctrines ; to suffer persecution, and to be sentenced to months of imprisonment ; to espouse the cause of Socialism and do battle in the ranks of Labour ; to float into the haven of Theosophy and be made the mouthpiece of invisible Mahatmas and of the by no means invisible Mme. Blavatsky; and finally to complete this quaint circle by becoming the high-priestess of a religious movement and the guardian of the herald of the coming Christ—such a career ought to satisfy the most picturesque ambition. Yet it would be unfair to doubt Annie Besant's sincerity. Having known her so long as I have I feel sure that she has been urged onward from point to point by a perfectly genuine mental evolution, largely directed no doubt at each turn of the road by some dominant mind whom she has met, and largely coloured by that naïveté of which we have already spoken—a naïveté indeed which has made it possible for her to take herself very seriously and to fulfil her adopted rôle always with a strong sense of duty and a comparatively weak perception of the humour of the situation.

From the hour when, alone in the pulpit of her husband's church, Annie Besant discovered her own great oratorical gift, her future career, one may say, was decided. With an excellent capacity for logical and clear statement she became the exponent in succession of large and important blocks of modern thought. She helped to batter down the ruins and remains of the stupefied old Anglican Church; she gave the general mind a wholesome shock on the Malthusian question; she dotted out clearly the main lines of the Socialist movement; she formed a new channel for religious thought by making the words 'Karma' and 're-incarnation' familiar; and she sought to bring the Western public into touch with the great agelong ideas and inspirations of the old Indian sages. In all these ways she has done splendid work, and helped vastly in the construction of that great twentieth century bridge which will in its due time lead us into another world. Only in the last item—her touch upon the ideas and inspirations of the ancient East—does she seem to me, curiously enough, to have failed. With all her enthusiasm for the subject, Mrs. Besant does not appear to have the intuitive perception, the mystic quality of mind, which should enable her to reach the very heart of the old Vedantic teaching. Her intellect, clear and systematic in its structure, has little of the poetic or original or inspirational in its composition, and it may be doubted whether it has ever quite fathomed the religious writings with which it has been so much occupied. Anyhow Mrs. Besant's own writings on these subjects are—unlike her general lectures—dull to a degree. She analyses the composition of the human personality, or the order of general creation, or the various life-rounds of our mortal race ; but in all she seems to be repeating or corroborating some pre-established formula, never to be describing something which she has herself perceived ; system and formula prevail, unseen 'authorities' are hinted at, the pages bristle with sanskrit jargon, but no living or creative *idea* moves among them, and the reader rises from their perusal void of inspiration or of any really vital impulse towards new fields of thought and life. Nevertheless, taking it all in all, and especially in her expositions of Socialism and Theosophy, Mrs. Besant has done, as I have said, a great work ; and one cannot sufficiently admire the courage with which she has carried it through, as well as her kindliness and helpfulness towards others, and—in later years—her own inner mental calm, contrasting with the somewhat restless bitterness of an earlier time.

In 1884 or so the founding of the *New Fellowship*

in London (from which afterwards the Fabian Society sprang) brought me into touch with Havelock Ellis and Olive Schreiner. As I think I have already said, Ellis discovered in the proverbial penny box of a second-hand publisher, and soon after its publication, the little first edition of my *Towards Democracy*; and rescuing it wrote to me. Thus began my friendship with him, and afterwards with the authoress of *The Story of An African Farm*. A prophet is seldom acclaimed in his own country; and the work which Ellis has done in that most important field of Sexual Psychology is even yet by no means recognized in England as it ought to be—even though the subject is becoming extremely 'actual' here in the present day, and though elsewhere over the world his pioneer work is most honorably received and respected. The six massive volumes of his *Studies in the Psychology of Sex* form a masterpiece of large-minded and yet extremely detailed observation and generalization, and provide a survey of the most impartial character over this vast realm, and such as can be obtained nowhere else. For though the Germans have written extensively in this field their books—*more Teutonico*—are generally overladen with detail, huge jungles through which it is difficult to find one's way. Ellis combines with the Englishman's perspicacity and love of order a remarkable erudition and command of particulars. And at the present juncture when the world is waking up to the absolute necessity of a reasonable understanding and frank recognition of sex-things, the appearance of his book may almost be characterized as 'providential.' This quality may indeed be suspected in the fact that the author began making notes for his *magnum opus* at a very early age, driven thereto by some sort of instinct, nor finished his work till he was about fifty. I know of few things in literature more touching than the postscript to his last volume—the *Nunc Dimittis* after some thirty years of toil: "It was perhaps fortunate for my peace that I failed at the outset to foresee all the perils that beset my path. I knew indeed that those who investigate sincerely and intimately any subject which men are accustomed to pass by on the other side lay themselves open to misunderstanding and even obloquy. But I supposed that a secluded student who approached vital social problems with precaution, making no direct appeal to the general public, but only to the public's teachers, and who wrapped up the results of his inquiries in technically written volumes open to few—I supposed that such a student was at all events secure from any gross form of attack on the part of the police or the government under whose protection he imagined that he lived. That proved to be a mistake. When only one volume of these *Studies* had been written and published in England, a prosecution instigated by the Government put an end to the sale of that volume in England, and led me to resolve that the subsequent volumes should not be published in my own country.[1] I do not complain. I am grateful for the early and generous sympathy with which my work was received in Germany and the United States, and I recognize that it has had a wider circulation, both in English and the other chief languages of the world, than would have been possible by the modest method of issue which the government of my own country induced me to abandon. Nor has the effort to crush my work resulted in any change in that work by so much as a single word. With help, or without it,

[1] They are published now in Philadelphia by the F. A. Dav s Company there.

I have followed my own path to the end. . . . He who follows in the steps of Nature after a law that was not made by man, and is above and beyond man, has time as well as eternity on his side, and can afford to be both patient and fearless. Men die, but the ideas they seek to kill *live*. Our books may be thrown to the flames, but in the next generation those flames become human souls."

The personality of Havelock Ellis is that of a student, thoughtful, preoccupied, bookish, deliberate ; yet unlike most students he has a sort of grand air of Nature about him—a fine free head and figure as of some great god Pan, with distant relations among the Satyrs.

Those early meetings of the New Fellowship were full of hopeful enthusiasms—life simplified, a humane diet and a rational dress, manual labour, democratic ideals, communal institutions. Indeed one or two little practical efforts towards colony groups were at that time made.[1] Herbert Rix, W. J. Jupp, Percival Chubb, Edith Lees (afterwards Mrs. Ellis), Mrs. Hinton, widow of James Hinton, Caroline Haddon, Ernest Rhys were among the early members.

Edith Lees was one of the most active and vigorous of this group. She helped to organize and to carry on for some time a joint dwelling or co-operative boarding-house near Mecklenburgh Square, where eight or ten members of the Fellowship dwelt in a kind of communistic Utopia. Naturally the arrangement gave rise to some rather amusing and some almost tragic episodes, which she has recorded for us in a little story entitled *Attainment*. After her marriage she took a farm near St. Ives in Cornwall,

[1] See *Seed-time*, a quarterly journal issued by the Fellowship ; which however was not started till 1890 and ceased publication in 1898. Editor, Maurice Adams, one of the earliest members.

which became a helpful retreat for her husband as well as herself from the strenuousness of London life. With her extraordinary energy and directness she plunged into and soon mastered all the details of cattle and pig breeding and farming; and I shall never forget the impression she produced on one occasion when staying with me at Millthorpe, when we took her round to the public-house in the evening. The delight and amazement of the farm men at finding some one more or less resembling a lady who really understood and would talk freely about such things, and her at-home-ness among that company were most refreshing. They were fascinated by the directness of her intense blue eyes, her sturdy figure, her vigorous gestures, and the evident equality of her comradeship with them. And to this day they not unfrequently ask us, "When is that little lady coming again, with that curly hair, like a lad's, and them blue eyes, what talked about pigs and cows? I shall never forget her."

Edith Ellis not only became a help to her husband in his literary work, but herself spoke and wrote on subjects of Eugenics and Sex-psychology. Of late years she has made a considerable study of James Hinton, and has done me the honour to associate my name with his and with Nietzsche's in a little book entitled *Three Modern Seers*.

One evening as we sat round a table (in Rix's rooms at Burlington House) I saw a charming girl-face, of *riant* Italian type, smiling across to me. It was Olive Schreiner. She had arrived from South Africa only a few months before, had published her *African Farm*, and though only twenty-one or twenty-two years of age was already famous as its authoress. Juvenile in some ways as that book was, somewhat incoherent and disjointed in structure, written by a mere girl of eighteen or nineteen, and with a title which gave no idea of its real content, yet its intensity was such that it seized almost at once on the public mind. The African sun was in its veins—fire and sweetness, intense love of beauty, fierce rebellion against the things that be, passion and pity and the pride of Lucifer combined. These things too Olive Schreiner's face and figure revealed—a wonderful beauty and vivacity, a lightning-quick mind, fine eyes, a resolute yet mobile mouth, a determined little square-set body. It was right—since alliances are so often knit by contrast—that she and Havelock Ellis should have become friends and maintained a close correspondence with each other for over thirty years; and it was a privilege to me to share in the friendship of them both.

Naturally, with such gifts of body and mind the arrival of the authoress of the '*African Farm* excited almost a *furore* of interest. Quite a procession of the young literary men of the day arrived in hansom-cabs at the door of her Bloomsbury lodgings to pay their homage to the new genius, and Olive herself often told me with considerable amusement of the dismay and severe disapproval of more than one of her landladies, who certainly were not inclined to believe that mere literary talent could cause so much attraction! Anyhow, at that time of day, before the suffragette had arrived, and when 'ladies' took the greatest care to bridle in their chins and speak in mincing accents, a young and pretty woman of apparently lady-like origin who did not wear a veil and seldom wore gloves, and who talked and laughed even in the streets quite naturally and unaffectedly, was an unclassifiable phenomenon, and laid herself open to the gravest suspicions! We may congratulate ourselves that the pioneer women of to-day have made a return to some of these inhumanities of the Victorian era impossible.

During that Bloomsbury period and afterwards I saw Olive Schreiner fairly frequently—that is, when she was in England (or Europe). I saw her in Paris early in '87, and at Todmorden and Whitby later in the same year; also at Alassio where she stayed for two or three months in '88. Those two years '87 and '88 were a period of considerable suffering for her. In 1893 she was in England again, and spent three months during the summer in a little cottage in my valley. After '93, what with her marriage to S. C. Cronwright, and what with the outbreak of the Boer War and all the tragedies attendant upon that, she did not come to England for a long period, and it was on the last day of 1913 that I saw her again, after a twenty years' absence.

Her father was a German Free Church Missionary—of the most tender self-forgetful type—the original doubtless of the German overseer in *The African Farm*. Olive herself has often told me how he would give away his last coin to any one he deemed to be in need. His wife would say to him:—

"John, where is that best Sunday coat of yours?" And he would say:—

"Is it not upstairs in the chest, as usual?"

"No, John, I have been looking for it everywhere."

"How very strange" was the reply.

"Now, John, I believe you have given it away!"

"No, surely, my dear, I could not have given *that* away—at least I think not."

"John! now tell me true, did you not give it to that *tramp* that came yesterday?"

"Well, my dear, now you mention it I think I *may* have done so; it is just possible you are right, but I am sure I hardly remember."

"Oh John! John! you are indeed incorrigible."

That was the picture of the father—soft, pitiful and dreamy. The mother, Rebecca Lyndall by her maiden name, was of English descent, keen, intellectual, fine featured and somewhat self-willed. The two types were combined in their daughter; and she again in writing her novel divided them up. 'Waldo' represented one side of her own character, 'Lyndall' the other.

Perhaps there was a tragic element in the combination of two such different hereditary strains in the one person; perhaps there were other causes. Certain it is that beneath the mobile and almost merry-seeming exterior of Olive Schreiner there ran a vein of intense determination, and that this again was crossed and countered by an ineradicable pessimism. *The Story of an African Farm,* despite its magical and beautiful pictures, is painful to read; and the same may be said of her other books. They realize and force the reader to realize almost *too* keenly the pain and evil of the world—too keenly I mean for truth and fact. Yet what is fact but what we feel; and if Olive Schreiner *feels* things so, so far her presentment is true. I have seen her shake her little fist at the Lord in heaven, and curse him down from his throne, with a vibrating force and intensity which surely must have been felt (and surely also with healthy result) in the Highest Circles.

A lady who had spent forty years of her life working in the Mission Schools of South Africa once said to me—and this was quite in her old age, when she was nearing eighty—"Ah!" she said, "the Kaffirs are the finest people on earth. You English think a lot about yourselves, but I tell you, you are not to be compared with the Kaffirs." Olive Schreiner was born in Basuto Land. She grew up and spent her early life among the natives, and in many ways her verdict was the same as that just quoted. She loved the dark folk and their land, and she has never ceased to love them. It has been one of the tragedies of her life that she has been compelled to stand by and witness the crushing of this free and fine-souled people beneath the sordid heel of Western Commercialism—or let us say "the attempted crushing," for indeed (thank heaven!) the process is not yet complete. It has been her agony to see them at every moment cajoled and betrayed of their lands, broken with labour in the mines, deceived with drink, and mowed down with machine-guns—and all this by the very Christian race that ought to have lent them a helping hand; and to have been able to do so little (as it would seem to her) for their salvation. But even though it would seem little, the fact that one woman in South Africa has thus prophet-like stood up and (much of the time) singly opposed Rhodes and the shoddy Imperialism of which he was the mouthpiece, *has* had an influence deep and wide reaching and such as will be felt far down the years.

Another thing that has formed almost a tragedy in Olive Schreiner's life has been her dedication to the Cause of Women. No one can read her *Three Dreams in a Desert* or her *Woman and Labour* without feeling how in the consciousness of the sufferings of Woman the iron has entered into her soul. If she had only been content—like some of the wilder spirits of the movement—to unload on *men* the vials of her wrath, and to saddle on *man*kind alone the responsibility for these sufferings, her strain in the cause would have had more of the delight of battle in it. But she was too large-minded not to see that if there is to be any blame in such a matter, the blame must be accepted by Woman herself just as much as by Man. The two sexes are joined together, and if Man has been unworthy has it not been because Woman his mother has made him so? If Woman has played the parasite has that not resulted in her injuring Man? Olive Schreiner's perception of the slow inevitable strain and suffering inseparable from Evolution itself in this matter of the emancipation of women, has had a complexion of tragedy in it. She has seen her dearest friends, like Constance Lytton and others, crippled and broken for life by their heroic struggles and undaunted resolution in face of prison-horrors ; and yet she has felt that the evil lay deeper than any accusation against men (taken by itself) could explain, or any mere reform of the suffrage could mend.

It is curious how South Africa, to those who know the country well, carries with it a fascination and an attraction which time and again draws them back to its soil. A friend of mine who lived for some years around Lake Nyassa told me that after his return to England he frequently dreamt at night of all that wild region and its primitive animal life. On more than one occasion he dreamed that he was wrecked at sea, and swam desperately to the African coast, if only he might die as it were in the arms of his beloved ; or he would make an imaginary pilgrimage from London to the very shores of the Lake, and there in a kind of ecstasy would take the water up in his palms and wash it over his face and head—only to wake up and find his features wet with his own tears.

This was Henry B. Cotterill—a schoolfellow of mine at the Brighton College—where indeed his father was headmaster. About the time (1875 or so) when I was lecturing Astronomy at Leeds, Livingstone's book came out exposing the horrors of the black slave traffic around Lakes Tanganyika and Nyassa—a region at that time entirely, except by Livingstone himself, unexplored by white men. The book bit deeply into Cotterill's heart and soul. It said that the only cure for the Mahomedan or Arabian trade in slaves would be the introduction of a trade by white men in the legitimate articles of commerce ; and from that moment Cotterill could not rest, goaded on by the thought that *he* must undertake this work. At the time he was acting as an assistant master at Harrow School. He started lecturing there and at other places round the country on the subject. He collected a fund ; the Harrow boys and masters gave him a steel launch or cutter which could be taken up country in sections and screwed together ; he came to Leeds and spoke there, as well as at places like Edinburgh, Manchester, Liverpool ; the fund grew ; and I remember going with him to some African warehouse in London City, where he bought bales of cotton cloth, and hundredweights of beads, and quantities of scarlet shell-jackets (especially coveted by African chieftains as their sole garment) for purposes of barter up country. Thus off his own bat, as it were, he got up this strange mission, and leaving Harrow and pedagogy behind, embarked on a career of considerable adventure and danger. The mission succeeded, ordinary traders followed in his footsteps, and within a few years the slave-trade engineered by Moors and Arabs died out in the land. It was followed, it is true, by the almost equal horrors of that commercial civilization which has since been introduced by Europeans ; but I suppose one must be thankful in the slow and age-long evolution of human affairs for even one small step towards better things.

At a later time Cotterill returned to England, but unable, like many another traveler and lover of the wild, to endure the smug Philistinism of British life, he ultimately settled on the Continent—or rather led a somewhat roving life there, chiefly in France, Germany and Italy—supporting himself and a small family by the not too lucrative pursuits of literature and the teaching of languages. He has written and edited many books, to which his encyclopædic knowledge and command of six or seven languages have contributed ; but undoubtedly his great and monumental work has been the translation of the Odyssey of Homer complete into English hexameters.[1] Daring is the man who ventures on that exceedingly boggy ground of the English hexameter, and many are those who have gone under and been gulfed in the attempt. By lightness and speed of movement only can one keep going ; but in those qualities—so characteristic of the Greek—this translation is supremely successful ; its verbal fidelity is amazing ; its presentation of the old warrior and tribal life (made possible as he himself says by his intimate knowledge of African customs) is such as no armchair scholar could attain to ; and the result is a gift to the whole English-speaking world—a rendering of the immortal classic that one may read with unflagging joy and zest from cover to cover.

[1] Published by George Harrap, 1912.

XIII

PERSONALITIES—II

THE part that Olive Schreiner played in trying to avert the Boer War, and to expose the scoundrelly commercial machinations which led to it, is well known. Curiously enough, while England was being worked up by a lying Press into a fury of indignation against President Krüger I knew already early in 1899 about the real state of affairs and the plot of the financiers to force on a reckless and selfish war—not only from Olive Schreiner herself but from a man who came at that time to Millthorpe from Johannesburg.

This was Lisle March-Phillipps—who afterwards wrote *With Rimington* and other books about the war. He was a young man of about thirty, who after an upper-class education on the usual lines had had the good sense to go abroad and see a little of the world for himself; had drifted out to South Africa, and had actually worked in the mines and shared the life of the miners. Disgusted with what he saw of the Beit and Joel and Rhodes and Barney Barnato gang—their meanness to their employees, their slanders against Krüger, their nonsense lies about British "women and children," and foreseeing the inevitable conflict, he hurried home—thinking doubtless also that he might do something to make the actual truth known in England. For some reason, not very clear to me as we had had no previous communication, he came straight to Millthorpe, and walking in one afternoon sat a long time telling me all about the affair. I saw at once that his errand was authentic and that he knew what he was talking about, and from that time did my best in my small way, at public meetings and lectures, to get the matter seen in its true light, and to check the rising war-tide. All of no use of course. The gulled sentimental sloppy British public poured itself out in a torrent of rubbish—as a broken reservoir might pour through the slums and alleys of a manufacturing town; and it was hopeless even to protest. It is one of the saddest things to find how easily the great majority of a nation may be caught and swept away by some trumped-up catchword, often of the most flimsy character. I wrote a warning leaflet entitled *Boer and Briton* and circulated some twenty thousand copies of it. I spoke with L. H. Courtney (now Lord Courtney) and others at a public meeting at Bradford, and at various other meetings. Mr. W. T. Stead did his best to warn the nation as to what was happening; Cronwright-Schreiner came over from the Cape, and later H. W. Nevinson also, in a crusade through England and Scotland. To no purpose: they only got mobbed and insulted for their pains. Finally March-Phillipps, anxious to see at close quarters all that was going on and unable to get a billet as war-correspondent, went out again and joined Rimington's Scouts; and after the war was over—returning to Millthorpe and taking a cottage there—remained near us a good part of the summer and wrote his very graphic and interesting account of the campaign as witnessed and taken part in by him.[1]

It was at an early period of the Socialist movement—in 1884 I think—that I first came across

[1] *With Rimington*, by L. March-Phillipps (Arnold, 1901).

Henry Salt and his gifted life-companion and wife, and it is to their initiative that I owe the gain of a close and long-enduring friendship. Salt and his brother-in-law, J. L. Joynes, were two young Eton masters who had in their time been collegers and scholars of Eton and afterwards graduates of King's College, Cambridge. Carried along on the rising tide of Socialism they both (much to their credit) broke away from the highly respectable traditions of these foundations. Henry George of Land Tax fame was in the country, and Joynes actually associated himself with George, and went with him in 1881 or '82 on a propagandist campaign to Ireland. This might well have passed unobserved at Eton, had it not happened that at some obscure place he and George were both temporarily arrested and had to spend the night under lock and key. The notoriety this gave to Joynes was fatal to his career, and he had to resign his mastership. Henry Salt and his wife about the same time gave almost worse offence. They adopted vegetarianism—a thing almost unheard of at Eton except in the dubious connection of Shelley; they revolted in their personal habits from the luxury and indulgence of the life there; and they protested against the coursing of hares, and other inhumanities favored by both boys and masters. It soon became clear to them that they could not remain in surroundings so uncongenial, and that they too would have to sacrifice a professional career and comparative affluence for the greater blessings of liberty and a simple living; and it was at the time when they were revolving their schemes of liberation and of migration into other spheres of life that I came—through Jim Joynes—to know them.

Joynes and his sister were singularly unlike externally, yet singularly alike in the depths of their hearts and in their devotion to each other. Both were tall and long-limbed: she dark, raven-haired, with large eyes and sensitive, somewhat sad, Dante-like profile; he red-haired, with high complexion, small bluish eyes, heavy features. She was intensely emotional, too emotional, but—as such people often are—highly musical; and her literary gift was certainly one of the most remarkable I have known—though unfortunately, except in her letters, rarely utilized. He was intensely logical, concentrated, determined—though underneath ran a strong current of poetic feeling—as witness his little book of excellent verses *On Lonely Shores* (1892). Both of them did good work in connection with the Socialist and Labour movement, he more especially by lecturing and writing for the Social Democratic Federation and other such organizations; and she rather more by personal sympathy and helpful friendship towards the rank and file of the workers; both of them were devoted lovers of Nature, and of a natural plain way of life; and their devotion to each other only ended with his too early death in 1893.

These two and Henry Salt were among the pioneers in the early eighties of the great Socialist and Humanitarian and Nature movements which are destined to play such an important part in the new Democracy. Henry Salt's work in founding the Humanitarian League (in 1891) and presiding over its very various activities has been so really extensive and far-reaching that it is difficult to estimate—the more so because unlike so many leaders of movements he has always kept his own name consistently in the background. As a matter of fact he has not only been the main originator of the important work done, but has been the guiding hand and inspirer of the many committees which have had to be formed in order to deal with the various subjects—with Vivisection, Blood Sports, 'Murderous Millinery,' Reform of the Prisons, the Game Laws, Slaughter-house Reform, Corporal Punishment, Diet Reform, Rights of Native Races, and so forth. Besides this the long list of his publications—on Shelley, on James Thomson (B.V.), on H. D. Thoreau, Richard Jefferies, Lucretius, etc., shows the trend of his mind and his liberating influence in the matters of religion and social freedom and a large-minded Nature-study.

At one time he and I composed jointly "A Church Service for the use of the Respectable Classes"—which I am afraid however has never yet been properly published. It consisted of a Preface, in the manner of our Prayer-book Preface of 1661, of a sort of Athanasian Creed (on the Trinity of Land, Capital and Interest) called the creed of St. Avaritius, of a Litany (on the lines of salvation through dividends and social advancement), and a final Processional Hymn. Of this last, as it has already been printed among some of Salt's verses, the two first stanzas may here be given :—

Respectables are we
And you presently will see
Why we confidently claim to be respected :
In well-ordered homes we dwell
And discharge our duties well—
Well dressed, well fed, well mannered, well connected.

We have heard the common cant
About poverty and want
And all that is distressing and unhealthy ;
Some cases may be sad,
But the system can't be bad
Which affords such satisfaction to the Wealthy.

And so on.

On one occasion a boy brought to Mrs. Salt a young rook which had been hurt (so he said) by falling out of its nest, and as she and her husband had been staying with us, the bird became for some time an inmate of our establishment. But though it became familiar, as was natural, with us, and would fly in and out of the door or window, and perch on hand or head quite freely, its devotion to Mrs. Salt was something almost uncanny. Indoors or outdoors it *would* be with her; and if she went into town for a few hours, or anywhere that she could not take the bird, she had to escape by ruse, or by simply caging the creature first. When she sat on the lawn it would delight to play and dance around, and to pick daisies with its beak and place them in her lap, or bright and shining pebbles from the gravel walk. Anything more like an engaging human child it would be hard to imagine. And it certainly seemed to know by some intuition of her return after absence along the road, and if caged would become very restless, or if free would fly to meet her. Once after a long absence, when she appeared once more—in the midst, as it happened, of a small crowd of people—the bird with a loud cry suddenly flew down from a tall tree and alighted forthwith upon her shoulder—much to the astonishment of the onlookers. Later, and after some months of this kind of life, the bird one day disappeared; nor could we ever find out what had happened to it—whether an accident or the mere "call of the wild" back to rook-land. It was seen no more, alive or dead; and one human heart at any rate felt the loss very deeply.

I have mentioned 1881 as the year in which *Towards Democracy* 'came to me,' and insisted on being given form and expression. It is curious that the same year (or 1882) saw the inception of a number of new movements or enterprises tending towards the establishment of mystical ideas and a new social order. Mother Shipton's prophecy with its strange prognostication of mechanically propelled cars and flying machines ended up with the words :—

> And the world to an end shall come
> In eighteen hundred and eighty-one.

The world did not come to an end, but in a certain sense a new one began ; and just in those two years quite a number of societies were started with objects of the kind indicated. Hyndman's Democratic Federation, Edmund Gurney's Society for Psychical Research, Mme. Blavatsky's Theosophical Society, the Vegetarian Society, the Anti-vivisection movement, and many other associations of the same kind marked the coming of a great reaction from the smug commercialism and materialism of the mid-Victorian epoch, and a preparation for the new universe of the twentieth century. Amongst these was one which especially claimed to fulfil the prophecies of Mother Shipton and to be the herald of a New Age. This was the Hermetic Society. It consisted practically of two people—Edward Maitland and Anna Kingsford ; for though there was a nominal membership I think it may be said that the other members had little or no voice in it. And its idea was to read into the stories of Jesus, and of Moses and Abraham and so forth, their inner significations, to interpret in fact much of the New and Old Testaments not as historical matter but rather as eternal truths, allegories and emblems of the drama of each human soul. Thus the miraculous birth of Jesus, his exile in Egypt, his temptation in the wilderness, his toils and sufferings, his Betrayal, Crucifixion, Resurrection and Ascension were not external histories of a certain man, but inner histories of you and me and all mankind.

This method of interpreting the myths of past days, which we now in the twentieth century so well understand, and which explains for us the origin of a vast number of legends and at the same time accounts for their popularity, was in 1881—except for some few previous hints by Swedenborg and others—quite unrecognized. And we owe much to Edward Maitland and Anna Kingsford that they gave it, as well as some valuable collateral matter, to the world. Of course they did not fully recognize—though they did in part—how much of the story of Jesus, for instance, *is* purely legendary and mythical. But even if they had known it to be entirely legendary, that would not probably have greatly altered their views—though it would certainly have deprived their gospel of the supernatural halo with which they delighted to invest it.

It was this affectation, if I may use the term, of a supernatural mission which rather spoilt the work of these two well-meaning people—as it has spoiled alas! the work of so many 'prophets' and teachers in the past. To the egotism of the human being there is no end; and if such an one can only persuade others that he has some supernatural source of knowledge and power, or persuade himself (or herself) of the same, there is no limit to the devilry or folly into which he will plunge—as witness the history of the priesthood all down the centuries. In the case of Anna Kingsford and Edward Maitland it was not devilry which was the trouble, but the other thing! Having reached a certain insight or intuition, or whatever you may call it, into the inner meanings of life, they both became so inflated with heavenly conceit over their discovery that they really grew quite foolish and intolerable. As it happened I had known Maitland since I was a boy. When I was eighteen or twenty years of age he a grown man, and known in the literary world as the author of *The Pilgrim and the Shrine*, used sometimes to come to my father's house at Brighton. He was an interesting talker, well up in literature and science, and always keen on some new idea or discovery; but even then somewhat egotistically absorbed in his own thoughts and conversation. When he met the lady, however, who became his great life-inspiration, it must be said that he submerged all his own claims to prophetic gifts in a whole-hearted recognition of hers. He laid his soul at her feet.

Anna Kingsford was certainly a remarkable woman. As a young girl she had had strange visions. When Maitland met her (she being twenty-seven) she must from all descriptions have been singularly beautiful. He describes her as "tall, slender and graceful in form; fair and exquisite in complexion; bright and sunny in expression. The hair long and golden, but the brows and lashes dark, and the eyes deep-set and hazel, and by turns dreamy and penetrating. The mouth rich, full, and exquisitely formed." While Mrs. Fenwick Miller says: "I thought her the most faultlessly beautiful woman I ever beheld; her hair is like the sunlight, her features are exquisite, and her complexion—I can use no other term than faultless—not a spot, not a flaw, not a shade."

Add to these natural gifts a good medical training in the Schools of Paris, a fair knowledge of Greek and Latin, considerable literary ability and a generous and undisguised use of cosmetics, and you have a strange but powerful combination. Edward Maitland met her in 1874 (he was then fifty and she twenty-eight), and practically thenceforward dedicated his life to her. (It must however be remembered that the intimacy caused no estrangement from Mr. Kingsford, the husband, who remained a close friend to them both.) The reinforcement of Anna Kingsford's intuitive and prophetic gift by Maitland's incisive and logical mentality certainly had a valuable result, and their combined work left a notable mark on the time. Jointly from 1881 (to 1888 when Anna Kingsford died) they carried on a strong Crusade against Vivisection—one of the earliest protests made ; and they published besides a series of works—*The Perfect Way, Clothed with the Sun, The Virgin of the World*, etc—bearing the esoteric and theosophic message to which I have already alluded. Of these *The Perfect Way*, which shows both the systematic clearness of the one mind and the inspiration of the other, is perhaps the most important. It embodies in fairly clear outline those ideas of Indian and Gnostic origin which were at that time curiously descending upon the Western world, and which no doubt quite independently began about the same time to be spread abroad by Mme. Blavatsky and the Theosophic Society. Portions of this book, and large portions of *Clothed with the Sun* were apparently spoken by Mrs. Kingsford under trance conditions, and have a certain fine quality and atmosphere about them. They seem to indicate things actually seen in the inner world of being ; but they suffer, as such communications must do, from the medium through which they come. Large portions of *The Perfect Way* degenerate into mere drivel, and large portions of *Clothed with the Sun* are offensive (as their authoress herself often personally was) with a kind of spiritual arrogance. It is curious that those two prophetesses Anna Kingsford and Sophie Blavatsky—though so very different in personal exterior—should have been so like each other in many respects. Both undoubtedly had access to trance-conditions and to some region of astral intelligence or earth memory ; both (as happens in such cases) dug out for us some shining jewels of truth, but mixed at the same time with a huge mass of rubbish. (No words can describe the general rot and confusion of Blavatsky's *Secret Doctrine.*) Both were emotional in their different ways to an abnormal degree ; and both were, fortunately for themselves, associated with coadjutors of cool and intellectual temperament—Mrs. Kingsford with Maitland, and Blavatsky with Mrs. Besant. Both had really great and remarkable gifts ; and both, notwithstanding their high calling, descended to strange and unworthy subterfuges—Blavatsky to common juggleries and Anna Kingsford to a most deliberate and disagreeable 'pose.' At the Hermetic Society's meetings the latter would take the chair in state—after the style of the Great Panjandrum—and if any humble member of the audience asked a simple question like "Do you think, Mrs. Kingsford, that the soul survives after death?"—she would draw herself up, close her eyes, and say "*I know,*" and sit down again! On one celebrated occasion I remember that at the close of the meeting, Edward Maitland rose and referring to the epoch-making speech of the Lady-president on "The finding of the Christ," pointed out that that very meeting was indeed a world-event. For just as the *Kings* of the East came across the *ford* of the Jordan to lay their treasures at the feet of the infant Saviour, so now the treasures of Eastern thought were being brought across the world for the birth of a new Redeemer in the West, and by one whose name was most appropriately and prophetically none other than *Kingsford* ! ! After that we could naturally do nothing but dissolve along our different lines—in tears, or laughter, or through the doorways and passages, as the case might be. We poor little mortals must be grateful for what illuminations we can get, however quaint or queer the mediating personalities may be.

The years from 1881 onward were certainly a new era for me. They not only brought me *Towards Democracy*, but they marked the oncoming of a great new tide of human life over the Western World, and so—partly through the book itself—brought me into touch with a number of people and movements. It was a fascinating and enthusiastic period—preparatory, as we now see, to even greater developments in the twentieth century. The Socialist and Anarchist propaganda, the Feminist and Suffragist upheaval, the huge Trade-union growth, the Theosophic movement, the new currents in the Theatrical, Musical and Artistic worlds, the torrent even of change in the Religious world—all constituted so many streams and headwaters converging, as it were, to a great river. To be in fairly close touch, as time went on, with these movements and their (English) representatives—with men and women like John Burns, Cunninghame Graham, Mrs. Despard, H. M. Hyndman, Bernard Shaw, Keir Hardie, the Bruce Glasiers, Pete Curran, Ramsay Macdonald, Walter Crane, Sydney Olivier, H. W. Nevinson, H. G. Wells, Annie Besant, F. R. Benson, Granville Barker, Iden Payne, Mona Limerick, Isadora Duncan,

Margaret Macmillan, Lowes Dickinson, G. P. Gooch, G. M. Trevelyan, Roger Fry, Rutland Boughton, Granville Bantock, Laurence Housman, William Rothenstein, R. J. Campbell, E. W. Lewis, the Sidney Webbs, Olive Schreiner, Isabel Margesson, Edith Ellis, Alfred Russel Wallace, Oliver Lodge, George Barnes of the A.S.E., C. T. Cramp of the A.S.R.S., Stephen Reynolds of the Fisheries, Raymond Unwin of Garden Suburbs, Cecil Reddie of Abbotsholme, James Devon of the Prisons Commission, Edward Westermarck, Havelock Ellis, and so forth—was indeed an extraordinary inspiration and encouragement. Practically all these (and I have not mentioned the foreign friends and coadjutors) were giving their lives to the furtherance of some tributary of the great movement, and each of them represented hundreds or perhaps thousands of others who were doing the same. One felt that something massive must surely emerge from it all.

It was no wonder that Hyndman—whose name I have put near the beginning of this list—becoming conscious as early as 1881 of the new forces all around in the social world was filled with a kind of fervour of revolutionary anticipation. We used to chaff him because at every crisis in the industrial situation he was confident that the Millennium was at hand—that the S.D.F. would resolve itself into a Committee of Public Safety, and that it would be for him as Chairman of that body to guide the ship of the State into the calm haven of Socialism! The S.F.D. was constituted in the early eighties; when 1889 was impending it was obvious that that year, as centenary of the first outbreak of the French Revolution would be the fateful date. I remember his telling me, not without gleeful rubbing of hands, that the whole Society of London Stevedores (whom he had been addressing at the Docks) was behind him to a man, and would come without fail to his support. 1889 however passed, with nothing more effectual than the Socialist Congress at Paris—at which a great deal of dissension and difference of opinion was manifested. Then came '99, the last year of the century and clearly big with destiny; and he piled his hopes upon that. But it alas! only gave birth to the Boer War—which put things back for many a year. And after that 1909 and other dates did but provide further material for disappointment. And yet all the time the Socialist clock was really going forward, and though there was no sudden revolution or conversion, the nation steadily and almost unconsciously became saturated with the new ideas. Hyndman—though no doubt disappointed from time to time—stuck gamely to his 'cause'—and it was largely through his personal exertions that the educational work begun by him in '81 was carried to such fruition that in 1914 with the German War the Government and the country suddenly adopted large sections of the Socialist programme (without calling them Socialist of course) as the most natural thing in the world!

That neither Hyndman in his time, nor Morris in his, nor the Fabian Society in theirs, nor Keir Hardie, nor Kropotkin, nor Blatchford, nor any other individual or body, succeeded in capturing the social movement during these years and moulding it to his or their hearts' desire, must always be matter for congratulation. For once pocketed by any clique it would have pined and dwindled into an insignificant thing; but, as I have just tried to show, the real movement of this period has been far too great for such a destiny. It is like a great river, fed by currents and streams flowing into it from the most various directions and gathering a force which no man can now control and a volume too great to be confined.

One regrets that Hyndman's efforts to get into Parliament have never been crowned with success. Not that he would have been any use in the House as a party-leader (Labour or Socialist). Much the reverse; for though personally the most good-natured man in the world he had an extraordinary gift for falling foul of all his friends in the political arena. But because it would have been a satisfaction—and there would have been a certain poetical justice in it—to see Hyndman face to face with the bogeys of his own propaganda, the representatives of the established order, and trouncing them to his heart's content. With an excellent command of statistics and finance, a good knowledge of political conditions and the diplomatic *personnel* over Europe, two great causes close to his heart in the championship of our colored subjects in India and our white wage-slaves at home, and with a vigorous and ready tongue, he would surely, off his own bat, have made the House sit up, and compelled its attention to some neglected things. Nevertheless he would never I think under any circumstances have been a great force in politics; for curiously enough notwithstanding his mental vigour and energy there was a certain want of *weight* about his personality which prevented his influence carrying very far. On the platform, with his waving beard and flowing frock-coat, his high and spacious forehead and head somewhat low and weak behind, he gave one rather the impression of a shop whose goods are all in the front window; and though a good and incisive speaker his frequent gusts of invective seemed out of keeping with the obvious natural kindliness of the man and rather suggested the idea that he was lashing himself up with his own tail.

The frock-coat and tall hat were always of course *de rigueur* with him—not I imagine that they were particularly congenial to his Socialist ideals, but because they were a necessary part of his outfit and 'make-up' on the stage of the Stock Exchange; for no doubt the Stock Exchange as the centre of our Commercial system will cling to these old symbols of the industrial capitalist era to the very last.

A young friend of mine, who was at one time clerk to Albert Grant of City fame, told me the following story. One day while he was sitting in Grant's office H. M. Hyndman was announced, and walked in, frock-coat and all. My friend left the room while the two conferred—the well-known Socialist with the even more well-known German Jew and Company-promoter. Grant's reputation was not of the highest—or if it could be called "high" at all it was only in the sense in which game is sometimes so called. When the visitor was gone and my young friend returned to the room, Grant said, rubbing his hands "Do you know who that is? Do you know who that is? That is Mr. Hyndman, the great Socialist. You see, you see, with all their talk, even *they* cannot get on without *me*."

I do not for a moment suppose that Hyndman's dealings on this occasion were anything to be ashamed of; but Albert Grant's transactions were commonly thought to be of a shady character. Perhaps to make up for that, he bought with some of his gains the site of Leicester Square, converted it into a public garden, and presented it to the public. In consideration of this, and possibly other things, he was made a Baron—Baron Grant. Whereupon some wag wrote the following distich :—

> Princes can Rank confer, but Honour can't;
> Rank without honour is a barren (Baron) grant.

I have mentioned Walt Whitman more than once in the foregoing pages, and I think I ought not to let this chapter pass without referring to the ardent little coterie at Bolton in Lancashire who for many years celebrated his birthday with songs and speeches and recitations, with decorations of lilac-boughs and blossoms and the passing of loving cups to his memory. J. W. Wallace was the president, and Dr. Johnston, Fred. Wild, J. W. Dixon, Charles F. Sixsmith, were some of the earlier members of this little club, which met quite frequently from 1885 onward for twenty years or more. If there was a somewhat Pickwickian note about its revels still no one could doubt the sincerity of its enthusiasm. It helped largely to spread the study and appreciation of Whitman's work in the North of England ; it welcomed Dr. Bucke on his arrival from Canada with congratulatory addresses and hymns of its own composing ; some of its members (the two first-mentioned) crossed the Atlantic on a pilgrimage to the good grey poet ; and Dr. Johnston wrote a quite excellent little book *A Visit to Walt Whitman* descriptive of Whitman's personality and surroundings, which I believe is now being reissued from the Press in conjunction with some Notes on the same subject by Wallace. In later years I have been able to count Dr. Johnston and Charlie Sixsmith among my own constant friends.

I will conclude this chapter with a few brief notes on my almost life-long friend Arunáchalam. I feel that I owe a great debt to him because long ago, in '80 perhaps or '81 he gave me a translation of a book, then little known in England, the *Bhagavat Gita*—the reading of which as I think I have said before, curiously liberated and set in movement the mass of material which had already formed within me, and which was then waiting to take shape as *Towards Democracy*. As when a ship is ready to launch, a very little thing, the mere knocking away of a prop, will set her going ; so—though it was something more than that—did the push of the *Bhagavat Gita* act on *Towards Democracy*. It gave me the needed cue, and concatenated my work to the Eastern tradition.

I first came across Arunáchalam at a meeting of the *Chitchat* or some such society at Cambridge, when he was an undergraduate of Christ's and I a newly made Fellow of Trinity Hall. As in the case of other Hindus his extraordinary quickness and receptiveness of mind had very quickly rendered him *au fait* in all our British ways and institutions. With engagingly good and natural manners, humorous and with some of the Tamil archness and bedevilment about him, he was already a favorite in his own college—and at that time these early comers to the Universities from India were certainly received by our students with more friendliness and sense of equality than they are to-day. His father having been a wealthy man and occupying a good position in Ceylon, Arunáchalam had received a good education and was fairly well up in Greek and Latin, French and German, and their literatures, besides his own Eastern languages, like Tamil and Sanskrit. Altogether he was a very taking, all-round sort of fellow, capable of talking on most subjects, and full of interested inquiry about all. Many were the afternoons or evenings we spent together—walking or boating or sitting by the fireside in College rooms —and I learned much from him about the literature of India and the manners and customs of the mainland and Ceylon. When he left Cambridge he went to London and studied Law for some years, and then going out to Ceylon joined the Civil Service there, and in due time became Judge, Registrar-General, and finally Member of the Legislative Council. In 1890 he wrote to me about the Gñani Ramaswamy whose acquaintance he had made, and asked me to come out and meet him; and I gladly went —for it just chimed in with my wishes at the time; and, as I have told in my *Visit to a Gñani* and elsewhere, for six weeks or so we called on the Guru every day and absorbed all he had to say on the traditional esoteric philosophy of India in general and of the Tamils in particular. After settling in Ceylon, Arunáchalam paid from time to time various visits to England, at one time to bring his wife over, at another to put his sons to College, and so on. The last occasion was in 1913 when he received a tardy recognition of his really important services to the Crown in the form of a knighthood.

On these occasions, whether he was conversing with the humblest of my friends at Millthorpe or at Sheffield, or with high officials and "great ladies" in London his manners had always just the same charming frankness and grace about them, which established at once the *human* relation as the paramount thing. And yet this man, whose artistic culture and practical knowledge of the world was miles above most people he met, had often to suffer from the boorish rudeness of Anglo-Indians in his own land, or of belated Britishers on board ship. Alas, for the vulgarity of my countrymen!

I cannot leave him without one little anecdote. Being a guest on some occasion at a Mansion House dinner he was duly of course introduced to the various bigwigs present, and took his seat with the rest; but immediately caused consternation (being a vegetarian) by refusing turtle-soup and other carnivorous dishes in favour of spinach, potatoes and the like, and finally nearly wrecked the whole show by asking for a glass of water! Such a thing had never been heard of before. Waiters hurried to and fro, but water could not be found; and at last, with many apologies, he was asked to put up with a bottle of Apollinaris ("Whiskey, sir, with it?" "No, thank you")!

XIV

LONDON AND LECTURES

HAVING many friends in London, and a good many relations, I naturally, during all the years of my sojourn at Millthorpe, have been in the habit of paying fairly frequent visits to the big city. It is good to have one's roots in the country, but it is also necessary to have one's branches in the great towns where one can come into contact with the winds and storms of human life.

A considerable social storm at which I was present was that of the so-called "Bloody Sunday" in November '87. A socialist meeting had been announced for 3 p.m. in Trafalgar Square, to protest against the Irish policy of the Government, and the authorities (for conscience doth make cowards of us all) probably thinking Socialism a much greater 'terror' than it really was, had vetoed the meeting and drawn a ring of police, two deep, all round the interior part of the Square. Of course the Socialists had to make an active protest, if only in order to bring the case into court; and three leading members of the S.D.F.—Hyndman, John Burns and Cunninghame Graham—agreed to march up arm-in-arm and force their way if possible into the charmed circle. Somehow Hyndman was lost in the crowd on the way to the battle, but Graham and Burns pushed their way through, challenged the forces of 'Law and Order,' came to blows, and were duly mauled by the police, arrested, and locked up.

I was in the Square at the time, and like most of the crowd there more as a sightseer than anything else. Indeed, though a large crowd it was of a most good-humored and peaceable kind; but the way in which it was 'worked up,' provoked and irritated by the authorities, was a caution; and gave me the strongest impression that this was done purposely, with the intention of leading to a collision. If this was not so the only explanation must be that abject *fear*, on the part of the authorities, was the moving cause. As I say, the crowd was a most good-humored, easy-going, smiling crowd; but presently it was transformed. A regiment of mounted police came cantering up. The order had gone forth that we were to be 'kept moving.' To keep a crowd moving is I believe a technical term for the process of riding roughshod in all directions, scattering, frightening and batoning the people—the idea no doubt being to prevent the formation of knots or the consolidation of organized bodies among the crowd. In this case there was really no sign of any organized movement on the part of the people against the police, nor had I heard of any plan to that effect, further than the march-up of the three leaders already mentioned. I was standing—with my friend Robert Muirhead, Cambridge mathematician and Smith's Prizeman, two peaceable enough members of society as may be supposed—on an island-refuge just where the Strand debouches into Trafalgar Square, when we found ourselves violently pushed about by mounted and foot police and told to 'move on.' Whether Muirhead did not move on fast enough, or what the trouble was, was never explained; but the next moment I saw him seized by the collar by a mounted man and dragged along, apparently towards a police-station, while a bobby on foot aided in the arrest. I jumped to the rescue and slanged the two constables, for which I got a whack on the cheek-bone from a baton (which distressed the more respectable members of my family for some weeks after), but Muirhead was released, and we soon regained our footing on the refuge, from which for some time we watched the police continuing, at considerable risk to life and limb, to circle round and insult the 'mob.' I mention these little details just to show the kind of thing that happens. Purely as the result of this ill-timed action there were one or two ugly rushes I believe and a few broken heads; but the damage of 'Bloody Sunday' did not after all amount to much.

The case came into Court afterwards, and Burns and Graham were sentenced to six weeks' imprisonment each for "unlawful assembly." I was asked to give evidence in favour of the defendants, and gladly consented—though I had not much to say, except to testify to the peaceable character of the crowd and the high-handed action of the police. In cross-examination I was asked whether I had not seen any rioting; and when I replied in a very pointed way "Not on the part of the *people*!" a large smile went round the Court, and I was not plied with any more questions.

At an early period of my Millthorpe days (about 1885 I think) two young Cambridge men who had only just taken their degrees, Lowes Dickinson and Roger Fry, came down to see me—two gentle, humorous and charming creatures, who have since

MORNING LEADER CARTOON, 13 MARCH, 1906.

"If Society people had to make their own clothes there would be some curious scenes in the streets, and many would go about attired in simply an Indian blanket."—Mr. EDWD. CARPENTER at the meeting of the **Humanitarian League** at **Essex Hall.**

(By courtesy of the *Daily News.*

made their mark in Literature and Art, and whose friendship has remained with me, I am happy to say, all these years. Dickinson as a writer of pure English is I should say far ahead of any of his contemporaries. In contrast with the Meredithian, Henry Jamesian, Chestertonian, and other literary gymnastics of the day, his style flows along, pellucid with pure grace and purpose, saying exactly what is needed, no more and no less. It has the quality of 'the absolute in style'—which is very different from, though sometimes mistaken for, absence of style. Nothing could be more charming and to the point than his *Letters from John Chinaman* (or *From a Chinese Official*) and his *Greek View of Life*. With regard to the former he told me an amusing story about W. J. Bryan, candidate more than once for the Presidency of the United States. Being an American Mr. Bryan, perhaps naturally, did not perceive (the English being so perfect) that no Chinaman could possibly have written the book, and being also somewhat shocked at some of the remarks in it about the common infidelities of matrimonial life in England and America, he quite innocently published an article rebutting these charges and explaining that if the author (the supposed Chinese official) had had the advantage of being brought up in an Anglo-Saxon household he would never have made such mistakes! Dickinson had consequently to write to Mr. Bryan, and, breaking his incognito, to inform him that the author *had* had the said advantage, and really knew what he was talking about!

From 1885 onwards I lectured pretty frequently in London, Edinburgh, Glasgow, Bristol, Leeds, Birmingham, Bradford, and so forth—chiefly at first in connection with the various Socialist societies and groups in those places. The subjects treated of were those which are now so well recognized and understood everywhere that there is no need to insist on them, though at that time they were only beginning to appear on the social horizon—the evils of Competition, Adulteration, Falsification of goods, Waste, the scramble for Dividends, the iron Law of Wages, and so forth. Afterwards the lectures branched out a little more widely into literary and philosophical subjects, and with more general audiences.

In 1891, as I have already said, the Humanitarian League was founded. And later on I gave addresses on various occasions in connection with the League's meetings; one at an early date (about '92 or '93) on Vivisection—in conjunction with Edward Maitland; another on the same subject some years later; one in '97 on the Prisons; one in '98 on what might be called "Humane Science"; and one in 1906 on "Simplification of Life," and others. In the last-mentioned lecture I referred to the complexity of life among our well-to-do classes which arises from the fact of their being able to *pay* servants for doing things for them, and pointed out (supposing the bottom ever fell out of the bucket of modern society, and these people really had to produce their own food, clothing, etc.) how *simple* their lives would probably become—and how interesting it would be to see them going about barefoot and clothed in flour-sacks, rather than do the hard work of cobbling and tailoring for themselves.

The *Morning Leader* took the idea up, and brought out a Cartoon illustration of the lecture, showing the London Club men promenading in Hyde Park with only Indian blankets and flour-bags for covering, though still clinging religiously to their old umbrellas and tall hats!

For the Theosophist societies I spoke occasionally, in Birmingham, Liverpool, Manchester, Sheffield, and elsewhere—weaving in some amount of Indian philosophy (the Upanishads, etc.) with talk on social subjects; also for the Ethical societies in much the same way; and for Charles Rowley's Sunday afternoons at Ancoats, Manchester. In 1905 I took up the question of Small Holdings and the Co-operative Colonization of the Land—a question which had by that time become actual through the Small Holdings Acts of 1892 and 1907, and which will have to be still more seriously considered in the future; and spoke on the subject in Holmesfield and other villages in my neighborhood, as well as in Oxford, Glasgow and other large centres. Joseph Fels was very keen at that time on the subject; and I went with him to view his group of a dozen or so five-acre holdings at Maylands in Essex. Unfortunately the experiment did not turn out a success. He had bought some very heavy clay land at an absurdly low price, £7 an acre, and had spent £20 per acre on it in breaking up and burning the clay and heavily manuring, thus making the real initial cost of the land £27 per acre; and had then planted the ground with fruit-trees and had suitable cottages built on it. Reckoning up the total cost of each holding he offered them at a low rental, some 3 per cent. or 4 per cent. on the capital invested, and took some care besides in the choice of tenants, feeling confident that with proper handling the places would prove remunerative. Unfortunately they did not do so. Probably it had been a mistake to speculate on such extremely poor land as this was to begin with. Anyhow it never yielded the crops expected; and one by one the tenants disheartened abandoned their holdings, and the whole scheme fell to the ground.

Having always a good many friends among the Railway-men I was not unfrequently asked to speak at their clubs and branch meetings. On one occasion in November 1907, in conjunction with George Barnes, C. T. Cramp, Pete Curran and Victor Grayson, I addressed an A.S.R.S. meeting of over three thousand in the Sheffield Corn-Exchange. George Barnes always strikes me as a fine, solid and sensible man; Charlie Cramp the same; and indeed the railway-men generally—perhaps from their close and constant contact with the flow of humanity—have a discernment and reasonableness of outlook which is quite peculiar. Victor Grayson, the course of whose political career was so brief and so meteoric, was a most humorous creature. His fund of anecdotes was inexhaustible, and rarely could a supper party of which he was a member get to bed before three in the morning. On the platform for detailed or constructive argument he was no good, but for criticism of the enemy he was inimitable—the shafts of his wit played like lightning round him, and with his big mouth and flexible upper lip he seemed to be simply browsing off his opponents and eating them up. His disappearance from public life has been quite a loss.

In some ways these large audiences are easier to speak to than small ones. Consciousness of personalities—either one's own or of members of the audience—disappears; the great broad human interests come forward; finesse and detailed argument are of little account; the reverberation of emotion is great, and that carries the speaker on; but of course much depends on conditions. To hold a large audience in the open air is difficult work, but it is good practice. Concatenation and logical continuity are of no great importance, but every word must be distinct, every phrase must tell, every point be made clear and attractive, else the congregation will evaporate even while you talk to it, and condense again round the nearest coster's barrow.

In a closed room or hall you have your hearers more at command. They cannot easily escape, and you may become dull without knowing it! But here again much depends on circumstances. I find a room (of the common type) with level floor and high raised platform at one end rather trying. It is difficult to get *at* an audience so much below you, and as the voice tends to rise the more *distant* listeners seem unreachable. Worse still is a flat room where you stand on the floor without *any* platform; for then you cannot see your flock, and you lose all command over it. Personally I like an amphitheatre lecture-hall with rising tiers of seats one behind the other; or best of all an ordinary theatre with pit and galleries, so that from the stage one is nearly on a level with the great bulk of those present. I have spoken (on *The Larger Socialism* or cognate subjects) to audiences of two thousand or more at various theatres—the 'Grand,' Manchester (November 1908 and November 1909), the 'Prince's,' Blackburn (October 1910), the 'Metropole,' Glasgow (November 1910), and others, and with a satisfactory sense in general of being able to reach my hearers.

On November 11, 1910, I gave an address to the Literary and Philosophical Society at Greenock on *State-Interference with Industry*, which was repeated afterwards at Cambridge,

Oxford, and elsewhere. The subject was much to the fore at that time, and from opposite points of view, owing to prevalent strikes and lock-outs. The Clyde shipping strike was on, and there was a good deal of indignation expressed up and down the country at the conduct of the men in the shipyards, who had refused to take up their tools and go to work again, even after their leaders had counselled and urged them to do so. I was as much in the dark as most others about the cause of this strange refusal—until I reached Greenock; and then I soon heard from various quarters, both of men and masters, the real reason. It was not a question of wages or of hours. Those matters had so far been settled satisfactorily. The real grievance was a personal one. The men had been affronted by the overbearing conduct of the Chairman of the Employers' Association, the insulting manner in which he had behaved to their representatives, and so forth; and they were not going to put up with this without a protest. They wanted to be treated in a gentlemanly way. It was encouraging and refreshing to find that this was so; and the fact that it was so lets a good deal of light into a frequent cause of labour troubles and dissensions. But of course in this case at Greenock, as in so many others, the Press all over the country had got on the wrong tack, and the public never knew the real rights of the matter.

On October 24, 1908, the Women's Suffrage party held a great demonstration in Manchester, which like others of their functions was a miracle of organization. There were to be ten platforms, and the mere getting together of ten distinct bodies of processionists at their respective starting-stations in the neighborhood of the Town Hall, and marching them off to the appointed time, was no light matter. However it was done; and with Mrs. Despard walking gallantly at the head, supported by Margaret Ashton, Miss Abadam, Dr. Helen Wilson, Isabella Ford, Mrs. Swanwick, Mrs. K. D. Courtney, Mrs. Billington Greig, Councillor James Johnston, Professor Chapman, Canon Hicks and myself, a solid phalanx nearly a mile long, with bands and banners complete, walked all the way to Alexandra Park, three miles out! The immense crowd which came forth to witness the demonstration, and which lined both sides of the road, did not say much; it did not cheer to any great extent, nor did it scoff; it was simply deeply impressed. A large part of it followed on the route and collected round the ten platforms—about a thousand listeners to each. Each platform dealt with a separate subject—mine, in conjunction with Mrs. Greig and Miss Margaret Robertson, took *Prison Reform*. A cornet finally gave the signal for a joint resolution to be proposed in favour of the Suffrage, which was of course carried by acclamation, and the crowd dispersed.

Mrs. Despard's work in the two related causes of Women and Labour has been splendid. Her ardour and indomitable resolution, despite the drawback of advancing years, have been almost miraculous, and I always see her in my mind's eye marching gloriously to some encounter, and resembling the horse (in the words of the book of Job) "who saith among the trumpets Ha! ha! and sniffeth the battle from afar!" It has been an honour and a pleasure to me to speak on many a platform with Mrs. Despard—in Trafalgar Square and elsewhere. In October 1912 I took the chair at a meeting of the Sheffield Women's Freedom League, when she lectured on the subject of Shelley's *Prometheus Unbound*. It is characteristic of her that this poem was a favorite of hers from earliest girlhood; and in a sustained address that evening she quoted very large portions of it by heart, holding her audience for nearly two hours in rapt accord and attention. Mrs. Despard was, I need hardly say, like Shelley himself, an ardent vegetarian—though Shelley, owing to circumstances and conditions, often probably found it difficult to live quite up to the mark of his wishes in this respect.

In October 1909 I was honoured by being made President of the Vegetarian Congress at Manchester for that year—notwithstanding my own occasional derelictions from the ideal standard—and I found myself in the chair at an interesting meeting supported by well-known pillars of the movement like Professor J. E. Mayor of Cambridge, Dr. E. A. Axon of Manchester, Dr. Lybeck of Helsingfors, and others. The thing that struck me most about the meeting was the extraordinary number of extremely ancient looking patriarchs present with long white hair and beards; and I very nearly disgraced myself in my opening speech by expressing a doubt whether in view of this result Vegetarianism was a thing really to be desired or recommended! Some kind presiding spirit however saved me from this ineptitude, and I reached the end of my discourse safely and without succumbing to the temptation.

A subject on which I have often spoken—though always with the sense of only touching the fringe of it—is that of the connection between Sun worship and Christianity. The existing books on the subject are quite unsatisfactory, being very limited in their outlook. Some day it will have to be worked out more thoroughly. It is a most interesting subject, but as it involves a good deal of historical and antiquarian information and some technical knowledge of Astronomy besides reference to early sexual rites, it is not a very easy one to put before a general audience. I gave a lecture on it for the Sheffield Ethical Society in December 1908 and for R. J. Campbell's "Progressive League" at the City Temple in November 1909, as well as in other places; but it really would require a series of lectures for anything like adequate presentment. The *continuity* of Christianity with the religions of the old world and its ordered evolution from them is the idea which we now require to realize. We have had enough of its portrayal as a miraculous and exceptional stage in human development; and now that the world is coming round again to a concrete appreciation of the value and beauty of actual life, and to a sort of neo-Pagan point of view, it is above all important that we should understand the sources from which Christianity sprang in the past, and what germs of a world-religion it may bear within itself for the future, when it shall have cast off the crude and gothic elements of its mediæval development.

My friend Edward Lewis, himself a writer on The New Paganism, was in 1912 and 1913 minister of the King's Weigh House Church, Duke Street, W., and he and R. J. Campbell not unfrequently interchanged pulpits at that time. Lewis persuaded me to speak at his church; and on two occasions (November 1912 and October 1913) I did so. His congregation, largely trained no doubt and educated by his discourses, was an intelligent and sympathetic one, and though I had some misgivings on my first visit in speaking on so abstruse a subject as "The Nature of the Self"—illustrated as it was by numerous quotations from the Upanishads and from *Towards Democracy*—I felt no misgiving on the second occasion, when my subject (similarly illustrated) was "Rest." These lectures were repeated at the Lyceum (women's) Club, Piccadilly, at Croydon, Eastbourne and elsewhere; and the fact that audiences like these, of a rather popular character, could listen with deep understanding and sympathy to the unfolding of innermost psychological teachings has convinced me that the germs of a new and democratic religion are only waiting among our mass-peoples for the day and the stimulus which will bring them to birth and development.

Edward Lewis, being vigorous in heart and brain, and a real man, naturally could not continue very long in a profession like "the ministry" which entailed his ascending the pulpit three or four times a week and not only giving 'edifying' counsel to his congregation but confining his own life within a corresponding circle of inanity. Such a career would inevitably have sapped and ruined his manhood; and with true instinct he threw up his five or six hundred a year and retired into the wilderness. The members of his congregation were duly shocked and grieved in their different ways, according to the views they took of his lapse or lapses from holiness; but if, as is likely, the quondam Christian minister should become the missionary and apostle of a new and vital Paganism, the world will be very much the gainer.

The War, now going on [1915] is not only acting already very directly on the industrial life of the nations concerned but is pointing pretty clearly towards a remodelling of our general conception of

Industry for the future. It is fairly certain that somehow or other the gloomy and depressing wage-slavery of the present day—so intimately bound up with the Commercial régime—will have to give way; and productive work will have to regain the characters of spontaneity and gladness which surely are of the essence of its nature, and which are the necessary roots of all Art and of all Beauty and Joy in life. With that transformation of industry all life will be transformed, and the neo-Pagan ideal will become a thing possible of realization.

For some years, from 1910 onwards I have spoken on this idea—entitling my lectures "Freedom in Industry," "Beauty in Civic Life" and so forth, and delivering them before various bodies and in various places—as at Caxton Hall, London, for the Humanitarian League; at Crosby Hall, Chelsea, for the University Settlement there; for the Fabian Society at Oxford; for the Arts Club at Leeds; for the Progressive and Town-planning League at Bolton; for the N.U.T. Association at Chesterfield; and for many Adult Schools, I.L.P. Clubs and Ethical and Theosophist societies in different parts of the country.

To produce for Use; that production should really take place for the benefit of the Consumer; to concentrate not on Profit to individuals, but on advantage and gain to the Community; to drop in one inspired moment the whole mad sequence of cut-throat Rivalry, insane Waste, disgusting Fraud, and inane Uselessness, which constitute modern Industry; all this would mean such an enormous liberation of Power, such an incalculable increase in general Wealth, that the spectre of poverty would be exorcised for ever, and the numbing anxiety which weighs so heavily now on the lives of millions would be lifted away like an evil cloud. Joy would descend upon life, and the ordinary occupations would become free, spontaneous and beautiful.

Our powers of production to-day are so immense that even in the midst of the present frightful War we (on this little island) can spare millions of our best men for fighting, and millions more for the work of providing those fighters with engines of death and destruction, and *yet* with the residue can calmly and easily keep the nation going. What our powers and our achievement might be if once those eight millions or so—whose work is now only destructive—were turned on to the great positive task of social reconstruction and sensible human emancipation, it really passes imagination to conceive. The age-long world-dream of Paradise Regained would at last be within our reach. We can see that the War is even now forcing the modern peoples to take stock of their boasted Civilization, to reckon up the gains to Humanity which it represents—and the losses; to find out and decide in what direction they are really moving, and in what direction they want to move. If an event so great, so colossal, as this does not shatter the old order of profit-grinding and wage-slavery and wake a new ideal of life in the heart of the nations, one would say there is little hope for the world. But surely it will do so.

XV

TRANSLATIONS AND TRANSLATORS

AMONG the many good things in my life which I owe to my books by no means the least has been my introduction through them to dear and valued foreign friends.

One day in March 1901 there called upon me a young Hungarian—Ervin Batthyány by name—a modest, sturdy and almost rustic-looking youth of about twenty-three. He proved to be a member of the well-known Batthyány family, whose influence in Hungarian politics, on the Liberal as well as on the Conservative side, has always been considerable; but he was by no means conservative in his outlook or ultra-aristocratic in his leanings.

It happened at the moment of his appearance that I was doing some gardening and trundling about a wheelbarrow. "Oh," he said at once, "do let me wheel that barrow for you; I do like so much to do that sort of work, but I have no chance at home—I am so *civilized* you know." For a moment I thought he was chaffing; then the next moment I saw he was quite sincere. I believe I let him trundle the barrow for a bit; then we sat down and talked.

It turned out that he was expecting in the following year to come into large landed estates in Hungary; that he had studied and thought about

Socialism to some extent; and that among other things he wanted to consult me about the administration of his property when he should have the management of it. It appeared that with the almost feudal system still prevailing in that part, the cottagers and labourers working on such estates were practically attached to the soil and frequently transferred with it from owner to owner; that they were employed by the farm-bailiffs in gangs for the benefit of the estate; that they received next to no monetary wages, but were paid in pork or flour or the poor tenements they inhabited—that is, they were paid by a small share of the wealth they had themselves created; that they had no means of earning anything independently; and that they had little or no education—the schools being all under the thumb of the Catholic priests.

We talked over possible reforms—of a mild kind of course, as anything drastic would be out of the question; and when he went away he said with the same charming simplicity as before "The next time I see you I hope I shall not be so *civilized*." The next time proved to be some three years later.

He returned to Buda-Pesth shortly after his visit to Millthorpe; and took as it happened a copy of *Towards Democracy* with him, which he gave to a lady friend there—a certain Madame Nadler—knowing that she was interested and indeed accomplished in English literature. Madame Nadler took warmly to the book, and before long it came about that she and the young Count, who was a frequent visitor at her house, spent a large part of their time together in reading and discussing it—with the not unnatural result that they became warmly interested in each other.

Meanwhile he, the young man, plunged into the

administration of his newly acquired estate, and in the course of two or three years made useful changes. He founded an undenominational school, with a workshop for instructing the peasants in various crafts, and a reading-room provided with more or less socialistic literature—an innocent enough proceeding as we should think, but it turned the whole Clerical party against him, and terrified the aristocratic landowners of the neighborhood out of their wits, as with the shadow of a coming revolution! All this, together with his journalistic work in connection with various anti-militarist and Anarchist papers brought him into conflict with his family and the authorities, with the result that a sequestration of his property took place, and for a couple of years he was subject to a good deal of annoyance. During that period, curiously enough, little Millthorpe became the chief means of communication between the two friends—for I was in touch with them both, while their local and more direct letters were liable to be intercepted. They were thus able to concert plans to frustrate the enemy, which they did with such success that at the end of the period mentioned Ervin resumed work on his estates—though not without some risk, as may be imagined, of renewed attacks.

After these events *Towards Democracy* became more than ever a link between the two friends. They determined to translate the book—not into Hungarian but into German (as being a more widely received language), and they set to work upon it in real earnest. Mme. Nadler's competence for this labour was quite exceptional. With a great enthusiasm for the book and a quick appreciation of its meanings, she combined a very fine literary sense and aptness of phrase; while Ervin with his rather encyclopædic brain was able to interpret all sorts of references to trades and Nature-processes. In 1906 the translation of Part I was published in Berlin; and Parts II, III and IV followed in separate editions in the three following years, 1907, 1908, and 1909.

But meanwhile (early I think in 1904) Mme. Nadler having decided to give her children the advantage of an English education, and at the same time to save them from the hatefulness of enforced military service, migrated to this country; and so it came to pass that I made the personal acquaintance of this remarkable and beautiful woman—an acquaintance which, I need not say, soon ripened into friendship. Ervin, too, finding his native land not very congenial came over to England; and thus it happened that after the lapse of three years he and I resumed the conversations which we had first begun over the wheelbarrow. I did not notice that he was notably less 'civilized' than before, but his experiences had very obviously altered his political and social outlook, and his general views were decidedly more anti-governmental than they had been at the earlier date.

These translations by Madame Nadler were, however, by no means the first to be made into German. In 1901 or so Herr Karl Federn had come over from Vienna and spent a day or two at Millthorpe. In 1902 he placed his translation of *Love's Coming-of-Age* with a Leipzig publisher, and the book almost immediately had a good reception. It passed through several editions, and when a few years later, in 1912, the first German Women's Congress was held in Berlin the book curiously enough became a sort of bone of contention, dividing the advanced party who took it as their text-book, from the more conservative party who anathematized it. In pro-

LILLY NADLER-NUELLENS WITH HER DAUGHTER.

portion as controversy raged around it the work became more notorious, a cheap edition was printed, and before the Great War broke out some fifty thousand copies had been sold.

Herr Federn was not very fortunate in his choice of a title. *Wenn die Menschen reif zur Liebe werden* is only a rather heavy paraphrase of *Love's Coming-of-Age*, and the text of the book itself suffers from a certain heaviness and diffuseness. Still to Herr Federn himself I feel I owe a considerable debt, not only for introducing my work to the German public, but for the general fidelity of his translations and the loyalty of his dealings on my account with the German publishers. In 1903 he published also in Leipzig his translation of *Civilization: its Cause and Cure*; and in 1905, in Jena, the translation of *The Art of Creation* (*Die Schöpfung als Kunstwerk*). This last was issued in rather elaborate *format* by the well-known firm, Eugen Diederichs, but has never reached the circulation of the other two.

In the Spring of 1909 I was at Florence for some weeks; and there—largely through my friend Professor Herron—I came into touch with an interesting circle of young Italian *literati* and artists; especially interesting to me because they represented a strong reaction away from the very bourgeois and commercialized Italian art-ideals of the later nineteenth century, and towards the ideals of John Ruskin and William Morris—ideals founded on the socialization of human activities and the intimate relationship of all true literary and artistic work to the actual life of the mass-peoples.

The group included such men as Riccardo Nobili, probably the best living exponent of Fourteenth Century Italian art, whose charming little story *A Modern Antique* delightfully exposes the fakes of Florentine art-dealers and the gorgeous gullibility of American globe-trotters; Roberto Assagioli, the young philosopher, editor of *Psiche*—a psychological Review—and author of an illuminating tract on the Talking Horses of Elberfeldt [1]; Guido Ferrando, author of a couple of tracts on *La Coscienza Universale* and *La Nuova Psicologia* (Florence 1908)—who has done me the honour to translate my *Love's Coming-of-Age* and my *Art of Creation* into Italian; Count Auteri, the Sicilian architect and sculptor; Giuseppe Rambelli, the artist, and others.

More or less associated with this group—and on a second visit—I made the acquaintance of Teresina Bagnoli, a gifted young woman who had already been in correspondence with me with regard to a translation of *T. D.* (of which she sent me batches from time to time for criticism and revision). I found her swift and penetrating and original, and verging on Anarchism in her political and philosophic outlook; and I have to thank her for her excellent little volume *Verso la Democrazia* [2] which has brought me into touch with Italian readers in that intimate field.

It is curious, but perhaps not unexpected, that my best translators have been women. To a third lady friend, Mademoiselle Senard, I owe a very excellent version of *Towards Democracy* into French (Parts III and IV only). After some little preliminary correspondence Mlle. Senard came over from Paris in the summer of 1913 and spent a couple

[1] Entitled *I Cavalli pensanti di Elberfeldt* (Florence, 1912).

[2] Part I only, published by Lanciani, 1912.

of months in the country in my neighborhood. Sprung from an old-fashioned and rather aristocratic family in Burgundy she had managed at a comparatively early age to emancipate herself from a convent school and education, and by her resolution had almost compelled her parents to find for her a way out into the great world. She had become a perfect linguist in English, German and Italian ; and I found her a fine-looking and attractive person of thirty-five or so, always, like a true Frenchwoman, perfectly dressed and *chic*, yet simply dressed and absolutely natural in her conversation and movements. It was a pleasure to spend many a morning or afternoon with her, looking over her translation work or rambling through the garden and the fields.

However well one may know a foreign language it is rarely possible to follow every *nuance* of meaning or to succeed entirely in avoiding errors ; and a foreigner dealing with English has perhaps all the more difficulty in that way on account of the idiomatic and irregular character of our language. I have not always cared so much about the other books, but with *Towards Democracy* I have been very anxious that the renderings should be faithful ; and it has been fortunate for me that in these three cases I have had such very competent translators, and been sufficiently versed myself in the languages concerned to be able to assist them in doubtful places.

Marcelle Senard wrote also a little brochure of her own on *Edward Carpenter et sa Philosophie*,[1] which shows the clearness and penetration of a well-balanced French mind. Then, on the outbreak

[1] Published by the *Libr. de l'Art indépendant*, 81 rue Dareau, Paris.

of the War in 1914 she took up Nursing work, and with extraordinary energy and devotion organized and helped to equip a new Hospital for the Wounded at Nevers, south of Paris, where she remained for a year as Manageress and Secretary, till exhausted with the incessant labour she was at last compelled to relinquish the post.

In connection with French translations I must not forget to mention my friend Paul Le Rouge who is now assistant judge in French Morocco, and who translated and published my *Prisons, Police and Punishment* in Paris some ten years ago. I am sorry to say I have not found an English judge or police-magistrate who has taken an equal interest in the original book!

Early in 1910 I received one or two letters from a young Japanese illustrating the sad state of commercial slavery and militarism into which Japan had fallen since the Russo-Japanese War. Women and children as well as men were being worked twelve hours or more a day in the factories which were springing up on all sides, and for a miserable pittance; there were no regulations to curb the greed of employers; and any public protest was treated as anti-governmental Socialism, with the result that papers were suppressed in the most arbitrary way, and speakers committed to prison. A Japanese lady, Mme. Fukuda, had been imprisoned for five years for thus voicing the wrongs of the workers; and my correspondent, Sanshiro Ishikawa, was awaiting trial on a similar charge. He had, being a fair English scholar, been interested in my work for some time; and told me (what I had heard before) that a translation of my Civilization book had circulated pretty widely in his country at a quite early date. That translation, however, had gone out of print, and he, Ishikawa, was preparing a new one for the press, when—the Japanese Censor interfered and forbade its publication!

This shows up pretty clearly the state of darkness which had descended on the land of the Rising Sun! It was not of course on account of his interest in my book that he had been arrested, but on account of his general work in the cause of Labour.

The result of his trial was that he was sent to prison for three months, and that on his emergence he had to keep rather quiet on account of the attentions of the Police. He retained however his interest in my writings, made translations of portions of them, and embodied these together with some biographical matter in a book of some three hundred pages beautifully printed in Japanese characters and published in Tokyo in 1912; but of course for the most part a sealed book to me. Some small portions, however, are printed in our language and characters, including a letter from myself written to him while he was in prison—which I may as well reproduce here as it serves to throw light on the situation :—

DEAR FRIEND ISHIKAWA SANSHIRO,

Just a line to cheer you in prison—though you will be nearly coming out when this reaches you. I received your letter of March 27 with much pleasure. You were to go to prison next day. They seem to be very severe and despotic in Japan, when one cannot even publish *Civilization: its Cause and Cure* there. But your countrymen are too sensible to bear this sort of treatment for very long. I suppose it is *patriotism* which is so very strong in the nation just now, and which forms an excuse for anti-socialism. King Edward VII's death is causing a great wave of patriotism here; yet the future of mankind is leading us beyond patriotism to *humanity*.

I cannot write much now, but thought I would send you a few

lines. I believe I did send you my photograph. If it did not reach you let me know, and I will send another.

With hearty greetings and thanks to you for what you have done in the great Cause.

Yours very truly,
EDWD. CARPENTER.

21 *May*, 1910.

After a time—I hardly know whether on account of troubles in Japan or of attractions towards Europe—Sanshiro determined to come to these Western lands; and one day in the autumn of 1913, as I happened to be in London, he came to call on me there. Anything less dangerous-looking as a revolutionary it would be hard to imagine. Small in stature, timid in manner, and with a very gentle voice, he seemed the embodiment of quietude and sympathy. It was not difficult however in his case, as in that of many Japanese, to discern, beneath that composed exterior, a strong undercurrent of resolution and courage.

He read English with ease, but spoke it rather slowly and with difficulty, was intelligent, and like many Orientals skilful with his fingers and apt at housework. We tried to find him employment and a means of living in our neighborhood or in Sheffield or Manchester, but without success, and after similar efforts in London he migrated to Brussels where he knew of a friend in Paul Reclus, son of Elie and nephew of Elisée Reclus, and where he obtained occupation in decorative painting. This was early in 1914. In August, of course, the War broke out, and a few weeks later the Germans entered Brussels. The Reclus family—before their entry I imagine—retired to Paris; but Sanshiro remained in Brussels—I believe as caretaker of their apartments. It was a somewhat risky position. The Germans drew a cordon round the city, and ruled severely within it. Once or twice only he got messages through to me. But as the weeks went by he began to feel that he must escape at all costs; and in the end he succeeded in doing so—by representations I believe to the Japanese Government, which led to his liberty being granted in exchange for a German prisoner taken at Kiao-chow; but of this I am not certain. I have not seen him since, but anyhow he got to Liancourt (near Paris) where he now is [1915].

Another Japanese friend, Mr. Saikwa Tomita, the youthful author of *The Matanjitenshô* or *Psalm of the Last Day*, has translated and published large portions of *Towards Democracy* in current Japanese magazines, and intends apparently to bring the whole out in book form—as well as versions of *The Art of Creation* and some of my other works. Speaking (in a letter) of the present War, he says: "Japan is at her crisis as well as Europe is. Here in this country, as you well know, he who is for the lower classes and vagabonds, or who is for [the] cosmopolitanism, is treated by the authorities under the name of ill-fame and has to suffer from a bitter experience." And Sanshiro Ishikawa above-mentioned speaks likewise: "Is not this a terrible epoch, that the violent force only holds the supreme power in this world, and humanity has no influence, at least in [the] international affairs. The present situation of Japan is in most dangerous step [stage]; many peoples are becoming admirers of militarism. Commercialism is already too powerful; and I feel a duty that I must fight with full-hearted spirit against them."

Let us pray that these true-hearted fighters for Internationalism may prevail—all over the world, and among all nations!

I am proud to find that among the Bulgarians—who are supposed just now to be our enemies—I have many friends. Messrs. Vaptzaroff and Dosseff, editors of the magazine called *Renaissans* at Burgas and Tchirpan, published in it shortly before the War various chapters of *Civilization,* including "The Defence of Criminals," "Custom," "Modern Science," etc., and later the whole of that book, and of *England's Ideal.* With the outbreak of the war however they retired to Maikop in the Kuban Territory (east of the Black Sea), being in touch there with another friend of mine, the Russian novelist and mystic, Ivan Najívin. M. Najívin, who makes his home apparently in the country near Novorossisk on the shores of the Euxine—working there among his bees, and in his vineyard and vegetable garden—has written to me for some years, chiefly about Cosmic Consciousness and Sandals! He is, as may be imagined, particularly interested in the Indian Sannyasis and mystics, and was lately much surprised to find that some of the Russian peasant sects (notably the *Stranniks*) among whom he had lived so long were all the time unbeknown to him holding views and favouring practices very similar to those of the Hindu mystics. "Bientôt je vous écrirai des choses extraordinaires à propos du *gñanam* et *samadhi,* etc. Tout cela existe parmi le bas peuple et les moines Russes!" (letter of May 1913). He has translated my *Visit to a Gñani* into Russian under the title *I Am,* also large portions of *Towards Democracy* and the whole of *Civilization.* Besides M. Najívin I am indebted to M. Sergius Orlovski and M. G. Rapoport and others for introductions to the Russian public.

To my young friend Illit Gröndahl of Kloften, Norway, I owe the circulation of my works in

MARCELLE SENARD.

(Photo : L. Fréon, Neuilly, Paris.)

Norway, especially in Bergen. In Amsterdam a translation of *Civilization* (*De Beschaving: hare oorzaak en hare Genesing*) was issued as long ago as 1899—with Preface by Leo Tolstoy (the same preface which Tolstoy wrote to the chapter on Modern Science [1]); and in the same city a translation of *Love's Coming-of-Age* (*Liefde's Meerderjarigheid*) was issued in 1904.

[1] But not of course to *Civilization* itself. M. Najívin, writing to me, says: "A propos de la 'Civilization' Tolstoy n'a pas écrit un préface—seulement il a beaucoup loué ce livre dans deux lettres à moi, et j'ai fait des extraits de ces lettres et je les ai publiés maintes fois. . . . L'exemplaire de la 'Civilization' *avec des notes de Tolstoy* est envoyé au Musée de Tolstoy à St. Petersbourg."

XVI

RURAL CONDITIONS

In contrast with the Artisans and Town-workers whom I had got to know so well, the farm-populations and rustics among whom I found myself embedded when I settled at Millthorpe were decidedly interesting. In the working masses of the towns—at any rate of the Northern towns—what attracted one was the ferment of the New Life coming on: the social dreams of a better future; the efforts to realize such dreams, even in a small way; the push towards independence; the greater alertness and education; the busy hum and activity of Trades Unions and all manner of Labour Associations. What interested me in the country was something quite different. It was in fact the Old Life—the old immemorial rustic existence still going on, still there though giving signs of passing of course. As it happened, I could hardly have found a more old-world, purely agricultural parish, if I had searched for it—certainly not in the North of England—than Holmesfield when I first came there. (Now—oh, irony!—it is already beginning to be civilized!) It was all in the old rural style—the leisurely long day with its varied occupations and interests, the life of the open air and the fields, the cattle and the crops, the barn and the public-house; the absolute acceptance of things as they are, complete non-interest in reform, positive indifference to anything not patently visible to the eye, or to abstractions of any kind. The good folk would talk about a particular field—and really with amazing detail about its history, its climate, its soil, its suitability for such and such crops, and so forth ; but if you broached any phase of the Land Question (however really important to them)—their eyes would soon glaze and their conversation revert to their pigs or potatoes.

A few years after my arrival at Millthorpe, having found out some facts about the Commons Enclosures in the neighborhood, I wrote a four-page tract entitled *Our Parish and our Duke*—giving some account of the circumstances under which our common lands were eaten up by our local landlords early last century—and circulated it around. It was printed in the London *Star* (July 8, 1889) and quoted and commented on in other papers ; and it sold and circulated in leaflet form some twenty thousand or more copies ; but in the Parish itself it elicited no response ! One old farmer whom I knew pretty well said " It's very well put together, Mister, and it's just exactly true "—and that was all the backing I got. Probably if there were others that approved they did not dare to say so. The fact that it challenged a Duke gave them pause ! The tract, somewhat enlarged and altered and under the title *The Village and the Landlord*, is now published by the Fabian Society (Tract No. 136, 1d.).[1]

Thus, as I think I have said before, on first coming to Millthorpe I experienced a certain sense of isolation among the people there. Whereas in Sheffield and even at little Bradway I was received

[1] There is also a little book called *Some Forgotten Facts in the History of Sheffield* (Independent Press, Sheffield, 2s. 6d.) which gives valuable information about the enclosures in that district.

as a friend and commonly called by my christian name, at Millthorpe I was a stranger—and like all strangers an object of suspicion—and was addressed as "Mister." It was a curious situation, and I found myself leading a double and divided life. How I came in the end to bridge the gulf and (so far) to overpass it I hardly know; but Time does wonders, and by slow degrees the rustics have accepted me almost as one of themselves and given me, some of them, their warm friendship. I am indeed bound to say that despite the great differences between them and the town-workers, and the greater general intelligence and alertness of the latter, I admire the character of the country-folk most—their extraordinary serenity and good humour, their tenacity, sincerity, and real affectionateness. Even their silent ways—though irritating at times—are a relief from the eternal gabble of the cities. Said a farmer youth to me one day—after we had been listening for some time to the rather cheap talk of an elderly and radical "citizen"—"They do talk, those townsfolk," he said; and then after a pause —"them as talks so much *they must tell a lot o' lies*." And I entirely agreed with him.

Talking about the gulf fixed between the Old and the New, and especially between the mentality of the downright manual worker and that of the artist—at one time we had an artist friend staying with us who was rather down on his luck and making only a poor living. He was working on a landscape picture, and every morning used to sit in one of my fields and close to the wall which divided it from the high-road. An old road-mender (the same who had told me years before how he remembered the Commons "going in" i.e. being enclosed)—

a good old man but bowed with age and labour—used to come that way every morning to his work; and every morning, as sure as Fate, made some patronizing remark to the painter, which at last enraged the latter beyond endurance. "That's a nice pastime for you, young man." And then the next morning, "I see you're amusin' yoursen again, young man"; and so on. ("Pastime, indeed! amusing myself! I wish the old fool had to do it instead of me. But I'll be even with him yet!") So the next morning the artist inveigled the old man into conversation, and after submitting meekly to more patronage, said: "Well you see I have to do this for my living."

"Do it for your livin', do ye?"

"Yes."

"Do you sell them paintin's, then?"

"Of course I do."

Old Man (a little taken aback): "And how much might you get for a thing like that?"

Artist (stretching a point): "Well I might get ten pounds."

Old Man (astonished): "Ten pun! well I never!"

Artist (following up): "Or I might get more of course."

Old Man (thoughtfully and with deep respect): "Ten pun! Well, I never—*and sittin' down to it too!*"

But Hodge is passing away. The old agricultural population (farmer and labourer) is changing under the pressure of modern life; and soon—for good or evil—will be a thing of the past. The motor-car and the cycle, the telephone and the daily paper, are ploughing up the country districts, torrents of townsfolk pour over the land on holidays, and the seeds of new ideas are being sown. Already I can see, even in this little corner of the land, a new type of native arising.

The great drawback of the country folk in England (worse here no doubt than in Ireland) is their want of initiative. Centuries of smothered life under the incubus of the Landlord and the Parson have had their inevitable effect. They never *will* speak their minds, or commit themselves to any action which is not entirely customary and approved by the powers that be. It may be different in other parts of the country, but here the one answer to any question of importance (especially if put by a stranger) is "I don't know—I don't know." So fearful have they been for generations lest their words should be by chance reported in ruling quarters that the habit of concealment has at last got into their blood. One sees from this how paralysing our land system is towards all manhood and resourceful initiative in the country.

Nor is the matter much different in many other lands. When in Sicily (in 1909) we found that among the peasants the children were systematically taught to *lie*, and punished by their parents for truth-speaking. And for a very simple reason. For if a stranger came along and asked questions of a child—"How much land has your father?"—"How many goats does he keep?"—ten to one that stranger was an emissary of the Church (the chief landlord of the old days), or a taxgatherer, and so an emissary of the State; and the truth would mean more rent or more taxes. Thus deceit was the only salvation, and lying the chief foundation of "Morality." Here in England the parson and the landlord have a similar paralysing influence; and whether they actively and consciously are conspiring against the people, or whether their questionings (as sometimes may happen) are inspired by pure kindness, the result is the same—namely the corruption of the people ; and perhaps a worse corruption in the second case than in the first.

Still the new life must come, and has to come, and is coming. Small Holdings—either freehold or with a secure tenancy under a public body—give perhaps the best chance of breeding a spirit of independence in the people. Co-operation trains them in adaptability and resource.

At one time—seeing the waste of energy resulting from the twenty or so small farmers in our valley each making their separate few pats of butter weekly (and bad butter at that !) I got a dozen or more of them together and put the case for co-operative milk-selling before them. They all agreed that it was the right thing to do, that milk-selling paid much better than butter-making and that the cost of transit to town (by motor-car or country cart) could be recouped with profit. We went into the figures and were satisfied. But when it came to actual operations the paralysis of lack of initiative was on them, and no one would stir a finger ! If *I* had arranged a whole scheme and set it in operation I have no doubt they would have fallen in with it. But, as I said, I had my own work to do, and had no intention of giving up a large part of the day to their affairs. The only one who volunteered to do anything practically—and this illustrates the difference between the agricultural and the other workers—was curiously enough a *navvy.* He had only a very small farm which he carried on side by side with his navvy work, but he immediately took practical steps and would I believe have carried a scheme through but for an illness which just then overtook him.

A supply of Small Holdings (holdings say up to thirty acres in size [1]) on a really secure basis would do an immense work in liberating the social life of the rural workers. For the first time in his history one of the most important types of man in the country would be able to hold up his head, face his 'superiors,' and give some kind of utterance and expression to his own ideals. At present agricultural life is hugely dull from its mere uniformity and want of variety under the all-pervading foot-rule of the landowner and his faithful servant the parson. A greater supply of small holdings would also, I need hardly say, be valuable from the economic point of view, and the greater variety it would encourage in the culture of the soil.

Of course what we now especially want, and what happily people are beginning to *feel* the want of, is the establishment of large co-operative farms over the face of the land—somewhat on the model of the Danish farms. When it is remembered what the Danes have done, with an originally quite poor soil, by their organized co-operative methods—how they have renewed the prosperity of their own country and created a new invasion of Britain by their agricultural products—it seems astonishing that we over here still remain in the muddy ruts of our old ways. Supposing for example that by co-operative or governmental purchase, or even (if it can be imagined) by gift from a large landowner, an extensive farm of some two thousand acres were acquired; supposing that suitable portions of the farm were broken up into twenty small holdings

[1] The Small Holdings Act of 1907 defines anything up to fifty acres as a small holding.

of ten or twenty acres each ; and that the remaining body of the land were farmed in thorough style under a skilled manager—the workers on the central farm being the small holders themselves, who would thus work partly for themselves on an individualistic basis and partly collectively for wages ; supposing that the manager was given by the co-operators a certain amount of authority for the purposes of work and organization, and that on the other hand he was there to *advise* the small holders to a certain extent as to their work and crops ; supposing that he organized co-operative arrangements for the members of the society, both for the purchase of necessary materials and the sale of their products ; suppose that a joint council arranged the matters of wages and dividends, and the establishment of creameries, cheese and butter-making apparatus, egg-collecting systems, and so forth ; surely it is not very difficult to see that in some such roughly indicated way a great new departure might be made in the agricultural development of the United Kingdom. If a thousandth, if a twenty thousandth part of what is spent in the mad destruction of a great war were spent on some such constructive work, ten times the number of people now employed in agriculture might be placed productively on the land, and the output of wealth and home-grown food (so important to our island) might be enormously increased.

About nine years ago—in 1906—I began to pull the farm lads and men together to form a little Club at Millthorpe. For some years we had a difficulty in finding a place for it, and had to be content with a very small room in a cottage. But here came in the advantage of the small holder. A silversmith who lives in the locality—the only man beside myself who has two or three acres of freehold and who is not tied to a landlord—having joined the Club, and seeing our difficulty, offered a fine and large barn belonging to him for our use. If it had not been for him we should have had to go, cap in hand, to some local owner or cleric and could never have developed freely. As it is, the place has been a great success. Managed in an easy-going sort of way by the men themselves (and I am happy to say that my share now of the management is very small) the Club has taken its own lines quite naturally. In order to avoid ill-feeling and competition with the public-house—which is close at hand—we have no drink, except tea and coffee. Whist, lectures, readings, whist drives, dances, socials, billiards, are the chief amusements, and the place serves occasionally for discussion of local affairs. Theatricals, in a small way, now and then. And the balance of our weekly subscriptions goes in winter to a Christmas supper, and in summer to an excursion by rail or brake.

With small people secure in their tenure, such Clubs would grow up pretty abundantly and would become the start-points of co-operative movements, creameries, agricultural Banks, and so forth. The great thing is that they should *not* be managed by benevolent superiors, for the management of their own concerns is after all the chief and most important item of a people's education. There is however a place in our countrysides—and a need—for people of a rather wider knowledge and outlook than the general rustics to come and live among them simply as friends (and not as benefactors). People of this kind can certainly contribute *something*—even though their 'wider knowledge' be as a rule rather vague and bookish. They have information about what is going on elsewhere, and they often are good at organizing. A new *kind* of parson, democratic-minded and really in touch with the people, and not attached to any 'church,' and a man with a *little* leisure at his command, might be greatly helpful. Why do not the thousands of young men (or women) who are thus qualified rush in to fill this void?

At one time, as I think I have already mentioned, I was a member of the Parish Council, but the hopelessness of getting any result therefrom, combined with the waste of time connected with it, caused me after a few years to abandon the position. The four or five farmers, all in terror of their landlords, and the parson (bound by golden chains to the Lord of the Manor) formed a solid phalanx against any progressive proposal. Perhaps I ought to have fought things out a little more, but wrangling is an occupation which I detest, and to fight questions to a practical finish always means the expenditure of much time—time which I with my agricultural, literary and other labours could ill afford. The one prevailing idea with the Council was not to spend *any* money if possible ; and even the few shillings necessary for the repair of a small length of public footpath would be debated over with a tenacity and miserliness of outlook which made one despair ; while the Vicar (not without laudable presence of mind) would resign himself to slumber in the Chair !

About the only thing of use I was able to do was to save from loss or destruction the Award Book—that is the book which records the enclosure, early last century, of the Common Lands of Holmesfield Parish, and specifies the details of their assignment to the various proprietors then holding land in the parish. And this I only did with difficulty and after the labours of many months. When the Award was completed (in 1820) the said Award Book naturally and rightly was handed over, not to the Church or the Squire, but to one of the Trustees who represented the Parish generally—a farmer, who of course kept the book at his farm under lock and key, but with permission to the parishioners to inspect it at convenient seasons. In course of time the farmer died, and his son following in the same farm, became custodian of the book. Later on and after many years, the son died, and the son's widow became custodian. By that time most people in the parish had forgotten, or were utterly ignorant of the existence of such a book. It might easily have happened that the widow or *her* son, migrating to another part of the country, should have taken the book with them among their household goods—in which case it might have been lost for ever to our Parish. Such or something similar *has* happened frequently of course. It happened to the Minute Book of the Courts Baron of Holmesfield—a manuscript record of the meetings of the said Court all the way from 1588 to 1800, and a most valuable and interesting document. In some unknown way the book disappeared ; but by a piece of good luck, it has now come into the possession of the Free Library at Sheffield, where it can easily be inspected, and where it is safer perhaps than it would have been in the village to which it refers.

To return to our Award Book, the Parish Councils Acts very wisely gave all such documents into the custody of the Parish Council to be kept in a Parish room or Chest. But the difficulty was to make our Council take any active interest in the fate of the book. Moreover it possessed no Parish Room or Parish chest, and when the question came before it of having a chest made, even that appeared to some of the members a serious and unnecessary expense. Questions of the dimensions of the chest, the material of which it should be constructed, the number of locks it should carry, the selection of the joiner who should be entrusted with the precious work and so forth, were endlessly debated; the Council meetings took place only at long intervals and it seemed at last as if the chest never *would* get made. I mention these details merely to show the kind of thing that happens in country villages. Meanwhile the Vicar went to the said widow and (not without remonstrance from her) succeeded in obtaining the Award Book; and placed it in the *Vestry*. A faction then arose in the Council who maintained that the book was quite secure in the Vestry safe; and that no Parish Chest was needed! It had then to be pointed out that the Act did not *allow* such books to be kept in the Vestry, and that the Council would be responsible if it did not keep the thing in its own custody. And so the game went on. Ultimately after a full year of similar imbecility, the chest really got itself made; the Award Book and some other documents were placed within, and now repose there in waiting for the Day of Judgment. Exhausted by the labours connected with the affair, and hopeless of ever getting any useful activity out of the P.C., I shortly afterwards retired from it.

Of course these conditions are not the same in all parishes. Where there are mining or artisan populations there is often a good deal of briskness and movement; but in the agricultural regions and the South of England affairs are somewhat as I have described. The District Councils are a shade better than the Parish Councils ; but the membership of them falls largely into the hands of small shopkeepers and a middling class of folk who are very philistine and wanting in æsthetic perception, and as a rule rather ignorant except in matters of business. They make hard and fast rules and regulations—often suggested by the conditions existing in the jerry-built slum-areas of the smaller towns—and by enforcing these regulations in country districts where they are not needed do seriously hamper the expansion of rural life. Such are some of the regulations about the height and cubic space of rooms, which desirable though they be in slum-tenements are quite out of place and the cause of needlessly high rents in country cottages ; such also the barring of wooden dwellings, on account of fire, in many rural and even isolated regions where there is no public danger from this cause ; and again the vexatious restrictions set upon the use of vans and tents. In these respects the work of the District Councils is really helping towards the increase of an existing evil, the depopulation of the country-sides.

On the other hand the composition of these Councils makes them absurdly deferent to big commercial and aristocratic interests, and the money of the ratepayers gets poured out like water on schemes in which under cover of public works private interests are largely concerned. As I have had occasion to explain in the Fabian Tract above-mentioned—*The Village and the Landlord*—our local District Council, having decided that a reservoir was needed, applied to the then Duke of Rutland for the purchase of a suitable area on the moors above us. The land in question had before 1820 been part of the Common Lands of the parish, and was now, as the ducal private property, paying rates on an *estimated rental* of less than 2s. 6d. per acre. It could not therefore be supposed to be worth much more than £3 per acre, capital value; and it might *almost* have been expected that in consideration of the history of the Enclosure transactions, and of the additional fact that the land was wanted for an important public purpose (water supply), the area necessary for the reservoir would have been granted free. Far from that happening, as a matter of fact the amount actually charged was at a rate of about £150 per acre! The sad thing about such a levy on the public purse is not only that the ducal people should have charged it, but that the District Council should have paid it! If the latter had had the gumption to offer a bold resistance, to decide for themselves what was a reasonable payment, and to bring the whole matter before the public, the case for the former would probably have collapsed. But there's the rub—the want of spirit and pluck in these public bodies; and considering these and similar things one seems to see very plainly that what really matters in the life of a nation is not so much the exact form of its institutions as the general level of education, alertness, and public spirit among its people. With these latter advantages defective institutions may still be made to serve; without them the best will soon become corrupt. It may however be said that some institutions are naturally more favorable than others to the growth of public spirit, and that is a consideration worth remembering.

One of the few native institutions of long standing in this locality is the Well-dressing—which takes place in some of the neighboring villages once a year, during the feast-week of the village, and is accompanied with dancing and other festivities. The village fountain or spring is decorated with flowers—sometimes in quite elaborate and ornamental designs—and the festival evidently dates from very early or pre-Christian times when the divinities of the streams and water-sources were recognized and worshipped. When I first came, in 1883, into these parts, there were along all the lane sides numbers of the most charming stone cisterns and water-troughs bubbling with clean water and overhung with maiden-hair ferns; and it was part of the habits of the country-folk to keep these places in order—a joy to human beings and to animals. Now we have a reservoir as above-mentioned. The Well-dressings truly remain as a yearly function; but the divinities whom they used to celebrate have fled. The cisterns and troughs all over the country are neglected. They are cracked and dried up and full of potsherds and salmon-tins; wayfaring men and animals go thirsty; and the public spirit and service of the water-gods has vanished. We are told that water conducted through miles of iron tubes and lengths of lead piping is much more 'sanitary' than the water from field springs and wells. It may be. But I prefer the latter. At one time there were so many cases of lead-poisoning in the Sheffield district, traceable to lead connections, that the matter excited serious attention. It was decided that the trouble was due to a certain acid in the moor water, which dissolved the lead, and consequently large filter-beds charged with chalk and lime were made in connection with the reservoirs, which neutralized the acid. The water was freed from this danger, but it became saturated with lime; and the people died from stone in the bladder instead of lead-poisoning! Personally I would prefer to take my risk of a microbe in a flowing cistern. And with an alert country-population, assisted by an occasional inspector, such a risk would certainly be small.

But we are told that public spirit ought to make us join these reservoir schemes ; and pressure is put on us by the 'authorities' to do so. I do not by any means agree. Though no doubt there are cases in which local storage is advisable or necessary, the unbridled transfer of water over immense distances is attended by serious evils. The beautiful Thirlmere is turned into a mere water-tank in order to supply Manchester ; the lovely dales of Derbyshire are disfigured beyond recognition so that they may quench the thirst of Birmingham. In other words, in order to encourage the growth of a hideous and dirty city with an unclean and poverty-stricken population a tract of clean and gracious land a hundred miles off is cleared of *its* population and also rendered hideous ! And all this at a huge and incalculable expense. We do not want these great congested and unhealthy centres, and we do want our streams and springs and the gods who dwell among them. Let the people come out for the water if they want it ; but let them come with forethought and reverence.

Another native institution managed, like the well-dressing, by the people themselves is the Ploughing Match. There *is* a Farmers' Association which of course ought to be a kind of Trade-union for the promotion and protection of farming interests. Perhaps once it was alive ; but now and ever since I have known anything about the matter it has become hopelessly futile and decadent. It has a dinner at some public-house once a year and gets thoroughly drunk—and that is about all it does !

But the Ploughing-Match Association, which was originally I suppose an offshoot of the Farmers' Association, *is* alive—possibly because it has nothing whatever to do with politics. The farmers and their sons and the small holders (such as there are) join in and organize the affair; and it is a pretty sight to see in two adjacent fields perhaps twenty teams of men or boys with their shining ploughs and their beribboned horses going to and fro each on their appointed strip of land; the turning of the animals at the extremities; the clicks and calls; the marvellous accuracy of the furrows; the groups of critics and the judges. Going among them all one perceives what splendid material there is here among the English country-sides; and also one grieves to think how it is paralysed from development and expansion by our absurd land-system and generally apathetic way of conducting ourselves towards the most important of all industries. We have at Holmesfield the champion ploughman of the neighborhood, who takes the prizes at the village matches for many miles round. He is a great friend of mine. And I am also proud to say that at our Association Committee meetings my professional opinion is sometimes consulted, and I may occasionally be seen amid the fumes of smoke and beer occupying the Chair and keeping a dozen or twenty farmers in order, or bringing them back to the practical point of discussion when (as they generally do) they wander afar from it—a sufficiently humorous situation for a so-called "poet and prophet"!

But the most important village institution after all—and more important perhaps than the Church—is the Public-house. Here is the natural centre of the Village life, and here the village Opinion—if there is any—is collected and consolidated. It is a great pleasure to me to sit occasionally in our "Royal Oak" among the rustics whom I know so well. Their quaint humour, their shrewd judgments, their shy silences, their naughty stories, are a continual recreation. Unfortunately, like so much else in rural life, the Pub. has in general been allowed to go to decay; and instead of being the village meeting-place and centre of sociability it has too often become a mere resort of drink and imbecility. "Tied" to a Brewery, and at an exorbitant rent, the Publican has no alternative but to sell as much as he can of the vile decoction supplied to him. He encourages booze but does not encourage sociable converse. The Brewer rises to wealth and obtains a seat in the House of Lords; the villager sinks slowly but surely poisoned in body and atrophied in mind, and dies in a ditch.

One of the very first things to be done for the restoration of the rural life is the reorganization of the Public-house—or rather its liberation. The clutch of the Brewers upon the drink trade should be cut off decisively and finally. The manufacture of beer ought either to be a State monopoly or it ought to be absolutely free, without licence, and subject only to a severe inspection. There has been a great deal of talk lately about the intemperance of the workers, and the abolition or serious restriction of the drink traffic; but the real root of the evil (certainly as regards beer) is the badness and poisonous character of the liquor supplied. See to it that that is clean and wholesome—that the lager-beers, small beers, teas and temperance drinks are not sophisticated with harmful chemicals—and for the rest leave the houses free. Leave the publican to use his good sense and authority, and make him responsible for not keeping order. If that policy is carried out there will not be much to complain of. The sale of actual *spirits* in drinking shops is another question, and that might well be restricted or abolished.

The village pub. ought to be a place where pleasant and decent refreshment of various kinds is provided—especially of drink which is a first necessity for tired workers. It ought to be clean and fairly comfortable and provided with games, papers, and similar means of recreation. On the other hand it should have no suspicion of genteel or missionary purpose about it. If the manual worker cannot talk freely and feel himself at home in the place he decidedly will not come to it ; and it is certainly better that he should be a bit rough and rowdy than that he should feel that he is being 'improved.' What the rural worker wants above all—and what it is very necessary that he should have—is a place where he can be at ease, converse freely, exchange ideas, and *develop out of his own roots*. The town worker has now, in his trade unions, his various clubs and societies, got something of the kind. The rural worker is a poor lost thing ; he has no centre of growth. The Church is absolutely of no use to him in that respect ; for the Parson practically paralyses his flock. The Chapel is better, for there the Chapel-folk organize themselves and carry out in an authentic way many a little scheme for their own satisfaction or entertainment. The Village Club and the Village Co-operative society are just beginning in many places to show an independent and progressive life ; but after all the Village Pub. strikes its roots deepest and widest, and if on a healthy basis is the natural meeting-place where all these other movements germinate and from whence they spring.

XVII

HOW THE WORLD LOOKS AT SEVENTY

I REMEMBER having often wondered, in earlier days, what would be the answer to this question. And now I have the privilege of myself standing on the pinnacle of age—and of being in the position where some kind of verdict may be given.

There are two verses about David and Solomon —whose origin I have not been able to trace, but which run as follows :—

King David and King Solomon
  Led very merry lives
With many many concubines
  And many many wives.

But when old age came on them
  With many many qualms,
King Solomon wrote the Proverbs
  And David wrote the Psalms.

Perhaps this gives the most general and accepted view on the subject—a view of old age as something a little dull, a little ineffectual, consoling itself with verses and good advice and other second-hand joys. On the whole perhaps a fairly correct view ; and yet I cannot but think that it misses something very important, something which in earlier days one does not associate with old age—the sense of adventure. Youth is full of acknowledged adventure ; the campaigns of Love and of War are thrilling and absorbing; but youth does not know—or at any rate only faintly surmises—how absorbing may be the great adventure of Death.

On the whole I am struck by the singularly *little* difference I feel in myself, as I realize it now, from what I was when a boy—say of eighteen or twenty. In the deeps of course. Superficially there are plenty of differences, but they relate mostly to superficial things like success in games, examinations and so forth. I used to go and sit on the beach at Brighton and dream, and now I sit on the shore of human life and dream practically the same dreams. I remember about the time that I mention—or it may have been a trifle later—coming to the distinct conclusion that there were only two things really worth living for—the glory and beauty of Nature, and the glory and beauty of human love and friendship. And to-day I still feel the same. What else indeed *is* there? All the nonsense about riches, fame, distinction, ease, luxury and so forth—how little does it amount to! It really is not worth wasting time over. These things are so obviously second-hand affairs, useful only and in so far as they may lead to the first two, and short of their doing that liable to become odious and harmful. To become united and in line with the beauty and vitality of Nature (but, Lord help us! we are far enough off from that at present), and to become united with those we love—what other ultimate object in life *is* there? Surely all these other things—these games and examinations, these churches and chapels, these district councils and money markets, these top-hats and telephones and even the general necessity of earning one's living—if they are not ultimately for that, *what are they for*?

At any rate that is how I feel about it now. I feel that the object of life at seventy is practically the same as it was at twenty. Only one thing has been added. One thing. Beneath the surface waves and storms of youth, beneath the backward and forward fluctuations, deep down, there has been added the calm of inner realization and union. I know now that these two primordial and foundational things (or perhaps they are one) *are* there. Our union with Nature and humanity is a *fact*, which—whether we recognize it or not—is at the base of our lives; slumbering, yet ready to wake in our consciousness when the due time arrives.

With this assurance one certainly discovers that life—even in old age—may be delightful. What one loses in the keenness and passion of sensual and external things one gains in the inward world—in calm and strength and the deep certainties of life. One can hardly expect to have it both ways. We may concentrate mainly (though not exclusively) on the outer life, or we may concentrate mainly on the inner life, but hardly on both at the same time. And the latter alternative has its advantages. Socrates, in reply to a friend who condoled with him on the waning of his sexual passion, asked whether he would not consider a man happy who had escaped from the clutches of a fierce tiger. "Certainly I should," answered the friend. "Then why," retorted Socrates, "do you not congratulate instead of commiserating *me*?"

I find there are compensations and consolations in old age. People feel kindly towards you—partly because they consider you harmless and not likely to injure them, partly because they are not envious of your condition. They pity you a little in fact—

which pleases them and does no harm to you. I find I am a little hard of hearing, and people are good enough—in fact they are compelled—to speak up and speak distinctly. They have the pleasure of helping me over my deafness, and I have the satisfaction of getting them out of their mumbling habits of conversation—a satisfaction so great that were I really not a bit deaf I feel that I should have to pretend to be! As I think I have said before[1] old people and infirm folk and chronic invalids and the like often get needlessly depressed over the impression that they are a burden and an affliction to their friends, whereas in very truth by calling out the sympathies, the energy, the resource and the consideration of those around them they are really conferring the greatest of benefits; and many a household is really supported and held together by the one who to all outward appearance seems to be the most frail and useless member of it. As Lâo-tsze says "The thirty spokes of a carriage-wheel uniting at the nave are made useful by the hole in the centre,[2] where nothing exists," and "To teach without words and to be useful without action, few among men are capable of this."

After the fuss and flurry of all the good folk who go about "doing good," to find that you can perhaps be most useful by being a "hole in the centre" is very refreshing.

Unfortunately the world is very unwilling to allow this privilege, and as a rule in a quite automatic way accords to the aged a good deal of respect and influence, pushing them up into positions of power and notoriety. This is all right if you are

[1] Chap. X, p. 180.

[2] By means of which, of course, the wheel turns on its axle.

E. C. (1910), AGE 66.

(*Photo: Elliott & Fry.*)

quite worthy of it, but dangerous if you are not. And naturally if you *desire* power (and notoriety) you are not likely to be worthy of it.

On August 29, 1914, being my seventieth birthday, some of my friends were good enough to present me with a congratulatory Address couched in very friendly and affectionate terms. Though I cannot say that I desired the thing beforehand—seeing that there is always something painful in the very idea of being singled out in any such way—yet I must confess that, being done, it was a consolation and a pleasure to me.[1]

There is one thing however that I think I have not sufficiently dwelt on as a valid and permanent object of Life—though perhaps in some subtle way it may be implied in what I have said before. I mean Self-Expression. Constructive expression of oneself is one of the greatest joys, and one of the greatest *needs* of life; and as long as one's Life exists—in this or any other sphere—so long I imagine will that need be present, and the joy in its fulfilment. It is a foundation-urge of all Creation. At first sight this seems contrary, and indeed hostile, to the hole-in-the-centre theory; but probably it will be found not to be so. Probably it is only a question of the *depth* at which the Self is functioning. Near the surface the self is very definite and constructive in *this* or *that* direction; it is limited in its aims and operations, and so far its activity seems to be at variance with other aims and operations. At the centre it is neither this nor that, because it is All. It vanishes from sight because it has become the Whole.

[1] The Address together with my Reply is printed in an Appendix at the end of this book.

Most healthy work is generated from a desire for, or an effort towards, self-expression. If one's feet suffer from cold and exposure to injury one makes boots to protect and cover them. If boots prove painful and confining one designs sandals in order to free them. Having made these for oneself first, other people desire them and adopt the same devices. One's work, begun for a private purpose and to satisfy one's own wants, is continued for public ends and becomes a kind of extended selfishness. It is the same with the institutions of society. Finding that they maim and confine you personally, the best thing you can do is to liberate yourself by reshaping them. In reshaping them you liberate others, and are accounted a reformer and general benefactor. But I imagine that no one is really a useful reformer who does not begin the work from his own private need, since that is the only way in which he can understand the true inwardness of the work to be done. And the accusation of selfishness, which may be preferred against him, saves him from the awful danger of becoming, or posing as, a public benefactor.

It is truly wonderful to see what activity, what enthusiasm, vast numbers of people throw into public work of one kind or another. Let us hope they all do so from the underlying ground of some personal need which makes them unhappy in the existing conditions and impels them for their own personal satisfaction to alter those conditions. If so their work will probably be healthful and successful. It will not wait on results but will bring its own results with it. Still there is a paradox in all such action. I cannot personally be comfortable in a society which makes a fetish, say, of what H. G. Wells calls The Misery of Boots. Therefore

I work for a future society where people shall go barefoot or freely wear such footgear as suits them. But by the time such state of society arrives, where shall "I" be? That is the question. What is the good of my working for a state of things which will certainly not come in my lifetime? What is the impelling force which *causes* me so to work when it would be so much easier not to work, and merely to let things slide? If, as one must suppose, it is something organic in Nature, it must be that I "myself" *will* be there. I, the superficial one, am working now for the other "I," the deeper one —who is also really present even at this moment (although he lies low and says nothing about it) and who in due time will consume the fruits which he is now preparing.

I find at the age of seventy that I am getting nearer to that place in the centre where nothing exists and yet all is done—and *that* I suppose is satisfactory. A very simple round of life contents me. As long as I can have my friend (or friends) and my little corner of Nature, and my little pastime of constructive work, I really do not know what to wish for more. (And surely every one ought to be able to command these.)

We are up—my friend and I—at about 7 a.m. in summer, about 8.0 in winter. In summer a wash and a sunbath on the lawn, for half an hour, are very much in the order of the day. Then, for me, there is my study to tidy up and dust and (in winter) my fire to light; there is the front of the house to sweep, wood to chop, and so forth. George has his kitchen to attend to, coals to get in, the chickens to feed, and preparations to make for the work of the day—baking or washing or whatever it may be.

I remember the time when I used to think that to get up early, perhaps by candlelight, go down into a dishevelled sitting-room, clean out the grate and light up the fire would surely be the most dismal of occupations; as a matter of fact I find these little preliminary duties quite interesting. They stir one's limbs and one's interest in the world, and help to peel off the thin but clinging veil of sleep.

By 8.30 I find I can settle down to work, either in my study or, if the weather allows, outside in my little veranda or porch. I thus get a couple of hours fairly undisturbed. At 10.30 we have breakfast—or what is called 'brunch,' a combination of breakfast and lunch—a good meal of coffee and milk, oatmeal porridge, an omelet, stewed fruit, or similar provender, and which one enjoys all the more for its being the first in the day. Brunch and reading the daily paper occupy an hour; and at 11.30 I am able to start work again and go on to 1.30 or 2.0. I thus get a good four hours or more in the morning for solid literary work, to some extent broken into at times by mere business matters and correspondence, but generally the most satisfactory period of work in the day.

At two or so one goes easy. By the ruse of 'brunch' one has avoided that deadly snare, the midday meal. Is it not Thoreau who says that one should pass by the one o'clock dinner "tied to the mast, like Ulysses, and deaf to the voice of the Siren"? Certainly George and I never cease to congratulate ourselves on this arrangement by which the painful density and lethargy of that period is escaped. It seems to place the day in its proper order and perspective; and we only regret that most people owing to professional hours and public duties are not able to conform to it. From 2.0 or

2.30 to 5.0 one can make a change. There are oddments of work to do in the garden, there are little outdoor renewals and repairs round the house, there are visitors and casual guests ; at 4.0 or so there is the sociability of afternoon tea. At 5.0 there are letters to get ready for the post, which goes at 6.30. At 7.0 there is supper, which is generally a rather more substantial meal than brunch. Sometimes tea and supper are combined in one intermediate meal, which of course goes by the name of 'tupper.' In the evening there are friends to see, books to read, notes to make ; there is the public-house, which is an unfailing joy, and the farm-lads' Club, which is always homely and cheering. What can one wish for more? It is hard to say.

Yet I ought to say—and it would be less than candid not to say—that there have been times all through my life when the necessity of escaping into an altogether bigger world than that provided by my native land has come upon me with a kind of Berserker rage. As I think I have said, I come of Cornish ancestry—and my private opinion is that I was left on the coast of Cornwall some three thousand years ago by a Phœnician trader. At any rate the leaden skies of England, and something (if I may say so) rather grey and leaden about the *people*, have since early days had the effect of making me feel not quite at home in my own country. I longed for more sunshine, and for something corresponding to sunshine in human nature—more gaiety, vivacity of heart and openness to ideas. But everything has its compensation, and the result of being pinned down so much to a limited and local life on the land has been that every three or four years I have been able to 'stick it' no longer, and have been compelled in the intervals of my work to make a dash for some warmer and brighter climate. In this way it has come about that I have seen quite a little of other lands—not only of the usual resorts in Switzerland and Italy, but of places like Morocco, Sicily, Corsica, Spain, besides (as already mentioned) the United States and Ceylon and India. Having a talent for economical travel I have been able to do this at singularly small expense. And my knowledge of agriculture and of the working life of the people at home has in such cases opened up a world of interest in the comparison of these with the corresponding things abroad—a world which as a rule is a sealed book to the ordinary tourist. In many cases my companions have themselves been manual workers, and I have found the vivacity of their interest in foreign fields and crops or in town-trades and workshops both encouraging and amazing.

At the age of seventy one does not bother so much about the exceptional feats, about great exploits, the climbing of the highest mountains. The ordinary levels of life seem sufficient. I confess that excessive cleverness and all that sort of thing bores me rather than otherwise. I seem to see in the general average of human life, in the ordinary daily needs, a steady force pushing mankind onwards, or rather, gradually unfolding through mankind—the liberation of a core of goodness and worth which is undeniable, impossible to ignore, and daily coming more and more into evidence. I say this deliberately and with full recognition all the time of the vast masses of cheap and nasty people as well as of cheap and nasty things which are washed up in the ordinary current of this our modern life, and with recognition also of the huge whirlpools of popular madness which occasionally arise, and which accompany crises like that from which we are now suffering [1915]. Perhaps the madness and the blind passion—the loosening of the torrents of hate and revenge, and of the pent-up waters of prejudice and ignorance—are, after all, better than the dreary stagnation of the cheap and nasty. The whole commercial period through which we, here in the West, have been passing for the last hundred years has undoubtedly bred, both in men and goods, a lamentable commonplaceness and cheapness—a low level and a paltry standard of human value. Perhaps even the madness of warfare is better than that.

It is curious that for the last twenty years or more there has been a general feeling—especially among the Socialists and Internationalists of the various countries—that society was approaching a critical period of transformation. It had become obvious that the existing order of things—in Government, Law, Finance, Industry, Commerce, Morality, Religion, the Capitalist Wage system, the Rivalry of nation with nation, the administration and cultivation of the Land, and so forth—could not continue much longer. In each one and all of these matters we have been heading towards an *impasse*, a block, a point at which further progress in the old direction must cease, and a new departure begin. We have seen this ; and yet we have been unable to say, for the most part, or even surmise, *how* the change would come, what catastrophe would upset the balance of our highly artificial Commercial Civilization, or in what way a new order of life, and a more human and rational order, might begin to establish itself. The Catastrophe has come. We are already in the welter of a World-war which in magnitude exceeds anything that has ever occurred in the past, or even been imagined. The nations are in the melting-pot; the institutions of society are threatened in every direction. But at present we are still unable to see the outcome, or even to guess what it will be. The lineaments of the new world are hidden from us. That the outcome will be far, far greater and grander than we now suppose, I do not doubt—also that it will take far longer than we generally think to define itself.

Beneath all the madness of the present conflict—the raging passions, the insane folly, the frantic delusions, the devilish concentration of all the wit and ingenuity of man towards purposes of death and torture, there is, I firmly believe, a method and a meaning. A new life is preparing to show itself—coming to the surface of society, as it were, out of the deeps, showing indeed the strangest and most violent agitation of that surface just before its appearance. Having lived so long as I have done among the downright manual workers of our towns and the agricultural rustics—primitives as they are in many ways and belonging to a period "before civilization"—I do not feel at all alarmed. I know that the lives of these good solid folk, founded as they are upon the primal facts of Nature, will not in any case suffer a very great change. If the whole of our Banking and Financial system collapsed and fell in, if world-wide Commerce came to a standstill, if the Capital necessary for huge armaments and general ironworks was not forthcoming, if Law and Government were paralysed, old-age insurances ceased to be paid, and Landlords were unable to collect their rents—if all this and much more happened, my friend who ploughs the fields near my cottage would go out next morning with his team to his usual work, and scarcely know the difference. *If anything he would decidedly feel more cheerful and hopeful.* Some other friend who forges and tempers table-knives by the score would continue to forge and temper them. The knives would still be wanted, the power to make them would still be there. And if at any point combined labour were needed, as to build a workshop or carry through a steel-making process, the men who do these things now in forced and servile toil under the Capitalist system would do them ten times better and more heartily in free co-operation.

No, if all this jerry-built cheapjack Commercial Civilization collapsed it would not much matter. The longer I live the more I am convinced of its essential pettiness and unimportance. The great foundational types, the real workers of the world—whether in England or Germany or France, or Turkey or Bulgaria or Egypt—will remain, and indeed must remain because the primal facts of Nature, the sun and the earth and the needs of human life, continually generate them. They will remain and, once freed (as one may hope) from the burden of the futile and idiotic superstructure which they have to support, will rise to a far finer standard of being than they can now realize. The cheap and aimless types belonging to the mercantile and middle classes will disappear with the world to which they belong.

Let me say however, for the consolation of some, that it is not necessary to suppose that the transformation of Civilization of which I speak—and which is even now preparing—must necessarily mean that all Law and Government, and world-wide Commerce and Finance and huge organization of Industry, and even present-day Art and Morality and Religion, will collapse and become non-existent. In a sense they will do so, and in a sense they will not. "In the twinkling of an eye they will be changed." In some sense the outer forms of these things will remain; but the Spirit will be changed; and so greatly changed that their shapes also will be profoundly modified. When Industry exists really for the supply of good and useful things and not for the manufacture of profit; when High Finance is not for gambling, but for the insurance and security of everybody; when Courts of Law are for the uplifting and not for the downcasting of criminals, and so on; then the forms of these institutions will be as different from what they are now as the organs of a Dragonfly are different from those of the Water-beetle from which it sprang.

But before this great and wonderful Transformation takes place, there must—it is abundantly evident—be great sacrifices. No such huge change could happen without. Some of the functions and activities of the present Society must perish; and with them must perish those who are engaged in these functions. Thousands and millions of individuals must die in the mere effort to create and establish a new collective order. Heroisms, exceeding those of the past, will be needed and will be supplied. We need not fear. We know the great heart of humanity.

It is amazing to see, in the present war, the high spirits, the courage, the devotion, the loyalty to each other of the combatants in each nation; and these things would be utterly unintelligible were it not for the fact that each people (and we need make no exception) thinks and believes in some obscure way that the cause for which it is fighting is a noble and an honorable one. Terrible as war is, and terrible the apparent folly of mankind which allows it to continue, still it is to my mind obvious that those engaged in it could not give their lives, as they so constantly do, not only with conscious devotion to some high purpose, but even with an instinctive exultation and savage joy in the very act of death, if they were not impelled to do so by the insurgence of a greater life within—a life within each one more vivid and even more tremendous than that which he throws away. The willing sacrifice of life, and the ecstasy of it, would be unintelligible if Death did not indeed mean Transformation.

In my little individual way I experience something of the same kind. I feel a curious sense of joy in observing—as at my age one is sometimes compelled to do—the natural and inevitable decadence of some portion of the bodily organism, the failures of sight and hearing, the weakening of muscles, the aberrations even of memory—a curious sense of liberation and of obstacles removed. I acknowledge that the experience—the satisfaction and the queer sense of elation—seems utterly unreasonable, and not to be explained by any of the ordinary theories of life; but it is there, and it may, after all, have some meaning.

APPENDICES

CONGRATULATORY LETTER

(*August* 29, 1914).

In offering you our congratulations on the completion of your seventieth year, we would express to you (and we speak, we are sure, the thoughts of a very large number of other readers and friends) the feelings of admiration and gratitude with which we regard your life-work.

Your books, with no aid but that of their own originality and power, have found their way among all classes of people in our own and many other lands, and they have everywhere brought with them a message of fellowship and gladness. At a time when society is confused and overburdened by its own restlessness and artificiality, your writings have called us back to the vital facts of Nature, to the need of simplicity and calmness; of just dealing between man and man; of free and equal citizenship; of love, beauty, and humanity in our daily life.

We thank you for the genius with which you have interpreted great spiritual truths; for the deep conviction underlying all your teaching that wisdom must be sought not only in the study of external nature, but also in a fuller knowledge of the human heart; for your insistence upon the truth that there can be no real wealth or happiness for the individual apart from the welfare of his fellows; for your fidelity and countless services to the cause of the poor and friendless; for the light you have thrown on so many social problems; and for the equal courage, delicacy, and directness with which you have discussed various questions of sex, the study of which is essential to a right understanding of human nature.

We have spoken of your many readers and friends, but in your case, to a degree seldom attained by writers, your readers are your friends, for your works have that rare quality which reveals "the man behind the book," and that personal attraction which results only from the widest sympathy and fellow-feeling. For this, most of all, we thank you—the spirit of comradeship which has endeared your name to all who know you, and to many who to yourself are unknown.

REPLY

MILLTHORPE, HOLMESFIELD,
DERBYSHIRE,
1st September, 1914.

In thanking my friends on the occasion of my seventieth birthday (29th August) for the many hearty letters of congratulation I have received, and in particular for the widely signed and very friendly Address which on the same occasion has been presented to me, I should like to say a few words.

At a moment like this when Europe is plunged in a monstrous war one naturally does not wish to dwell on one's own affairs. Yet some of us who have worked for thirty years or more in connection with the great Labour Movement at home and abroad may perhaps be excused if we cannot help looking on the strange events of the last few weeks in a somewhat personal light. For those events surely connect themselves by a kind of logical fatality with that very Labour Movement. They seem to point to the break-up all over Europe of the old framework of society, and (like the Napoleonic wars of a century ago) to bear within themselves the seeds of a new order of things.

Insane commercial and capitalistic rivalry, the piling up of power in the hands of mere speculators and financiers, and the actual trading for dividends in the engines of death—all these inevitable results of our present industrial system—have now for years been leading up to this war; and in that sense indeed all the nations concerned are responsible for it—England no less than the others. But the mad vanity of the Prussian military clique, and its brutal eagerness for imperial expansion at all costs, have precipitated the fatal move. The German Government is now involved in a conflict which the more socialistic section of its population absolutely detests, and for which its masses have little desire or enthusiasm; it is alienating from itself the loyalty of the warm-hearted and very human and brotherly folk whom it professes to represent; and is sowing the seed of its own destruction. Curiously enough too, by supplying the Russian Autocracy with an excuse for gratifying *its* lust of conquest (an excuse which is welcome no doubt as a means of discounting the revolutionary movement at home) this action of Germany is destined to lead to a disorganization of Russia similar to that which awaits herself.

On the other hand, the same action has already caused an extraordinary and astounding development of solidarity and enthusiasm among the more pacific peoples of Western Europe—this partly no doubt in sheer self-defence, but even more, I think, as an expression of their hatred of militarism and bullying Imperialism. The enormous growth during the past few years of democratic and communal thought and organization on the Continent generally is well known; and the events of which we are speaking have suddenly crystallized that into definite consciousness and into a fresh resolve for the future—the resolve that never again shall the peoples be plunged in the senseless bloodshed of war to suit the ambition or the private interests of ruling classes. Furthermore, in Britain, where, for so long, the forward movement has seemed to hang fire and fail to define itself, we have developed—most swiftly and in almost miraculous fashion—a whole programme of socialist institutions, and (what is more important) a powerful and democratic sentiment of public honour and duty.

In view of all this it is impossible, as I have said, not to hope for a great move forward—when this present nightmare madness is over—among the Western States of Europe towards the consolidation of their respective democracies and the establishment of a great Federation on a Labour basis among them; as well as to expect a sturdy reaction, perhaps amounting to revolution, among the Central and Eastern peoples against the military despotism and bureaucracy from which they have so long suffered. In both these directions, in aiding the Federation of the democracies of the West and in hastening the disruption of the military bureaucracies of the East, England—if she rises to her true genius, and to a far grander conception of foreign policy than she has of late years favoured—will have a great work to do. Nor is it possible to doubt that the new order thus arriving will largely be the outcome of those years of work all over Europe in which the ideal of a generous Common Life has been preached and propagated as against the sordid and self-seeking Commercialism of the era that is passing away.

If in my small way I have done anything towards the social evolution of which I speak, it is I think chiefly due to the fact that I was born in the midst of that Commercial Era, and that consequently my early days were days of considerable suffering. The iron of it, I suppose, entered into my soul. Coming to my first consciousness, as it were, of the world at the age of sixteen (at Brighton in 1860) I found myself—and without knowing where I was—in the middle of that strange period of human evolution the Victorian

Age, which in some respects, one now thinks, marked the lowest ebb of modern civilized society: a period in which not only commercialism in public life, but cant in religion, pure materialism in science, futility in social conventions, the worship of stocks and shares, the starving of the human heart, the denial of the human body and its needs, the huddling concealment of the body in clothes, the "impure hush" on matters of sex, class-division, contempt of manual labour, and the cruel barring of women from every natural and useful expression of their lives, were carried to an extremity of folly difficult for us now to realize.

As I say, I did not know where I was. I had no certain tidings of any other feasible state of society than that which loafed along the Brighton parade or tittle-tattled in drawing-rooms. I only knew I hated my surroundings. I even sometimes, out of the midst of that absurd life, looked with envy I remember on the men with pick and shovel in the roadway and wished to join in their labour; but between of course was a great and impassable gulf fixed, and before I could cross that I had to pass through many stages. I only remember how the tension and pressure of those years grew and increased—as it might do in an old boiler when the steamports are closed and the safety-valve shut down; till at last, and when the time came that I could bear it no longer, I was propelled with a kind of explosive force, and with considerable velocity, right out of the middle of the nineteenth century and far on into the twentieth!

My friends speak of gratitude, and I am touched by these expressions, because I do indeed think the genuine feeling of gratitude is a very human and lovable thing—blessing in a sense both him that gives and him that takes. Yet I confess that somehow, when directed towards myself, I find the feeling difficult to realize. After all, what a man does he does out of the necessity of his nature: one can claim no credit for it, for one could hardly do otherwise. I have sometimes, for instance, been accused of taking to a rather plain and Bohemian kind of life, of associating with manual workers, of speaking at street corners, of growing fruit, making sandals, writing verses, or what not, as at great cost to my own comfort, and with some ulterior or artificial purpose—as of reforming the world. But I can safely say that in any such case I have done the thing primarily and simply because of the joy I had in doing it, and to please myself. If the world or any part of it should in consequence insist on being reformed, that is not my fault. And this perhaps after all is a good general rule: namely that people should endeavour (more than they do) to express or liberate their *own* real and deep-rooted needs and feelings. Then in doing so they will probably liberate and aid the expression of the lives of thousands of others; and so will have the pleasure of helping, without the unpleasant sense of laying any one under an obligation.

And here I think I ought to say (lest by concealing the fact I should seem to be laying my friends under an obligation and obtaining their seventieth-birthday congratulations under false pretences) that only two or three years ago a horny-handed son of toil—a gold-miner from the wilds of South Nevada—came all the way direct to Millthorpe on purpose to tell me that I should yet live for four hundred years! He stayed, curiously enough, but a very few days in this country, and having delivered his message set sail again the next morning but one for his gold-mines and his quartz-crushing. The prophecy I confess was one of rather doubtful comfort either to myself or my friends, but in order to avoid disappointment in case of its fulfilment I think perhaps I ought to mention it.

Anyhow, referring back to those early Victorian days, I now seem plainly to see that if what was working then in my little soul could have been realized in society at large there would have been no need for you to address me the special letter or letters which I have just received—pleasant though they are to me—because you would have understood that in all reason letters equally grateful and full of recognition ought to be addressed to the joiner, the farm-labourer, the dairy-maid, and the washerwoman of your village, or to the soldier fighting now in the ranks. You would have realized that the lives of all of us are so built and founded one on the work of another that it is impossible to assign any credit to one whose name happens to be known, which is not equally due to the thousands or millions of nameless and unknown ones who really have contributed to his work. We literary folk, I need hardly say, think a great deal too much about ourselves and our importance.

This is of course so very obvious that I am persuaded that most of the signatories on this occasion will understand the matter so. And on that understanding I may say to my friends: I accept your expressions with the greatest pleasure. I appreciate the extraordinarily tender and gracious wording of the Address, and I thank you from my heart.

EDWARD CARPENTER.

ADDENDUM TO CHAPTER VII

In dealing with the Sheffield Socialists in Chapter VII, I omitted accidentally all mention of the gallant work they did, in 1887 and the following years, by waging a crusade against the Sheffield Smoke. Though situated in a most picturesque district of wooded hills and moors and streams, Sheffield had at that time become a by-word, almost throughout the world, for its filthy, soot-begrimed streets and impure air. Our little band of reformers, not content with merely warring against economic evils, set out boldly to purify the air and slay the Smoke-dragon, whose devastating wings over-spread the city.

We got a table out into the street, gave little talks on the subject, and distributed leaflets and pamphlets. The Sheffield workers were amazed. They had never heard of anything so preposterous! "They want us to do without smoak," they said. "But how can we live without smoak?—Why, if there were no smoak there would be no tra-ade." The argument was irrefutable, and for a time our efforts were only greeted with laughter. At last, however, the tide turned. A few more thoughtful and influential men (including the, then Editor of the *Sheffield Daily Telegraph*) joined the crusade, and the cause began to move. During the ensuing years more lectures were given; regulations on the subject were framed and issued by the City Council, smoke inspectors were appointed, exhibitions of smoke-consuming apparatus instituted. And a considerable improvement was already noticeable when the Great War broke out.

The War, it need hardly be said, put the clock back in this as in so many other matters. In the wild outbreak of profiteering which occurred during that period all restraining regulations were cast aside, and for a time the defilement of the Sheffield air became worse than ever. It was only at a later date that things began to mend again. Curiously enough it was the great Coal Lock-out of 1921 which set the public back into the right path. After twelve weeks of almost entire non-consumption of coal—either in domestic or in factory chimneys—people were astounded at the purity and magic beauty of the skies over their heads. It was a revelation. Their eyes were opened to the fact that the drab and dismal character of their climate was largely or chiefly due to their own folly and neglect. They realized that if only proper pre-cautions were taken against the production of smoke, our vast stores of coal might still be utilized (in the form of electricity, etc.) with a substantial gain in economy, a positive gain in the health of our people, and a great gain to their joy in life and in the beauty of Nature.

Thus, the labours and enthusiasm of our little Socialist coterie had a valuable result in leading to the more refined and efficient means of developing power, light, and heat, which are in operation at the present day.

October 1921.

BIBLIOGRAPHY

The Religious Influence of Art: being the Burney Prize Essay for 1869. Cambridge, Deighton, Bell & Co., 1870. [*Out of print.*

Narcissus and other Poems. London, Henry S. King & Co., 1873. [*o. p.*

Moses: **A Drama in Five Acts.** London, E. Moxon, 1875. [*o. p.*

THE SAME. Reprinted with alterations and republished as *The Promised Land.* Sonnenschein, 1910. George Allen & Unwin, 1916.

Syllabuses of University Extension Lectures. (Astronomy, Sound, Light, Pioneers of Science, Science and History of Music, &c.) 1874–1881.

Towards Democracy (Part I). First edition. John Heywood, Manchester, 1883.

THE SAME (including Parts I and II). John Heywood, Manchester, 1885.

THE SAME (including Parts I, II, and III). Fisher Unwin, London, 1892.

THE SAME (with new Title-page). The Labour Press, Manchester, 1896.

THE SAME (Part IV only, "Who Shall Command the Heart"). London, Swan Sonnenschein; Manchester, S. Clarke, 1902.

THE SAME (Four Parts complete in one vol.). London and Manchester, Sonnenschein and S. Clarke, 1905.

THE SAME. Complete Library Edition, with two portraits. Same publishers, 1908.

THE SAME, on India paper (pocket edition), without portraits, but with Note at end, 1909.

Later issues the same as the last two. Thirtieth Thousand, 1921.

American Edition: T.D. complete. New York, Mitchell Kennerley, 1912.

England's Ideal and other Papers on Social Subjects. London, Swan Sonnenschein (Social Science Series). First edition, 1887.

THE SAME. Sixteenth Thousand. London, George Allen & Unwin, 1919; New York, Charles Scribner's Sons.

Civilization: its Cause and Cure. And other Essays. London, Swan Sonnenschein (Social Science Series). First edition, 1889.

THE SAME. Seventeenth Thousand. London, George Allen & Unwin, 1919; New York, Charles Scribner's Sons.

New and Finally Complete Edition. Fourth Thousand, 1921. London, George Allen & Unwin.

Chants of Labour. Edited by Edward Carpenter. With music; and Frontispiece by Walter Crane. First edition. London, Swan Sonnenschein, 1888.

THE SAME. Seventh Thousand. London, George Allen & Unwin, 1916.

From **Adam's Peak to Elephanta**: being Sketches in Ceylon and India. With illustrations. First edition. London, Sonnenschein, 1892; New York, Macmillan Co.

THE SAME. Second edition, enlarged, 1903. Third edition, revised, 1910.

A Visit to a Gñani: being four chapters from the above, in separate volume, with two photogravure portraits. George Allen & Co., 1911.

THE SAME. Third Thousand. George Allen & Unwin, 1920.

THE SAME. Authorized American edition. Published by A. B. Stockham & Co., Chicago, 1900.

THE SAME. Pirated and mutilated. Published by the Yogi Publication Society, Masonic Temple, Chicago, 1905.

Love's Coming-of-Age : A Series of Papers on the Relations of the Sexes. First edition. The Labour Press, Manchester, 1896.

THE SAME. Second edition, 1897.

THE SAME. Third edition. Swan Sonnenschein, London; S. Clarke, Manchester, 1902. Fifth edition, enlarged, 1906.

THE SAME. Fourteenth Thousand. George Allen & Unwin, 1916.

THE SAME. Note on Preventive Checks omitted. London, Methuen. Shilling edition, 1914.

THE SAME. American edition. Stockham Publishing Company, Chicago, 1902. [*Out of print.*

THE SAME. Published by Mitchell Kennerley, New York, 1911.

Forecasts of the Coming Century : by Alfred Russel Wallace, Tom Mann, H. Russell Smart, William Morris, H. S. Salt, Enid Stacy, Margaret McMillan, Grant Allen, Bernard Shaw and Edward Carpenter. Edited by E. C., and published by the Labour Press, Manchester, 1897.

The Story of Eros and Psyche from Apuleius, and the first book of the Iliad of Homer, done into English by Edward Carpenter. London, Sonnenschein, 1900. [*Out of Print.*

Angels' Wings: Essays on Art and its Relation to Life. With nine full-page Plates and Appendix. First edition. London, Sonnenschein, 1898; New York, Macmillan Co.

THE SAME. Second edition, 1899. Third edition, 1908.

THE SAME. Fourth edition, 1917. Fifth edition, 1919. George Allen & Unwin.

Ioläus : an Anthology of Friendship, in old Caslon type, with red initials and side-notes. First edition. London, Sonnenschein, 1902; Boston, U.S.A., Ch. A. Goodspeed.

THE SAME. Author's edition, 1902, bound in white and blue calf; 150 copies only. [*Out of print.*

THE SAME. Second edition, enlarged. Forty pages added; black initials and notes. Sonnenschein, 1906.

THE SAME. Third edition. Title changed to **Anthology of Friendship (Ioläus)**. Published by George Allen & Unwin, 1915.

THE SAME. Fourth Edition, 1920.

The Art of Creation: Essays on the Self and its Powers. First edition. London, George Allen, 1904. Second edition, enlarged, 1907.

THE SAME. Third edition, 1916. Fourth edition, 1919. Fifth edition, 1921. George Allen & Unwin.

Prisons, Police, and Punishment: an Inquiry into the Causes and Treatment of Crime and Criminals. London, Fifield, 1905. [*Out of print.*

The Simplification of Life: being selections from the writings of E. C. by Harry Roberts. Published by Anthony Treherne, London, 1905. Second edition. George Allen & Unwin, January 1915.

Days with Walt Whitman: with some Notes on his Life and Work, and three Portraits. London, George Allen, 1906.

THE SAME. Second edition, 1906. Reprinted, 1921. George Allen & Unwin.

Sketches from Life in Town and Country: Some Verses, and a Portrait of the Author. London, George Allen, 1908. [*Out of print.*

The Intermediate Sex: a Study of some Transitional Types of Men and Women. First edition. London, Sonnenschein; Manchester, Clarke, 1908. Second edition, 1909.

THE SAME. Third edition. George Allen & Co., 1912.

THE SAME. Fourth edition. London, George Allen & Unwin, 1916. Reprinted, 1918 and 1921.

THE SAME. American edition. New York, 1912.

The Drama of Love and Death: a Study of Human Evolution and Transfiguration. London, George Allen & Co., April 1912.

THE SAME. Second edition, August 1912.

THE SAME. American edition. New York, Mitchell Kennerley, 1912.

Intermediate Types among Primitive Folk: a Study in Social Evolution. London, George Allen, 1914. Second edition. George Allen & Unwin, 1919.

THE SAME. American edition. New York, 1914.

The Healing of Nations: and the Hidden Sources of their Strife. First edition. London, George Allen & Unwin, March 1915. Reprinted April and October 1915, July 1916, September 1917, and September 1918.

The Story of My Books. London, George Allen & Unwin, March 1916.

My Days and Dreams: being Autobiographical Notes by Edward Carpenter. With Seventeen Portraits and Illustrations. George Allen & Unwin, May, 1916. Second edition, October 1916. Reprinted February 1918. Third edition, September 1921.

PAMPHLETS.

Modern Science: a Criticism. Pp. 75. John Heywood, Manchester and London, 1885. [*o. p.*

Co-operative Production: with reference to the experiment of Leclaire. A lecture given at the Hall of Science, Sheffield, 1883. Published by John Heywood, Manchester, 1883. Pp. 16. [*o. p.*

THE SAME. Second edition. The Modern Press, 13, Paternoster Row, London, 1886. [*o. p.*

England's Ideal. A Tract reprinted from *To-day*, May 1884. Pp. 22. John Heywood, Manchester and London, 1885. [*o. p.*

Modern Moneylending, and the Meaning of Dividends. John Heywood, 1883.

THE SAME. Second edition, 1885. Pp. 28. [*o. p.*

Desirable Mansions. A Tract reprinted from *Progress*, June 1883. Pp. 16. John Heywood, 1883.

THE SAME. Second edition. The Modern Press, London, 1886.

Third edition, 1887. [*o. p.*

Social Progress and Individual Effort. Reprinted from *To-day*, February 1885. Pp. 13. The Modern Press, London, 1886. [*o. p.*

The Enchanted Thicket: an Appeal to the "Well-to-do," by Edward Carpenter, late Fellow of Trinity Hall, Cambridge: being a reprint by permission from the book *England's Ideal.* For private circulation, 1889. Pp. 12.

Civilization, Exfoliation, and Custom. Published by Humboldt Library of Science, New York, 1891. Pirated from *Civilization: its Cause and Cure.* Pp. 65.

Modern Science and Defence of Criminals. Humboldt Library, 1891. Also pirated from *Civilization: its Cause and Cure.* Pp. 53.

Our Parish and our Duke: a Letter to the Parishioners of Holmesfield, in Derbyshire. Four-page leaflet, published by the author, 1889. (Two editions about 10,000 each.) Also printed in full in the London *Star*, July 8, 1889. [*o. p.*

The Village and the Landlord. An adaptation of the foregoing. Published by the Fabian Society (Tract No. 136). London, 1907.

A Letter Relating to the Case of the Walsall Anarchists. Four-page leaflet. Reprinted from *Freedom*, December 1892. [*o. p.*

Intorno alla Protezione degli animali (four-page leaflet). Reprinted from *Il Lavoro* (Genoa) of May 18, 1906.

Empire: in India and Elsewhere. Pp. 20. London, A. C. Fifield, 1900.

THE SAME. New edition, 1906. Published by Fifield, for the Humanitarian League.

A Letter to the Employees of the Midland and other Railway Companies. Four-page leaflet. Fillingham, Sheffield. Signed "E. C., on behalf of the Sheffield Socialist Society, Commonwealth Café," November 1886. [*o. p.*

Boer and Briton. Four-page leaflet. Labour Press, Manchester, January 7, 1900. (? Two editions 5,000 each.) [*o. p.*

Proof of Taylor's Theorem in the Differential Calculus. By Edward Carpenter and R. F. Muirhead. Four-page pamphlet, with orange cover. Extracted from the Proceedings of the Edinburgh Mathematical Society, vol. xii. Session 1893–4.

Sex-love: and its Place in a Free Society. Pp. 24. Labour Press, Manchester, 1894. Second edition, 1894. [*o. p.*

Woman: and her Place in a Free Society. Pp. 40. Labour Press, Manchester, 1894. [*o. p.*

Marriage in Free Society. Pp. 48 (5,000 copies). Labour Press, Manchester, 1894. [*o. p.*

Homogenic Love: and its Place in a Free Society. (Printed for private circulation only.) Pp. 52. Manchester, 1894. [*o. p.*

An Unknown People. Reprinted from the *Reformer*. Pp. 37. London, A. and H. B. Bonner, 1897. (Brown and gold cover.)

THE SAME. Second edition, 1905. (Plain brown cover.) [*o. p.*

Fly, Messenger! Fly: being a reprint (8 pages) from *Towards Democracy*, by permission. For private circulation only. Tring, 1894.

The Wreck of Modern Industry: and its Reorganization. Pamphlet, pp. 16. National Labour Press, Manchester, 1909.

Non-Governmental Society. Originally a chapter in *Forecasts of the Coming Century*, 1897; afterwards in *Prisons, Police, and Punishment*. Pp. 32. Reprinted separately, and published by A. C. Fifield, London, 1911.

Vivisection. By Edward Carpenter and Edward Maitland. Two Addresses given before the Humanitarian League. Fifty-four page pamphlet. London, W. Reeves, 1893.

Vivisection. By Edward Carpenter. Pp. 12. Another Address given before the Humanitarian League. Published at 53, Chancery Lane, London, 1904.

Vivisection. Two Addresses by Edward Carpenter (being the above two Addresses). Revised edition. London, Fifield, 1905.

The Art of Creation. Being the second Anniversary Lecture of the Larmer Sugden Memorial, delivered at the William Morris Labour Church, at Leek, by Edward Carpenter, and printed at Hanley, in Staffordshire, 1903.

The Inner Self. Report of a lecture given at King's Weigh House Church, London, November 7, 1912, and published (pp. 8) by the Christian Commonwealth Company, 1912.

St. George and the Dragon: a Play in Three Acts for children and young folk. Dedicated to the I.L.P. clubs. Labour Press, Manchester, 1895. Second edition, 1908.

The Need of a Rational and Humane Science: a lecture given before the Humanitarian League. Published at 53, Chancery Lane, London, 1896. Pp. 33.

THE SAME. Reprinted as a chapter in *Humane Science Lectures* by various authors. London, George Bell, 1897, and incorporated in *Civilization: its Cause and Cure*, edition 1906.

British Aristocracy and the House of Lords. Pp. 36. Reprinted from the *Albany Review* of April, 1908. London, Fifield, 1908.

The Smoke-Nuisance and Smoke-Preventing Appliances. Pp. 8. Being report of a lecture given at the Firth College, Sheffield, October 27, 1889. Publishers, Leader & Sons, Sheffield.

SOME MAGAZINE ARTICLES.

(*Not* including those already [1916] republished in book form.)

The Value of the Value-Theory. *To-day*, June 1889.

On High Street, Kensington, in the *Commonweal*, April 26, 1890.

Lawrence Oliphant, critique in the *Scottish Art Review*, February 1889.

November Boughs, critique in same Review, April 1889.

The Smoke-Plague and its Remedy. *Macmillan's Magazine*, July 1890.

Love's Coming-of-Age: a Reply to Mr. Rockell. The *Free Review* (Sonnenschein), October 1896.

Two Gifts: a Poem. The *Adult*, February 1898.

On English Hexameter Verse. Two articles in the *Cambridge Review*, February 22 and March 1, 1900.

An Open-Air Gymnasium, *Sandow's Magazine*, January 1900.

The Awakening of China. In the *Co-operative Wholesale Society's Annual*, Manchester, 1907.

Morality under Socialism. The *Albany Review*, September 1907.

Four Articles, **Sketches in Morocco.** The *New Age*, November 1906, and May, June, and July 1907.

The Taboos of the British Museum. By E. S. P. Haynes (and E. C.) in *English Review*, December 1913.

The Meaning of Pain. *English Review*, July 1914.

Does Pain on one Plane mean Pleasure on another? The *Epoch*, July 1914.

The Great Kinship. Translated from the French of Elisée Reclus ("La Grande Famille") by E. C. The *Humane Review*, January 1906.

Sport and Agriculture. In the *Humanitarian*, November 1913.

Conscription and National Service. Letter to the *Daily Chronicle*, London, August 12, 1915.

Two articles on **The Music Drama of the Future.** The *New Age*, August 15 and 22, 1908.

Two articles on **The New South African Union.** The *New Age*, August 27 and September 3, 1909.

Two articles on **The Minimum Wage.** The *New Age*, December 21 and 28, 1907.

Drawing-room Table Literature. Article in the *New Age*, March 17, 1910.

Le Philosophe Meh-ti. Book-review in the *New Age*, February 1, 1908.

Beauty in Civic Life : report of a lecture. The *Humanitarian*, January 1912.

TRANSLATIONS.

GERMAN.

Wenn die Menschen reif zur Liebe Werden (*Love's Coming-oj-Age*). Translated by Karl Federn; published by Hermann Seemann, Leipzig, 1902.

Die Civilisation: ihre Ursachen und ihre Heilung. Translated by K. Federn; published by H. Seemann, Leipzig, 1903.

Towards Democracy. Translated by Lilly Nadler-Nuellens and Ervin Batthyány.

(Part I), "Demokratie," published by H. Seemann, Leipzig, 1903; Berlin, 1906.

(Part II), "Freiheit," same publishers, 1907.

(Part III), "Der Freiheit Entgegen," published by Freier Literarischer Verlag, Berlin, Tempelhof, 1908.

(Part IV), same title and publishers, 1909.

Die Schöpfung als Kunstwerk (*The Art oj Creation*). Translated by K. Federn, published by Eugen Diederichs, Jena, 1905.

Das Mittelgeschlecht (*The Intermediate Sex*). Translated by L. Bergfeld, published by Seitz und Schauer, München, 1907; afterwards, Reinhard, München.

England's Ideal. Translated by Sophie von Harbon; published by Wilhelm Borngräber, Berlin, 1912.

Articles and Pamphlets.

Die Homogene Liebe. Pamphlet. Translated by H. B. Fischer, published by Max Spohr, Leipzig, 1894.

Three separate pamphlets, "Die Geschlechstliebe," "Das Weib," and "Die Ehe," all published in 1895. Same translator and publisher as above.

Article "Ueber die Beziehungen zwischen Homosexualität und Prophetentum" in the *Vierteljahrs-berichte des Wissenschaftlich-humanitären Komitees*, July 1911, published by Hirschfeld, Berlin.

Pamphlet **Die Gesellschaft ohne Regierung** (*Non-governmental Society*). Translated by Pierre Ramus, published by W. Schouteten, Brüssel, 1910.

ITALIAN.

L'amore diventa maggiorenne (*Love's Coming-of-Age*). Translated by Guido Ferrando; published by frat. Bocca, Torino, Roma, etc., 1909.

L'Arte della Creazione. Translated by G. Ferrando; published by Enrico Voghera, Roma, 1909.

Verso la Democrazia (Part I). With biographical notice and note from *Labour Prophet*. Translated by Teresina Campani-Bagnoli; published by R. Carabba, Lanciano, 1912.

FRENCH.

Prisons, Police, et Châtiments. Traduit et annoté par Paul Le Rouge et Alain Garnier, avocats à la Cour d'Appel de Paris. Published by Schleicher Frères, Paris, 1907.

Vivisection. Par E. C. Traduit de l'anglais par E. F. Satchell; published by St. Catherine's Press, Bruges, 1910.

L'Amour Homogénique et sa Place dans une Société libre. Published in *La Société Nouvelle*, Brussels and Paris, September 1896.

Vers l'Affranchissement (being Parts III and IV of *Towards Democracy*). Translated by Marcelle Senard. Published by the Librairie de l'Art Indépendant, 81 rue Dareau, Paris, 1914.

Also **E. C. et sa Philosophie.** Par M. Senard. Published same year and place.

La Régénération des Peuples (*The Healing of Nations*). Translated by M. Senard; published by . . .

DUTCH.

Liefde's Meerderjarigheid (*Love's Coming-of-Age*). Translated by Meezen brock; published by Holkema, Amsterdam, 1904.

Die Beschaving: hare Oorzaak en hare Genezing (*Civilization: its Cause and Cure*). Translated by P. H.; published by Elsevier, Amsterdam, 1899.

RUSSIAN.

Civilization: its Cause and Cure. Translated by Ivan Najívin, with biographical Note, and Portrait, Moscow, 1906.

Modern Science: a Criticism. With Introductory Note by Leo Tolstoy, 1904.

Prisons, Police, and Punishment. Translated by A. M. (without Appendix). Large 8vo, light green cover. Moscow, 1907.

A Visit to a Gñani (four chapters) entitled *I Am*. Translated by Ivan Najívin, Moscow, 1907.

Towards Democracy (*I arise out of the Night*). Being selections from T. D., with Note on E. C. by Sergius Orlovski. Moscow.

Love and Death. Translated by P. D. Ouspenski. With **Introduction.** Petrograd, 1915.

The Intermediate Sex. Translated by P. D. Ouspenski. Petrograd, 1915.

See also article on E. C. by S. E. Rapoport in *Russian Thought* for January or February 1914. Petrograd.

BULGARIAN.

Modern Science: a Criticism. With Introduction by Leo Tolstoy. Translated from the Russian by D. Jethkoff and Chr. Dossieff. Burgas, 1908.

Also **Civilization** and **England's Ideal.** Translated by D. Vaptzaroff, Burgas, 1908.

Articles in *Renaissans* (Burgas):—

On Rational and Humane Science. 1909.

England's Ideal. 1910.

Defence of Criminals. (2 numbers.) 1914.

SPANISH.

Defensa de los Criminales. Critica de la Moralidad. Translated by Julio Molina y Vedia; published by P. Tonini, Buenos Aires, 1901.

El Matorral Encantado (*The Enchanted Thicket*). Translated by Peter Godoi Perez, por el Grupo "Los Precursores." Santiago, 1911.

JAPANESE.

Sections I to XIX of **Towards Democracy** by Saikwa Tomita in *Tokyo Magazine* of July 1915.

Also **After Long Ages** and many shorter poems.

See also **E. C.: Poet and Prophet.** By Ishikawa Sanshiro: being a series of chapters on E. C. with long quotations from his works, also portrait and letter from E. C. Yokohama, 1912.

MUSIC.

See **Chants of Labour.** Edited by E. C. First edition 1888.

Also **Three Songs** ("Men of England," by Shelley, "The People to their Land," and "England, Arise"). Set to music by E. C. Published by the Labour Press, Manchester, 1896.

England, Arise. Arranged by John Curwen as four-part song for male voices. Staff and sol-fa notation. Published by J. Curwen and Sons, Berners St. London, W., 1906.

The City of the Sun. Words and music by E. C. Published by the Labour Press, Manchester, (?) 1908.

Die Stadt der Sonne. Worte und Musik von E. C., "dem Kämpfenden Proletariat gewidmet." Verlag "Wohlstand für Alle." Vienna XII. Herthorgasse, 12, (?) 1909.

SOME BOOKS, PAMPHLETS, ARTICLES, ETC.

E. C.: The Man and his Message. Pp. 40. With two portraits. By Tom Swan. Manchester, 1901. Second edition, 1902.

THE SAME. Third Edition. London, Fifield, 1905. Fourth edition, 1910.

E. C.: Poet and Prophet. By Ernest Crosby. 50 pp. Second edition, Fifield, 1905.

The Gospel according to E. C. By G. H. Perris. In two chapters. Article in the *New Age*, April 23 and 30, 1896.

Three Modern Seers (Hinton, Nietzsche, and E. C.). With Portraits. Pp. 228. By Mrs. Havelock Ellis. London, Stanley Paul, 1910.

E. C.: Poet and Prophet. Expositions of and quotations from his works. Pp. 300. In Japanese script. By Ishikawa Sanshiro. Yokohama, 1912.

E. C.: an Exposition and an Appreciation. By Edward Lewis. Pp. 310. With Portrait. London, Methuen, 1915.

Modern Science. A reprint in English of Leo Tolstoy's Introduction to that Essay. Published by Wm. Reeves, Charing Cross Road, London.

E. C. and his Message. By Leonard D. Abbott in the *International Socialist Review*, Chicago, November 1, 1900.

E. C. ein Sänger der Freiheit und des Volkes. Von Pierre Ramus, verlag Schouteten. Brussels, 1910.

E. C. et sa Philosophie. Par M. Senard. Libr. de l'Art Indépendant, Paris, 1914.

Chapter on E. C. in *All Manner of Folk*. By Holbrook Jackson. London, Grant Richards, 1912.

And various articles :—

See the *Dublin University Review*, April, 1886; *Seed-time*, London, April, 1893; the *Friend*, January 4, 1895; the *Twentieth Century*, New York, June 25, 1898; the *Inquirer*, London, May 13, 1899; the *Westminster Review*, December, 1901; the *Pioneer*, London, January, 1901; the *Humane Review*, July, 1903; the *Literary Digest*, New York, February 25, 1905; the *Craftsman*, New York, October, 1906; the *Millgate Monthly*, Manchester, April 1907; the *Forum*, New York, August 1910; the *Christian Commonwealth*, London, December 11, 1912; *Bibby's Annual*, 1913; the *Bystander*, March 18, 1914; the *Epoch*, November 1915; the *Herald of the Star*, August 11, 1915; etc.

ADDENDA

ADDITIONS TO BIBLIOGRAPHY, 1921.

Towards Industrial Freedom: Essays in Social Reconstruction. Pp. 224. George Allen & Unwin. First edition, 1917; second edition, 1918.

Never Again! a Protest and a Warning addressed to the Peoples of Europe. Pp. 24. George Allen & Unwin, 1916. Second impression, 1916. Price 6d.

THE SAME. Pp. 12. National Labour Press. Price 1d.

The Story of My Books: being a Chapter from **My Days and Dreams.** Pp. 16. Allen & Unwin, 1916.

Three Ballads: an Intermezzo in War-time. By E. C. October, 1917. Pp. 12. Limited edition. Printed in Manchester. No publisher's name.

War and Peace in Human History: an Address delivered at a Peace Conference in the Caxton Hall, London, July 8, 1915, and published, with other Addresses under the title **Towards Ultimate Harmony,** by Headley Bros.

Pagan and Christian Creeds: Their Origin and Meaning. First edition, January 1920. Reprinted April 1921. London, George Allen & Unwin.

SOME MAGAZINE ARTICLES.

Article on genesis of **Towards Democracy,** in *The Labour Prophet*, edited by John Trevor. May 1894. Manchester and London.

The Language of Domestic Fowls. By E. C. and G. Merrill, in *Country Life*, September 10, 1910; also, with additions, in the *Humanitarian*, September 1913.

The Great Kinship: a Translation by E. C. of "La Grande Famille," by Elisée Reclus. Mag. Internationale, 1896. Published in the *Humane Review*, January 1906, and the *Humanitarian*, October 1913, and reprinted in pamphlet form by the Humanitarian League. Pp. 12.

TRANSLATIONS.

FRENCH.

Avènement de l'Amour (L. C. of A.). Translated by M. Senard. Librairie Art Indépendant, Paris, 1918.

Drame de l'Amour et la Mort. Translated by Georges Bazile. Librairie Art Indépendant, Paris, 1918.

NORWEGIAN AND DANISH.

Mot Solrenning. Being Selections from E. C.'s works. With Introduction by Illit Gröndahl. Kristiania, 1917.

Civilisationen, dens Aarsag og Helbrederlse. Translated by B. C. Gad. Peter Hansen, Copenhagen, 1913.

SWEDISH.

Karlekens Myndighets Ålder (L. C. of A.). Translated by O. H. D. Hugo Geber, Stockholm.

JAPANESE.

Love's Coming-of-Age. Translated by — Sakai. Pp. 115. With portrait. Japan, 1916.

MUSIC.

The City of the Sun. With new Musical Setting. By E. C. Published by the Author, at Holmesfield, 1918.

SOME BOOKS, PAMPHLETS, ARTICLES, ETC.

Simplification of Life. Selections from the Works of E. C. By Harry Roberts. Pp. 124. Antony Treherne, 1905.

THE SAME. New edition, 1915. George Allen & Unwin.

E. C.: His Ideas and Ideals. By A. H. Moncur Sime. Kegan Paul, Trench & Co., 1916.

Poets of the Democracy. By G. Currie Martin. Headley Bros., 1917. Chapter on E. C.

Tom Maguire: A Remembrance of a Socialist Pioneer. Manchester Labour Press, 1895. Memoirs by E. C. and others.

Beethoven. By Romain Rolland. English translation published by Kegan Paul, Trench & Co., 1917. Introductory Note by E. C.

INDEX

Printed in Great Britain by
UNWIN BROTHERS, LIMITED, THE GRESHAM PRESS, WOKING AND LONDON

Printed in the United States
102554LV00003B/50/A

9 780766 146297